MISS AMERICA
In Pursuit of the Crown

"Ann-Marie Bivans has *really* done her homework...! Her work should be 'required reading' for armchair authorities, as well as the novitiate. The recent passing of Adrian Phillips and Al Marks makes her work even more significant."

—Robert Arnhym, President and CEO,
Miss California Scholarship Pageant, Inc.

"Bravo! This is an excellent, factual book explaining the Miss America program. Ann-Marie does a beautiful job of describing the system from the local level to becoming Miss America. The book provides humor and is very interesting. It should be required reading for all contestants. It is the best book I've read about the Miss America Pageant!"

—Brenda Thornton, formerly Executive Director,
Miss Idaho Scholarship Pageant, Inc.

"Fascinating, informative, and a 'must read' for everyone, especially pageant people! Anyone at all interested in the Miss America program should have a copy. Most highly recommended."

—Kenn Berry, Field Director,
Miss New York State Scholarship Pageant, Inc.

"I have walked many miles on the road of this history—its people, its places, its pageantry.
"*Miss America: In Pursuit of the Crown* ... is right, real, and refreshing! It strikes a note of nostalgia in perfect pitch. Ann-Marie Bivans, thank you for a beautifully rendered orchestration."

—Evelyn Ay Sempier,
Miss America 1954

"Ann-Marie's book is interesting, factual, and most of all will be a tremendous help to the public to understand what we, the Miss Americas, are all about...."

—Marian Bergeron Setzer,
Miss America 1933

"From the spirit and dedication of the thousands of grass-roots volunteers to the hard work, talent, and intelligence of the contestants across the country, the Miss America Pageant embodies qualities which endure and enrich our lives. Chevrolet, the 'Heartbeat of America,' is proud to be a corporate sponsor of the Miss America Pageant."

—Danielle Colliver, Manager,
Chevrolet Motor Division

"Thanks for the first accurate, warmly written work on our program.
"Your book is 'alive' and took me through each era and phase as if I were on a personally conducted tour of a 'family' history. Congratulations! Your efforts are appreciated."

—Nathan Zauber, Executive Director,
Miss New Jersey Pageant Organization

"At last, a book we can call 'our own'! Not another generic book that we have to adapt for our use, but rather a comprehensive inside look at the Miss America Pageant by those of us who have been there. Precise, timely, and thoughtful. Great reading from cover to cover."

—Jeffrey J. Quin, Executive Director,
Miss Pennsylvania Scholarship Pageant, Inc.

"With warmth and humor, Ann-Marie captures the many-faceted feelings and experiences that comprise the Miss America experience."

—Marilyn Van Derbur,
Miss America 1958

"At last, a responsive, readable, concerned, and caring chronicle!

"Congratulations, Ann-Marie, you deserve high praise. I wish I had written it. It's great fun to read.

"The Miss America Scholarship Pageant, of course, has a precious place in my heart. Thank you for sharing with us the memories of so many women whose lives were changed overnight."

—Lee Meriwether,
Miss America 1955

"As a longtime Pageant sponsor, we have always been concerned that contestants receive the best advice and the best care on their journey through the Miss America Pageant system. *Miss America: In Pursuit of the Crown* is a guidebook for contestants and their families and should be required reading for anyone who envisions herself wearing the Miss America crown."

—Brian McFarland, President,
Personal Care Division,
The Gillette Company

"Good job! Everyone would benefit from the 'hints' given. This seems to be good advice for people not even in the pageant business. Can't wait for the publication!"

—Nora Chapman, Executive Director,
Miss Alabama Pageant

"This wonderful book, with its true-to-life stories of young women who dedicate themselves to being the very best, reconfirms my reasons for providing Quintessence sponsorship to the Miss America Pageant."

—Joe Aramanda, President and CEO,
Quintessence

"The Miss America Pageant stands apart from all its competitors. The Pageant has a sense of history and tradition. It has roots. It is part of the culture of America. . . . These are attributes that all the other pageants covet, but never achieve."

—Arthur Schriebam, President,
Clifford A. Botway Inc., National Media Buyers
for Chesebrough-Pond's, Ltd.

MISS AMERICA
In Pursuit of the Crown

MISS

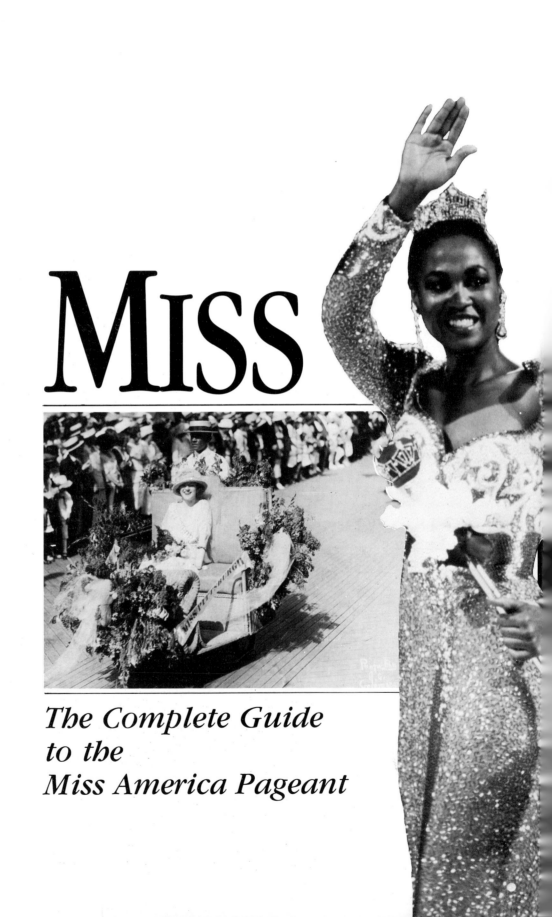

The Complete Guide to the Miss America Pageant

ANN-MARIE BIVANS

AMERICA

In Pursuit of the Crown

MasterMedia Limited · New York

Library of Congress Cataloging-in-Publication Data

Bivans, Ann-Marie.
    Miss America: In pursuit of the crown: the complete guide to the Miss America pageant/Ann-Marie Bivans.
        p.   cm.
    Includes index.
    ISBN 0-942361-27-X
    1. Miss America Pageant, Atlantic City, N.J.   I. Title.
HQ1220.U5B58   1991
791.6—dc20   90-63421
                                                                                     CIP

Manufactured in the United States of America

10   9   8   7   6   5   4   3   2

Designed by Antler & Baldwin, Inc.

Production services by Martin Cook Associates, Ltd.

Title page, left to right:

The Miss America Boardwalk Parade began as a wicker rolling chair parade in 1921. Seventy years later, the parade draws a quarter of a million spectators. MISS AMERICA PAGEANT

Marjorie Vincent, Miss America 1991. JOHN FRANK, CP NEWS

In 1988, Gretchen Carlson became the first violinist to capture the Miss America title. GEORGE SORIE

The form-fitting swimsuits of the 1950s showed off the voluptuous physiques of the era. Georgia's Neva Langley was so abundantly blessed that contestants' mothers accused her of illegal padding. Vindicated, Neva won both a swimsuit trophy and the 1953 crown. FRED HESS & SON

During the forties, the dramatic "Everglaze" wardrobes provided each winner by sponsor Joseph Bancroft popularized hooped ball gowns as the blueprint for Pageant attire in the next decade. Bess Myerson models an original Everglaze design. MISS AMERICA PAGEANT

To my husband, Karl,
whose love, faith, and unceasing encouragement
made this book a reality.

Contents

Acknowledgments

I would like to express my gratitude to the Miss America Pageant "family," which so graciously cooperated with my research, particularly to chairman Leonard C. Horn, without whose support this book could not have been completed. My deepest appreciation for his willingness to assist my efforts to share the fascinating history of the Pageant, and for sharing his contagious vision about the future of this great American institution. My profound gratitude as well to Lenora Slaughter Frapart, the late Adrian Phillips, and the late Albert Marks, Jr., for sharing their wealth of memories.

I would also like to acknowledge the contributions of the following officials, volunteers, judges, etc.: Karen Aarons, Bill Caligari, Ellen Plum, Robert Bryan, Ruth McCandliss, Gary Collins, Jane Kubernus, Dr. Leonard Hill, Jayne Bray, Mary Pat Feehan, Connie Fitzgerald, Betty Frisch, Eleanor Ross, Margaret Stevenson, Anita Puhala, Robert Arnhym, Jeff Bell, Kenn Berry, Adair Brown, Ada Duckett, Vernon DeSear, Richard Cardone, Nora Chapman, Joe Dickens, Marie Finnell, Phyllis Goldhammer, Sam Haskell, Tom Hensley, Irv Kaar, Roger Knight, B. Don Magness, William Marcotte, Tim Mason, Mike McMahan, John Moskal, Nancy Prince, Jeffrey Quin, Joseph Sanders III, Bettie Sorie, Sid Stoen, Vicki Trimble, Bernie Wayne, Bob Wheeler, Peggy White, Bill Wolfe, Nathan Zauber, and Robert Zettler.

My deepest appreciation to the Miss Americas who graciously reminisced about their reigns: Marjorie Vincent, Debbye Turner, Gretchen Carlson, Kaye Lani Rae Rafko, Debra Maffett, Cheryl Prewitt, Dorothy Benham, Shirley Cothran, Rebecca King, Terry Meeuwsen, Laurel Schaefer, Phyllis George, Pamela Eldred, Judith Ford, Donna Axum, Vonda Kay Van Dyke, Jacquelyn Mayer, Mary Ann Mobley, Marilyn Van Derbur, Marian McKnight, Lee Meriwether, Evelyn Ay, Neva Langley, BeBe Shopp, and Marian Bergeron. Also to: Wylie King, Eleanor Schaefer, Ron and Nonnie Maffett, and Marie Boyd and Dian Spitler of the Atlantic City Library.

My thanks as well to the state titleholders who were interviewed. While space limitations precluded incorporating many of their comments, their input was nevertheless invaluable: Sandy Adamson, Melissa Aggeles, Lee Beaman, Kris Beasley, Kim Boyce, Debra Cleveland, Christina Chriscione, Kathleen Cryan, Sarah Evans, Sandy Frick, Carrie Folks, Carla Haag, Mary Donnelly, Regina Hopper, Lori Lee Kelley, Michele Passarelli, Marlise Ricardos, Jennifer Sauder, Mia Seminoff, Sophia Symko, Christi Taunton, Maya Walker, and Janet Ward Black.

For the photographs in this work, I am grateful to the following sources: The Miss America Pageant; the *Atlantic City Press;* Paul Abel, Jr.; Irv Kaar; Terry Chenaille, P & W Graphics; George Sorie, Picture Takers, Inc.; Michael Kurtz; W. Earle Hawkins; Doug Rumburg; Phyllis Wayne; Joe Profetto, Pro Photographics; John and Kathleen Frank, CP News Service; Atlantic Foto Service; Candid Camera of Atlantic City; Central Studios; Fred Hess & Son; Ron Cohen for Clairol, Inc.; John Reilly; Sid Schrier; Associated Press; Fruit of the Loom; Randy Brooke; and K. Bivans.

Finally, my deepest gratitude to my dear friends Mary Di Stefano-Diaz and Anne St. Pierre for their unfailing support and encouragement. Special thanks to Beth Greenfeld, James S. Baumann, my literary agent, Marlene Connor, and my publisher, Susan Stautberg, for their belief that a *positive* book on the Miss America Pageant would be welcomed by Pageant fans around the nation.

Introduction

The Miss America tradition has always reflected the best of American ideals and today, more than ever, is working to support the wholesomeness, intelligence, and achievements of young women.

Over the past two years as chief executive officer of the Miss America Organization, and during my twenty-year tenure as a member of the Organization's board, I have been part of the many progressive changes within the Miss America system. As we move toward the twenty-first century, we have taken a proactive approach that reflects the characteristics, interests, and concerns of today's women in general and the Pageant's contestants in particular. These changes are recognizable within the Pageant's three entities—the Miss America Scholarship Fund, the Miss America Pageant, and the Miss America Foundation.

The Miss America Scholarship Fund is the largest scholarship foundation in the world for women. We have enlarged the scholarship base for all contestants competing in Atlantic City to reemphasize our commitment to personal growth and achievement. We have established the first Miss America Scholarship, which is awarded to the college or university the reigning Miss America attends. We have also expanded the scope of the Allman Medical Scholarship program to include national, state,

and local contestants (previously only state winners were eligible). As a result, scholarship continues to grow as a vehicle for these young women to achieve their goals.

The Pageant provides a forum for Miss America to communicate to the public her commitment to specific social issues. In addition to the actual Pageant structure, we are proud to have established the national Women's Achievement Award to honor women whose contributions to society have improved the visibility and prestige of women in general.

We have also created the Women's Advisory Council, a panel of successful businesswomen who provide guidance to the Organization and serve as liaison for the Pageant with other women's organizations, enabling us to respond to the changing concerns of women. The overall changes made reflect suggestions made by all of our Pageant officials, as well as sentiments expressed by volunteers at the state and local Pageant levels. These thousands of volunteers are the lifeblood of the Miss America Organization. We rely upon them to keep us in touch with what really matters across our country, and in America's heartland, and to keep us ever broadening the scope of our mission.

The Miss America Foundation is being established to extend both tangible and intangible benefits of the Miss America program not only to our contestants, but also to those who do not compete and to communities at large. By using donations made to the Foundation for projects that will be identified and developed, we will be able to provide financial assistance for education to girls and women in need.

The most important message we can communicate to the public is that the Miss America Organization exists to recognize the capabilities of young women and to provide them with a support system that encourages the development of their talents. It does so by providing them with new opportunities for intellectual growth and additional career options. Indeed, we are especially proud of the many contestants, who have not been crowned Miss America, who have gone on, because of opportunity provided by the Pageant, to achieve important goals and career success.

The Pageant of the nineties is concerned with individuality rather than conformity. With the achievement of goals more than the meeting of standards. Miss America has long been a role model for young women. Today, that role has been enlarged to embody not only femininity and family values, but achievement and social involvement. The positive image of Miss America continues to represent the highest ideals and to attract many who aspire to achieve the status and recognition made possible through participation in the Miss America Organization.

Miss America: In Pursuit of the Crown is a living chronicle of this great American tradition, replete with little-known facts about its history, as well as a guide to would-be participants. It is for everyone who has ever shared—or hopes to share—the Miss America dream.

Leonard C. Horn
Chairman, CEO
Miss America Organization

MISS AMERICA
In Pursuit of the Crown

The first "Miss America," Margaret Gorman. MISS AMERICA PAGEANT

PART I

THE BACKGROUND

CHAPTER 1

There She Is—
Miss America!

The eyes of a nation are riveted on the faces of six beautiful young women. The contestants nervously clutch at each other's hands as they await the announcement that will dramatically alter one of their lives. For several suspenseful moments television cameras scan their expressions as a hush settles over the huge Convention Hall audience. A drumroll thunders expectantly in the background as the master of ceremonies pauses and turns toward the quivering semifinalists. Suddenly he shouts, *"And our new Miss America is . . . Miss Michigan— Kaye . . . Lani . . . Rae . . . Rafko!"* The audience roars with excitement as the winner gasps in disbelief and buries her face in her hands. Nearly overcome with emotion, she extends her trembling hands toward the judges in a poignant gesture of gratitude. The new Miss America glides to center stage, where she embraces her predecessor and pauses gracefully to receive the glittering crown and rose-adorned scepter.

"Ladies and gentlemen—meet your new Miss America!" proclaims the emcee, as Kaye Lani Rae Rafko begins her long-anticipated victory walk. As she maneuvers the famous 125-foot runway, she waves at the cheering audience and smiles brilliantly through her tears. A wave of photographers surges forward to capture the scene on film, sending a cascade of photographic flashes twinkling throughout the hall. In the background echoes the melody that has etched itself into the nation's soul:

There She Is, Miss America
There She Is, your ideal.
The dreams of a million girls,
Who are more than pretty
May come true in Atlantic City.
For, she may turn out to be,
The queen of femininity!

There She Is, Miss America,
There She Is, your ideal.
With so many beauties,
She took the town by storm,
With her All-American face and form—
And There She Is,
Walking on air, she is,
Fairest of the fair, she is,
Miss America!

© Bernie Wayne. Reprinted by permission.

Kellye Cash, Miss America 1987, crowns her successor, Kaye Lani Rae Rafko. ASSOCIATED *PRESS*

It is a moment of which millions of girls have dreamed. One which Kaye Lani Rae Rafko has worked half a decade to achieve—and she is clearly relishing every second. For the radiant beauty, who has somehow edged aside an army of determined competitors, the victory is literally a dream come true!

"THE DREAM OF A MILLION GIRLS"

Since the first Miss America accepted her crown in 1921, sixty-six teary-eyed winners have come and gone, mesmerizing generations of spectators. The advent of Pageant-side radio broadcasts, and then movie newsreels and television coverage, steadily intensified the nation's romance with Miss America. In fact, since the Pageant's first live coast-to-coast television broadcast in 1954, the coronation of Miss America has drawn audiences of 35 million to 80 million viewers. Yet, after seven decades, a depression, a world war, and feminists' protests, the annual tradition has never lost its charm.

Apparently, its enduring popularity with the public is due to Miss America being not only a long-standing national tradition, but the personification of a modern-day fairy tale. "It's a Cinderella story," Albert Marks, the Pageant's late chairman emeritus, once theorized. "It's the fact that a little, unknown youngster from Brownsville, Texas, can begin with perhaps a dozen other young women and move up the ladder to a night in September when she becomes an instant celebrity." Terry Meeuwsen, who experienced that dreamy moment in 1972, explains, "It's the whole mesmerizing mystique of the fact that this *was* a girl next door, but now she is—*ta da!! Miss America!*" She adds with a laugh, "In some ways, it's America's answer to Princess Di!"

In fact, it has long been conjectured that the public's perception of Miss America is at least partially influenced by society's latent longing for American royalty. "A lot of people say that the proliferation of pageants in the United States is our quest for some type of royalty since we don't have our own Royal Family," affirms Karen Aarons, the Pageant's executive vice president. "When they don't know all the hard work that has gone into getting up to that point, I think they can view Miss America as being anointed rather than as being part of an arduous selection process and competition. When, in the space of two hours, someone who is unknown goes to being Miss America it *does* appear to be a Cinderella story."

Generations of newly crowned Miss Americas have discovered the reality of that public perception as they have embarked on their whirlwind tours of the nation. And, year after year, they have returned to Atlantic City with touching recollections of awestruck children inquiring in whispered tones, "Do you *really* live in a castle?" Dorothy Benham, Miss America 1977, remembers their reverent expressions: "They'd look at you, at the gown, at the sparkling crown on your head, and they would be in awe. Their little eyes would become so wide. It was just amazing." Eleanor Ross, one of Miss America's official traveling companions, interjects with a laugh, "Oh, *Lordie,* the little girls just idolize her! Their mouths just hang open. To the little girls, it's like *Cinderella!*"

Over the years, the fairy tale has woven itself into the fabric of American society. "I don't think there is a person in the country today over five years of age who has not heard the term 'Miss America,'" remarks attorney Leonard C. Horn, the Pageant's chief executive officer. "It's ingrained in the language. It's ingrained in what we call 'Americana.'"

And the program's popularity is not limited to any particular social strata. It seems that everyone from the man on the street to the man in the White House tunes in for the an-

"I think keeping the ideal of Miss America being crowned is very important," says Laurel Schaefer, Miss America 1972, "because it demonstrates that the American Dream comes true." EARLE HAWKINS

nual extravaganza. "I've always been a fan," confesses Merv Griffin. "I don't think I've *ever* missed a Miss America Pageant." Eva Gabor, who served as a national judge in 1988, also admits to being a longtime fan. "I must say that I watch Miss America every year—and when those beautiful girls get their crown and cry—*I cry with them*." Even former president Richard Nixon revealed an appreciation for Miss America back in 1972, when he remarked to then-reigning queen Laurel Schaefer, "We only allow our two girls to stay up late to watch TV for one program—the Miss America Pageant."

Clearly, the Pageant has touched the collective heart of America. "I have learned that this program is a lot more popular, and has a lot more intrinsic value, than even I thought it

had," says Leonard Horn. "Millions of people across the length and breadth of this country share a love for the Miss America Pageant. This thing has been pretty popular since 1921. It's one of the oldest live events in the history of television, and our ratings are among the highest of any television special during the course of the year." He adds with a proud smile, "It's a tradition, and I think people enjoy traditions."

In the case of Miss America, the tradition serves as an annual affirmation that the American dream endures. "I think keeping the ideal of Miss America being crowned is very important," says Laurel Schaefer, "because it demonstrates that the American Dream comes true— that with hard work and tenacity you can truly attain absolutely anything your heart desires. I think that's the best part of what the Miss America title stands for. It is an affirmation that we have in the United States the opportunity to have a definite dream as well as the opportunity to attain that dream."

THE WORLD SERIES OF WOMANHOOD

Not surprisingly, in a nation that cherishes the ideal of the American Dream, a victory at the Miss America Pageant is tantamount to winning the "World Series of Womanhood." Although the odds against taking the title are long—approximately 80,000 to 1—the dream endures. Since the inception of Atlantic City's "National Beauty Tournament" in 1921, the "dream of a million girls" has been to capture the elusive Miss America crown. To date, sixty-six ambitious young women have achieved that dream—and multitudes are waiting in the wings to join the elite sorority.

It isn't hard to figure out *why*. These enterprising competitors realize that when the television cameras are unplugged, the new Miss America glides off the runway with a king's ransom: a $35,000 scholarship, the keys to a snazzy Chevrolet Corvette, a spectacular "Made in the U.S.A." wardrobe, an assortment of gifts too numerous to detail, and the opportunity to bank close to $200,000 in personal appearance fees. Not bad for a college kid from Cut 'n Shoot, Texas, or Elk City, Oklahoma. Is it any wonder that legions of red-blooded American girls have their eyes on the crown?

MORE THAN A BEAUTY CONTEST

While the dream of floating down the runway with 55 million people watching may be a major attraction for contestants, they realize that there is far more to Miss America than crowns, banners, roses, and runways. What contestants know, and the general public sometimes fails to comprehend, is that the Miss America Pageant is not a "beauty contest." It is a scholarship pageant system that makes available over $5 million in scholarship funds each year. In fact, the program's generous financial assistance has made a major—if often unrecognized—contribution to the lives of thousands of American women by providing them with the finances to achieve their educational goals.

The list of former national contestants who benefited from their participation in the program reads like a volume of *Who's Who in America:* judges, attorneys, physicians, dentists, educators, Academy and Emmy Award recipients, authors, executives, a nuclear technologist, an aerospace engineer, a state senator, and a mayor. Clearly, Miss America alumnae are not vapid beauty queens, but talented, determined achievers who have utilized the Pageant as a springboard to educational and career success.

In fact, the program's role in the development of such feminine leaders has been likened to the impact collegiate sports programs have traditionally had upon young men. These gutsy contestants are the female equivalents of the ambitious college football player—and the Pageant is their competitive arena. Marilyn Van Derbur, a former Miss America and award-winning educational film producer, points out, "When some of the boys are going out for football scholarships, young women are going out for Miss America scholarships, and they are funding their educations by doing that." She adds, "I must tell you, I think that these girls are very wise to look at it that way. In that regard, I think young women are much more educated as to what they can *gain* from doing it."

Gary Collins, whose unique perspective on the issue has included his marriage to former Miss America Mary Ann Mobley and a decade as the Pageant's emcee, agrees that the program has forged a pathway of opportunities for women where opportunities were extremely limited. "For many years this Pageant was one of the few areas women could compete in and receive scholarship money. You can't ignore the fact that women *do* enjoy competing, and they *do* have ambition. It's a basic tenet of life that one does not have to be male to want to compete."

Despite its record of providing millions of dollars in scholarship funds to girls since 1945, the program continues to be plagued by misunderstanding and criticism from feminists and reporters. Such carping, Leonard Horn explains, usually comes from individuals or organizations that have not taken the time to familiarize themselves with the Pageant's benefits. If critics would only set aside their preconceived ideas and take a fresh look at what the program offers, he says, "they would recognize that the program is a valuable program." Not earthshakingly important, Horn concedes, but certainly of value. "It isn't going to change the world, but it does substantially help those who participate. On a scale of trivia, with the most important trivia being a ten, this would be a ten!"

For a piece of "trivia," the Pageant certainly attracts a lot of attention. Journalist Peter Mattiace once wrote, "The fact of the matter is that more people are interested in Miss America than what's going on at Camp David." Is it any wonder—particularly in light of some of the thorns that have sprouted from Miss America's roses in the not-so-distant past? Vanessa's resignation. The dismissal of longtime host Bert Parks. The feminist infiltrator at the Miss California Pageant. While the hailstorm of controversy left Pageant officials blushing, the incidents also generated enormous amounts of publicity, and ironically gave the Pageant a much-welcomed boost in popularity. "As far as the Miss America Pageant is concerned," Horn remarks with a hint of a grin, "indifference is

our worst enemy—and people are *not* indifferent to this program."

Frankly, they never were. The Pageant has not only survived the widely publicized incidents of recent years, but it has also lived to laugh about some of the colorful moments of bygone eras: the newly crowned queen who ran off with her dashing escort, a bogus Miss America, an invasion of stink-bomb-tossing feminists, a host of hilarious talents, and an unforgettable appearance by Marilyn Monroe, to name a few. In fact, the history of this splendid tradition is bursting with legendary characters, poignant moments, and hilarious escapades—none of which, incidentally, has succeeded one iota in dampening the nation's romance with Miss America. If anything, her racier moments have fueled public interest. A review of the Pageant's seven-decade history reveals that this *grande dame* of pageants is a lady with a surprisingly flamboyant past.

CHAPTER 2

A Great American Tradition

... Thus a year or more, we may
all adore
This Queen of a Nation's flower
Whose "Royal Crest" is
"Democracy's Best,"
Cradled in "Liberty's Bower."

And as years roll on, God grant
each one
May enhance our "Pageant Day"
With the beauty and spleen of the
land whose queen
Is—Miss America!

Mary Carroll Potter
Atlantic City Press,
September 1925

In early 1921, the seeds were sown for the emergence of one of our nation's most enduring annual traditions, when a group of New Jersey entrepreneurs met to discuss a promising publicity gimmick. The businessmen couldn't possibly have guessed that their idea would evolve into a renowned American institution. On that frigid winter afternoon, it simply seemed like a clever idea to boost local tourism.

Their community, the famed vacation mecca of Atlantic City, would host a gala fall festival or "pageant" to extend tourism past Labor Day weekend, which traditionally closed the summer season. The "Atlantic City Pageant" would feature a host of events, including a beachfront bathing beauty contest. Chamber of Commerce president Samuel Leeds embraced the idea, convinced the Hotelmen's Association to house the beauties, and appointed a committee of prominent business leaders to organize and promote the festival.

Soon after, a pair of local newspapermen, Harry Finley and Herb Test, attended a convention of East Coast newspaper executives and suggested that their papers sponsor entry-level contests as a gimmick to increase circulation. Readers would submit photos of pretty girls to editors, who would in turn select winners to represent their respective communities in Atlantic City's bathing beauty contest. There, a panel of distinguished artists of the era would select "The Most Beautiful Bathing Beauty in America." Herb Test added the crowing touch to the idea. "And let's call her 'Miss America'!" he exclaimed.

That first Miss America Pageant, then titled a "National Beauty Tournament," took place on September 7, 1921, with a mere eight contestants. The beauties were divided into appropriate divisions: "Professional Beauties" (models, stage and screen), "Civic Beauties" (amateurs), and "Inter-City Beauties." Historical sources list New York's Virginia Lee as the sole "professional" candidate, with seven "civic" and "Inter-City" contenders: Margaret

Gorman, Miss Washington, D.C.; Kathryn Gearon, Miss Camden; Thelma Matthews, Miss Pittsburgh; Hazel Harris, Miss Ocean City; Emma Pharo, Miss Harrisburg; Nellie Orr, Miss Philadelphia; and Margaret Bates, Miss Newark. Miss Atlantic City, Ethel Charles, graciously withdrew to serve as "hostess." The beauties were judged in several events: the Rolling Chair Parade, Bathers' Revue, and final judging.

During the opening ceremony of Atlantic City's pageant, as cannons boomed and yacht whistles sounded, the festival's amphibious mascot, "King Neptune," floated to shore on a Viking barge. Neptune—portrayed by eighty-one-year-old smokeless gunpowder inventor Hudson Maxim—was a fanciful sight, with his towering crown gleaming in the sun and his seaweed robe and white beard blowing in the

Atlantic City's "Pageant" included a popular "Bathers' Revue," where huge crowds watched contestants parade along the beach. By the mid-twenties, the contest was so well known that over seventy entrants representing thirty-six states and Canada competed. MISS AMERICA PAGEANT

King Neptune crowns Miss America 1926, Norma Smallwood, of Tulsa, as Miss America 1925 and Princess America II look on. ATLANTIC FOTO SERVICE

ocean breeze. As His Majesty disembarked to greet the cheering crowds and introduce the candidates, a retinue of mermaids and sea monsters danced around him, showering him with a cascade of flowers—unscented, due to Maxim's renowned aversion to fragrances. "While I am exceedingly strong and rugged," he assured reporters, "if I were placed next to someone smelling to high heaven with perfume, I'd collapse and fall in a heap."

After greeting the dignitaries, King Neptune presided over the spectacular Boardwalk Rolling Chair Parade. Poised on a giant shell that was carried by "sea monsters," His Oceanic Majesty led a procession of bands and floats along the parade route, as bombs ex-ploded in midair and airplanes showered the crowds with confetti and flowers. Trumpets then heralded the arrival of the contestants, who were perched on elaborately decorated wicker rolling chairs and nearly smothered with freshly cut flowers—not to mention the admiration of onlookers.

However captivating the beauties appeared in the parade, it was the boisterous Bathers' Revue that showed them off to best advantage. There, contestants strolled down the beach between the Garden and Steel Piers accompanied by the mayor, city officials, firefighters, and a band—all clad in bathing attire. Even the police force joined in the spirit of the day by patrolling the parade route while garbed in bathing suits accessorized with officer's caps, badges, and police clubs. The usually strict rules governing beach attire were officially loosened for the duration of the pageant, leaving lifeguards who doubled as "beach censors" gaping in shock. After all, women had been arrested for wearing more at other times. Even the usually shockproof _New York Times_ noted that censors weren't the only people who were astonished by the display of feminine charms. "Thousands of spectators gasped as they applauded the girls . . . ," its reporters tattled.

The late Adrian Phillips, a past Pageant president who observed the original contest, disagreed that contestants' bathing dresses were daring. "From the earliest days, girls were in swimsuits. We're a beach resort, so we take swimsuits as part of the normal scenery. We didn't see anything risqué or anything out of order about a swimsuit." Besides, he argued, "Back in the 1921 pageant, their swimsuits were wool. They wore long pants with an over-jersey. If somebody thinks a swimsuit is sexy—the outfits they wore in those days certainly wouldn't classify. Although," he admitted with a grin, "relatively, they may have been—I don't know."

Margaret Gorman, a sixteen-year-old schoolgirl attired in a suitably demure swimming dress, won the hearts of the judges and the first Miss America crown. One spectator, seventy-two-year-old Samuel Gompers, president of the American Federation of Labor, publicly hailed the judges' choice. "She represents the type of womanhood America needs," he informed the _New York Times,_ "strong, red-blooded, able to shoulder the responsibilities of homemaking and motherhood. It is in her type that the hope of the country rests." As Margaret's victory was announced, officials inaugurated her with great fanfare, bestowing upon their queen the predictable trappings of American royalty—a replica of Lady Liberty's

pronged tiara and a coronation robe fashioned from a huge American flag.

As the victor, she also received a monstrous trophy featuring a gilded mermaid reclining upon a teakwood base. According to Phillips, "The 'Golden Mermaid' was actual gold," and reportedly valued at $5,000. It was announced that Gorman, or any other young lady, who managed to win the Miss America title three consecutive years would be allowed to keep the trophy. Margaret, however, didn't accomplish the feat, and by the end of the decade the Golden Mermaid had vanished into the annals of Pageant history. "Nobody knows what actually happened to it," Phillips reported. "It just disappeared, so that's sort of a mystery."

There was no mystery, however, about the success of the festival and beauty tournament. The events captivated the public, generated massive amounts of publicity for the resort, and increased profits for merchants by encouraging thousands of tourists to prolong their vacations. Excited city leaders promptly decided to continue the successful event throughout the decade.

As the festival and beauty tournament achieved nationwide fame in the years that followed, the roster of candidates swelled from eight girls to over seventy entrants representing thirty-six states and Canada. In 1923, for the first and only time in Pageant history, a contestant won back-to-back Miss America titles when Ohio's Mary Katherine Campbell, who had defeated reigning champion Margaret Gorman the previous year, returned to recapture her title. Unfortunately, Campbell's winning streak abruptly ended in 1924, when she narrowly lost the Miss America crown to Philadelphia's Ruth Malcomson.

Despite its popularity with the public, the beauty tournament's success was interrupted by a series of embarrassing incidents that focused an unflattering media spotlight upon the event. First, after officials forgot to include a no-marriage clause in the original set of rules, Mary Campbell's first runner-up, Ethelda Kenvin, turned out to be *Mrs.* Everette Barnes, wife of a Pittsburgh Pirates player. Then, "Miss" Boston, Mildred Prendergast, showed up with her attorney husband and seven-month-old baby in tow, and officials discovered that Miss Alaska, Helmar Leiderman, was not only married, but a resident of New York City! After being barred from competition, Helmar filed suit for $150,000, citing "humiliating discrimination." The pageant's reputation was further tarnished when several women's clubs labeled the competition "indecent" and the *New York Graphic* ran a series of inflammatory articles that were later retracted.

By the late twenties, the detrimental aftermath of such publicity, compounded by early effects of the Great Depression, eroded critical financial support from the resort's business community, and the fall festival and National Beauty Tournament were discontinued in 1928.

THE 1930S—THE REVIVED PAGEANT

In September 1933, an attempt was made to revive the beauty tournament. Despite the determined efforts of pageant director Armand T. Nichols, its revival was brief—and memorable. First, the preliminaries were delayed when judge Gladys Glad overslept; then Miss New York State collapsed onstage from an abscessed tooth, Miss Oklahoma was rushed to the hospital for an emergency appendectomy, Miss New York City dropped out, Miss Arkansas was revealed to be married, and three western contestants were disqualified for residing in other states.

After much ado, the final competition was staged on the Steel Pier and judges awarded the Miss America title to fifteen-year-old Marian Bergeron. As the petite Miss Connecticut

stepped forward in victory, she was dwarfed by the mammoth crown. "It was so big it came right down over my eyes," Marian recalls with a laugh, "and it made me look retarded!" Then, she says, during the rush of post-coronation activities, the crown was stolen from Miss America's suite at the Ritz-Carlton. "It just vanished," she pouts.

The pageant nearly followed suit, after lingering bad press and lukewarm support from Atlantic City's business community doomed the 1933 tournament to financial failure. Amidst rumors that the production would be moved to another city, the competition was discontinued until 1935, leaving the youthful Miss Bergeron to unofficially reign for two years.

In 1935, showman Eddie Corcoran, promotional director for the Steel Pier, persuaded his boss, Frank P. Gravatt, to sponsor a reorganization of the defunct competition. Hotelman John Hollinger, Chamber of Commerce president Louis Johnson, and city commissioner William Casey offered their assistance. The Variety Club of Philadelphia, to which several of the men belonged, accepted the challenge of conducting entry-level contests in other Variety Clubs and theaters across the nation. The reorganized national pageant, which would be staged in the largest ballroom on the Pier, would be called "The Showmen's Variety Jubilee."

Successfully reviving the contest would take wholehearted community support, and Corcoran turned his attention to finding an individual qualified to organize the event and gain the cooperation of civic leaders. As if on cue, he happened upon a news release lauding the nation's only woman pageant director, Miss Lenora Slaughter, a Chamber of Commerce civic events coordinator and assistant to Florida's baseball commissioner, Al Lang.

Convinced that Slaughter was the ideal candidate for the job, Corcoran contacted Lang with a request to "borrow" her for six weeks

When the defunct beauty tournament was revived in 1933, fifteen-year-old Marian Bergeron earned the crown. When the contest was discontinued until 1935, Marian unofficially reigned for two years. ATLANTIC FOTO SERVICE

preceding the upcoming contest. When Lenora skeptically asked her boss what *he* thought of the offer, Lang cracked a grin and responded, "Well, you ought to go up there and show those damn Yankees how to do a *real* job with a pageant!" Spurred on by curiosity, and by the $1,000 fee that came with the project, Lenora accepted the "temporary" position that would become her life's passion.

Slaughter's strategy for bolstering the contest's reputation included both concentrated efforts to convince the town's business com-munity to support plans to revive the pageant and efforts to attract the "finer types" of young ladies as contestants. Regulations were imposed banning titles representing commercial interests such as newspapers, amusement parks, and theaters, and requiring contestants to compete under the title of a city, region, or state. Participation was limited to girls between the ages of eighteen and twenty-eight who had never been married, a 1:00 A.M. curfew was enforced, and contestants were prohibited from frequenting bars or nightclubs during pageant week. Miss Slaughter's endeavors to polish the contest's reputation were soundly applauded by city leaders such as Mayor White, who proclaimed to reporters, "We are past the time when beauty parades are in the nature of floor shows. This is a cultural event seeking a high type of beauty."

One of the most significant changes implemented during the era was the addition of "talent" as a competitive factor in 1935. Despite talent being an optional competition, Lenora recollects that "at least half of the girls would get out there on the Steel Pier and sing or dance or do something—badly." She attributes the initially unimpressive performances to a clash of musical styles. "They usually had big-name bands performing to draw the crowds, so I'm sure the music wasn't right for them and naturally the girls didn't do too well—and they *still* picked the pretty girls." Nevertheless, Lenora was convinced that talent was a worthwhile trait which warranted more emphasis. "I knew that a pretty girl was a pretty girl—but while it was worthwhile being a pretty girl, you had to develop *talents, too.*"

In 1938, she promoted talent to a mandatory phase of competition valued at a hefty one-third of balloting—a move that effected an improved pool of talent and a slicker production. "It gave us a big advantage," Adrian Phillips once said. "We had a real good show, something to really *stage*. It broadened the scope of the pageant and brought opportunities for women with talent. It was just a very good move."

Pageant organizers were busy making all the right moves and increasing the program's momentum when their newly crowned Miss America 1937, Bette Cooper, jolted them by vanishing only hours after her victory. "We were astonished," Phillips recalled, "as was the general public. We had no idea where she was. We had the state police and everybody looking for her."

Later, the startling news surfaced that the new queen had run off with her handsome Atlantic City chaperon—but for "very proper reasons," Phillips hastened to explain. "At the time, we had young men, who were very respectable young men of the community, driving the cars for the girls. Bette's driver was a man named Lou Off, the son of a city commissioner and hotel owner. He was a very fine guy." Her escort was not only a fine fellow, but a suave, socially prominent bachelor who owned his own airplane and cabin cruiser—and whose father owned the Brighton Hotel, where Bette was staying.

As it turned out, when seventeen-year-old Bette won the Miss America title that night, she was stunned by her unexpected victory, and unwilling to leave school to fulfill the demands of the reign. Her father, Le Brun Cooper, fretted to the *Atlantic City Press,* "She's so young and we feel it's not right to shove a kid into Vaudeville. Her mother doesn't want to lose her 'baby.' So considering everything, she slipped out a side door of the hotel to escape the terrible crowds."

With her parents' approval, Lou Off became a willing accomplice to her predawn departure. "When they called him and roused him out of bed at two or three o'clock in the morning," Phillips reported, "he came with a buddy of his and picked her up and put her on his boat at the end of the Steel Pier, where they could watch all the hubbub." He added, "They were within sight of what was going on, but of course, nobody knew that until much, much later."

As dawn broke Sunday morning, a mob of reporters and photographers gathered on the Steel Pier for the customary photo session with the winner. Photographer Sid Stoen, who has covered the Pageant for half a century, recalls the commotion that ensued when the media learned of Miss America's mysterious disappearance. "When they couldn't find Bette

Miss America 1937, Bette Cooper, ran off with her handsome chaperon only hours after her coronation, creating an uproar. As officials and police frantically searched for the missing queen, photographers recorded the unprecedented scene. MISS AMERICA PAGEANT

Cooper, all of us photographers and writers were really upset! People were amazed that somebody would enter into a pageant and then not accept the crown as Miss America!" Dumbfounded by the unprecedented development, reporters simply recorded the events as they unfolded, and hours later, newspapers across the nation carried front-page photographs of the startling sight—Miss America's throne occupied by nothing more than a beautiful, but unclaimed, crown.

Exasperated by this unfortunate turn of events, Slaughter took immediate steps to guarantee that her girls were protected not only from charming chauffeurs, but from unscrupulous New York "talent agents," as well. "I went to the board and pleaded with them to appoint a hostess committee to serve as chaperons and to take care of the girls when they came to Atlantic City." Lenora suggested that the most socially prominent woman in town should organize and oversee the committee. Mrs. C. D.

"Borrowed" from the St. Petersburg, Florida, Chamber of Commerce to help reorganize the defunct pageant, Lenora Slaughter elevated the Pageant from cheesecake to the largest private scholarship program in the world for women. She retired in 1967.
CANDID CAMERA OF ATLANTIC CITY

White, the mayor's wife, seemed the obvious choice. The distinguished Quaker socialite agreed to undertake the challenge on the condition that her hostesses be granted complete control over contestants when they were not in rehearsals or competition. "When she accepted, we were all delighted," Lenora reports, "because now we had the one lady who could command anybody in town to serve on the committee, and they'd be flattered."

Mrs. White developed the impeccable hostessing system that would become an integral part of the Miss America Pageant not only at the national level, but at the local and state levels, as well. "She set rules that were iron-clad where the girls were concerned," Lenora explains, including the now famous "no men"

regulation. "You've probably heard a lot of laughs about the rule that men—even a girl's father—couldn't go in a girl's hotel room while she was there. And you can understand *why!* You can't print on a man's back, 'Hey, I'm her father!,' so we kept men out." She grins. "We guard the Miss America contestants in Atlantic City so well that their mothers say that we guard them better than they're guarded at home."

Indeed, White's hawk-eyed hostesses have performed their functions so effectively that they have removed virtually any chance that a Miss America could vanish into the night again. "Mrs. C. D. White deserves a tremendous amount of the credit for the reputation of the pageant over the first few years," Slaughter affirms. "Her hostess committee preserved the dignity of the girls in Atlantic City—and, as a result, there hasn't been a word of scandal written about a contestant in Atlantic City."

While major scandals have spared Pageant week since, one notable exception occurred in 1938, when Miss California, Claire James, was passed over for the Miss America crown because judges disapproved of her use of mascara. Incensed over placing second to Miss Ohio, Marilyn Meseke, James complained to reporters, "I can't stand it. I've had one insult after another heaped upon me since I came here." Her promoter, theatrical producer Earl Carroll, denounced the judges as incompetents and charged that Miss California was the rightful winner. Carroll called a press conference and announced that he was going to personally crown her the *"real"* Miss America—"The People's Choice"—the next morning in New York City. Apparently, Miss James took the pronouncement to heart and toured the country for several years as a "former Miss America."

Despite the occasional turbulence of the 1930s, the Miss America pageant closed the decade on a decidedly upbeat note. The contest's popularity with the public was soaring as millions of Americans viewed the competition for the first time in movie newsreels, and the long-awaited move from the Steel Pier to massive Convention Hall was, at last, at hand. Unbeknownst to pageant organizers, the program was about to enter an era when the biggest threats to its survival would not be vanishing queens and bogus Miss Americas—but the ominous winds of an approaching Second World War.

THE 1940S—THE WAR ERA

Miss America had survived the critical decade of the 1930s to emerge into the forties with a new confidence and a determination to keep the Pageant's momentum growing. A variety of changes were implemented to ensure its continued growth and to enhance its reputation. The official title, "The Showmen's Variety Jubilee," was changed to "The Miss America Pageant," as suggested by Press Club member Nick Carter, Convention Hall became the new home of the Pageant, restrictions were imposed governing the composition and conduct of judging panels, and the Pageant sorority, Mu Alpha Sigma, was organized. Then, after the first runner-up to Miss America 1940 returned to Atlantic City the next year and effortlessly walked off with the 1941 crown, a rule was invoked prohibiting contestants from competing in the national competition more than once.

In 1941, another significant change occurred when Lenora Slaughter was promoted to national executive director after director George Tyson clashed with officials. "He worked for Dunn and Harris and the Ice Capades," Lenora recalls, "and he got the idea that he was going to run Miss America on Ice, using the Miss America name, but my board hit

The Pageant moved to Convention Hall in 1940, where a sell-out audience watched as Philadelphia's Frances Burke became the first winner to walk the now-famous runway.
MISS AMERICA PAGEANT

the ceiling. . . ." Tyson resigned over the spat and Lenora assumed leadership of the program's national operations. Seven days after her promotion, the Japanese bombed Pearl Harbor and the United States entered World War II.

As America's involvement in the war escalated, Atlantic City was placed under military occupancy. The glamorous Boardwalk hotels were transformed into barracks housing thousands of soldiers, and Convention Hall became an Army Air Force training site. During one month in 1942, even the glittering lights of the Boardwalk were ordered dimmed when it was suspected that Nazi submarines lurked offshore. Despite the Pageant's newfound temporary housing in the Warner Theater, the military conditions in town made it nearly impossible to conduct the production effectively and much thought was given to discontinuing it until the conclusion of the war. However, city leaders decided that the program should be continued because, as Lenora Slaughter put it, Miss America was "emblematic of the spirit of America—a spirit that continued through war and peace, good times or bad."

During the early 1940s, the director struggled to achieve full state representation in the program. After approaching the United States Junior Chamber of Commerce with an invitation to stage local and state competitions, she gained the cooperation of the Jaycee organizations in North Carolina, Texas, and Georgia. "That was all I could get," she concedes with a shrug, "but I kept trying." From that humble start evolved the nationwide network of 300,000 community volunteers who conduct approximately 2,000 Miss America preliminaries from the Hawaiian Islands to the New England coast.

In addition to her expansion of the program, Slaughter was also responsible for the development of its celebrated scholarship program. "This is a story I want told," she emphasizes, "because this is the *true* story." Jean Bartel, Miss America 1943, and the first college girl to win the national title, was a member of the Kappa Kappa Gamma sorority at UCLA. During a Lever Brothers War Bond tour of the Midwest, Bartel attended a tea given in her honor by her sorority sisters at the University of Minnesota, while Miss Slaughter met with student government leaders. "I was *delighted* to talk with them," Lenora recalls, "because I was trying to reach the nicest girls in the country, and I knew that through them I would get to the nicest girls." There, the director shared her vision for the Miss America program. "I don't want my Miss Americas to have to take Hollywood careers," she told them. "I want them to *become* something." Lenora recollects that it was "a little girl with her hair pulled back and dark glasses on, never a potential beauty but apparently smart," who offered the suggestion that altered the course of Pageant history. "Why don't you give her a scholarship?" the student leader inquired. "If you want to get the support of schools and colleges, it would be wise to offer scholarships to girls. There are a lot of scholarships offered to boys, but very few offered to young women in this country. You can do something worthwhile with this!"

Lenora was so enthralled with the idea that she "walked out of that room singing"— and oozing with determination to implement the unprecedented concept. When she arrived back in Atlantic City, she pitched the idea to her board of directors. Their skeptical response was that while she couldn't solicit funds in town, if she managed to round up the money elsewhere, she could bring the idea back to them "for discussion." Fuming, Lenora countered, "How do you expect me to go out and tell a nation of businessmen to give me a thousand dollars for a scholarship program when you won't even have approved it until I raise the money?! You expect them to have confi-

Bess Myerson, Miss America 1945, was the first Jewish winner, the first to hail from New York, and the first Pageant scholarship recipient. Myerson's later achievements in television and public service, and her so-called "Bess mess" trial and acquittal, distinguish her as one of the most famous Miss Americas.
CENTRAL STUDIOS

dence in it, when _you_ don't have confidence in it." The iron butterfly prevailed and the board voted unanimously to sanction the scholarship program.

With the backing of her directors assured, Lenora began contacting corporate executives with requests for $1,000 contributions to build a $5,000 scholarship fund. "I sat down and wrote two hundred and thirty-six letters—by hand!" she recalls with a groan. "I didn't have a secretary during the winter because the Pageant didn't have enough money, so I wrote every one myself." Those 236 letters produced the program's original scholarship patrons: Joseph Bancroft & Sons, Catalina, F. W. Fitch Company, Harvel Watch Company, and the Sandy Valley Grocery Company.

By September 1945, the fund was established, and New York's Bess Myerson became the first recipient of a Miss America scholarship. A graduate of Hunter College, Bess later used her $5,000 award for graduate studies at Columbia University. In 1946, the scholarship kitty had grown to $25,000, which was shared by Miss America and fifteen national finalists. A year later, state scholarship programs developed totaling $16,500, with local pageants joining the effort in 1948 with $50,000 in awards. Although Lenora couldn't have foreseen it, her efforts during the war years to scrape together a scholarship fund for her titleholders would develop into a nationwide program providing millions of dollars in scholarships annually.

In 1945, World War II concluded victoriously, and Atlantic City reverted to its former status as a vacation mecca. The postwar years ushered in a myriad of changes that increased public support for the program. The Pageant returned to Convention Hall, where the stage productions mushroomed into spectacular extravaganzas, the judging system was improved by the addition of a fourth ballot for intelligence and personality, and the scholarship fund grew rapidly.

By 1946, the national scholarship fund had expanded to $25,000, which was shared by fifteen finalists and Miss America 1946, Marilyn Buferd. State and local pageants soon joined the scholarship program, contributing over $50,000 in awards. CENTRAL STUDIOS

However, one change implemented during the forties met with hearty resistance from the press. In 1948, in an effort to dignify Miss America's selection, officials altered the coronation scene so that the winner would be crowned in an evening gown rather than a swimsuit. When reporters balked over the change and threatened to boycott the Pageant unless the swimsuit coronation was reinstated, officials thanked the press for their support over the years, but refused to budge. The newsmen made good on their threat, dismantled their newsreel platforms, packed up their cameras, lights, and equipment, and left Convention Hall—while Lenora Slaughter retired to her hotel room "to sweat it out."

At dusk, Pageant publicity chief Mall Dodson called her. "Congratulations!" he bellowed. "You won. The press are all back!"

Apparently, as the sulking reporters and photographers were traveling back to their respective cities, they stopped to phone their editors—and were promptly tongue-lashed, "You get *back* there in a hurry and get those pictures!" That night, an initially unenthusiastic press corps observed the crowning of Miss America 1948, BeBe Shopp, who was attired in a suitably demure evening gown. Soon after, the newsmen approached Miss Slaughter and sheepishly conceded, "Okay, now this is the type of pageant I would be proud to have my own daughter take part in!"

It was a milestone in Pageant history and an important victory for the reputation of the Miss America Pageant. "I was just thrilled to a peanut that we had won," she reports with a triumphant smile. "And Miss America was never again crowned in a swimsuit!"

THE 1950S—THE GOLDEN AGE OF TELEVISION

Like the war era, the fifties ushered in revolutionary changes, the first of which involved Miss America's title, which was officially postdated to allow most of the queen's reign to take place during her actual title year. Thus, in September 1950, Alabama's Yolande Betbeze was crowned Miss America 1951, eliminating a 1950 title.

Shortly after her coronation, Yolande made a startling pronouncement that bolstered Lenora's endeavors to dignify the Pageant. At the time, Catalina featured each Miss America in an annual swimsuit style-show tour of the United States, but Yolande brazenly announced that she had no intention of modeling swimsuits, and preferred to be scheduled for appearances where her extensive operatic training could be utilized. Chagrined, Catalina president E. W. Stewart demanded that she be forced to go on with the tour or be disqualified. The Pageant, however, backed Yolande's conviction that Miss America should be presented with the dignity befitting her title, and ruled that future queens would not appear in swimsuits during their reigns. Catalina promptly withdrew its sponsorship of the Miss America program and formed its own contest as a promotional vehicle for its swimwear fashions. "I understand," Lenora asserts with a grin, "that that little devil Jacque Mercer [Miss America 1949] told him, 'Why don't you go run _another_ pageant?' And he did—and that's Miss Universe!"

Four years later, another significant change altered the course of Pageant history when Miss America was courted by the new-fangled television industry. ABC executives had

During the 1940s and 1950s, judges "interviewed" contestants over meals, swapping tables every few minutes as officials rang a dinner bell. "As I look back on it"—Evelyn Ay laughs— "it was comical that they even thought of trying to serve meals at those occasions... because nobody really ate!" FRED HESS & SON

Twenty-seven million viewers watched Lee Meriwether crowned Miss America 1955 during the Pageant's first live coast-to-coast broadcast on ABC. MISS AMERICA PAGEANT

previously attempted to secure rights to broadcast the national finals for a $5,000 fee, but Pageant organizers rejected their offers, fearing a huge financial loss if the Convention Hall audience stayed home to view the telecast.

However, a chance meeting between Pageant president Hugh Wathen and Paul Whiteman, a renowned band leader and entertainment consultant for the American Broadcasting Company, led to the first live telecast of the competition in 1954. As the men chatted in a Penn-Atlantic Hotel lounge, they discussed the possibility of an ABC broadcast. Realizing that a corporate sponsor would be necessary, Whiteman pitched the idea to the president of the Philco company during a golf game the next day. The executive wisely recognized the benefits of his firm sponsoring the historic event, purchased the television rights for $10,000, contracted to have ABC broadcast the event, and promoted its sponsorship with a new line of Philco "Miss America" television sets.

The first live telecast of the Miss America Pageant couldn't have been timed more splendidly. The broadcast of Queen Elizabeth II's Coronation the previous summer had enchanted viewers around the world and created an epidemic of royal mania in the United States. On the evening of September 11, 1954, a huge viewing audience of 27 million people tuned in to observe the coronation of an *American* queen. Kenn Berry, a Pageant volunteer for over four decades, recalls public reaction to the historic transmission. "The first broadcast of the Miss America Pageant was considered to be one of the big, big stepping stones for the Pageant. Everybody and his mother tuned in to see that Pageant. To think that folks out in Idaho could see this on television was amazing! It just knocked everything off the airwaves."

Pageant officials were delighted with the results of their gamble. The broadcast not only broke records for television viewership, but sold out tickets in Convention Hall as well. "The end of this was that we had more money than we had ever had to pay our bills and have a few dollars extra," says Lenora. To no one's surprise, she reports, "Philco was down there bright and early after the Pageant ready to buy again." While executives insisted they wanted the Pageant "very badly," they bemoaned that they "couldn't *possibly* afford anything more than ten thousand dollars." Then, Lenora recalls, "this young upstart, this new board member Al Marks, got up and made the best speech I ever heard. He was as smart as a whip! Al Marks had his say about what Philco got out of it, what we got out of it, and so forth, and that we could not consider any sum less than twenty-five thousand dollars." Despite their earlier pleas of poverty, Philco's president immediately bellowed, "I'll *buy* it!" So, Lenora grins, "Al Marks became our television hero. After that, he took over television for the Pageant and did one remarkable job!"

Marks once modestly suggested that his involvement in the marriage of Miss America and television began "more by accident than design" after he was approached by Whiteman and invited to assist him in overseeing the broadcast. "I wore the hat of executive producer for stage and television," said Marks, "because then you *could* have absolute control—veto power, if you will." He added with a laugh, "I suppose you could call it a 'benevolent dictatorship.'" At any rate, he reminisced, "television was very much in its infancy. I had no concept of the impact it would have as the years rolled by."

The Pageant's second live telecast introduced two new features—both of which would indelibly etch themselves into the hearts of viewers. The first, ebullient master of ceremonies Bert Parks, was an instant hit—particularly with contestants. "He *wanted* to do a good job," reminisces Lee Meriwether, the reigning queen during Parks's debut, "and he was so endearing. Bert really *cared* about the girls. He worked very hard to be helpful to each one of

The 1958 pageant produced two future celebrities: actress Mary Ann Mobley, who won the Miss America 1959 title, and singer Anita Bryant (second from left)*, who finished as second runner-up.* MISS AMERICA PAGEANT

Perennial television host Bert Parks was hired as Pageant master of ceremonies in 1955 and remained for a quarter of a century. During his debut, Parks inaugurated the theme song There She Is—Miss America. MISS AMERICA PAGEANT

hour." When Wayne submitted his tune to the Pageant in 1954, the producer and music conductor adored it, but arrangements had already been made for the emcee to perform his own composition. Dejected, Bernie nearly gave up—but fate soon intervened.

Months later, as Wayne performed a medley of his tunes at a Park Avenue reception, screenwriter Paul Dudley asked him to play *There She Is*. As the lyrics "Walking on air, she is, fairest of the fair, she is, Miss America ..." fell on a suddenly hushed room, a male voice demanded, "Why haven't I heard this song before?" When Wayne inquired why he *should*

The Pageant's famous theme song, There She Is—Miss America, *by composer Bernie Wayne of* Blue Velvet *fame, was introduced to the public in 1955, when Johnny Desmond serenaded Lee Meriwether, Miss America 1955, with the song during a Philco Playhouse program on Miss America.* PHYLLIS WAYNE

them, to show *them* off, to make them as comfortable as possible. That is what impressed me about Bert," she reminisces with a sigh. "Of course, he sang like gangbusters, but the personality of the man is what I remember as endearing!"

During Parks's debut as television host, he inaugurated the second new feature—a soon-to-be-legendary coronation song, *There She Is—Miss America*. Its composer, Bernie Wayne (of *Blue Velvet* fame), recalls that his inspiration for the song occurred a year earlier when a newspaper article announced the Pageant's upcoming live broadcast. "Although I had never seen a Pageant before," he says, "somehow the words and melody for the song suddenly came into my mind. I wrote it in one

have heard it, the distinguished gentleman retorted, "Because I'm the Miss America *sponsor!*"

With that timely twist of fate, Philco executive Pierson Mapes rescued *There She Is* for posterity. At his insistence, the song was introduced to the nation months later, first when Johnny Desmond crooned it to Lee Meriwether during a *Philco Playhouse* program on Miss America, and again when Bert Parks serenaded Lee's successor, Sharon Ritchie. "The audience reacted to it very well," Adrian Phillips reported. "So well that they just kept it in the show from then on. The more you hear it, the more you realize that it is an extremely *appropriate* piece of music." Indeed, *There She Is* proved so appropriate that, to this day, the tune remains deeply ingrained in the public's perception of Miss America.

The golden era of the fifties proved to be an enormously successful decade for the Pageant. Full state representation had finally been achieved, the scholarship program had reached the $250,000 mark, and television viewership had nearly tripled in five years. "In the 1950s, the Miss America title was at its peak," affirms Neva Langley, the 1953 titleholder. "It was a wonderful time to be Miss America. They hadn't burned their bras yet and there was still some hero worship left. It really was an ideal time for the Pageant."

THE TURBULENT 1960S AND 1970S

The turbulent years that followed weren't such an ideal time for the Pageant. It was an era when society was experiencing the upheaval of radical cultural change. The Vietnam War, antiwar protesters, "hippies," the sexual revolution, and the women's and civil rights movements were carving their messages into the pages of American history, as the nation—and Miss America—struggled to maintain their equilibrium.

The late Albert Marks, Jr., the Pageant's long-time chairman, CEO, and executive producer, was instrumental in ushering the Pageant into the television era. He retired in 1987, after over three decades of volunteer service.
MISS AMERICA PAGEANT

Albert Marks, who was appointed Pageant chairman in 1965, was slapped with accusations that the Pageant was exploitative and degrading to women. During the 1968 Pageant, Atlantic City was invaded by a mob of about two hundred angry feminists who staged a protest in front of Convention Hall. "We were picketed by a number of wild-eyed females out of New York," Marks recalled. "They needed a publicity vehicle to climb aboard that dealt with women—and believe me, they *got* it!" The group, which called itself the "Women's Liberation Front," marched on the Boardwalk, where they refused to speak with male reporters, chanted anti-Pageant slogans, and tossed bras, girdles, makeup, and hair curlers into a "freedom trash can." Marks tried to handle the incident with a touch of humor when he quipped to the press, "It appears that . . . we will be visited by the 'ban the bra' girls. For some reason, these people seem bent upon making women seem less attractive through the questionable process of doing away with underwear."

During the broadcast, despite the presence of heavy security, a cluster of protesters invaded Convention Hall and attempted to disrupt the telecast. "They had security men in every corner who rounded 'em up as they were shouting 'Down with pageants! You're being exploited!'" recalls Irv Kaar, a veteran photographer who observed the scuffle. But before they were hauled outside, he says, the demonstrators managed to toss a stink bomb onto the runway. Fortunately, the disturbance wasn't audible to television viewers, and the broadcast continued without incident.

As the Pageant entered the seventies, the attacks continued to plague the program and its winners. Laurel Schaefer, who won the Miss America title in September 1971, reveals that feminists threatened her life on one occasion and dogged her during her reign. "Back then, the feminists were so rampant. They would start literally bra-burning in front of my motorcades and burning me in effigy. It wasn't *me*," she concedes. "It was what I was representing with the title. But I took it very personally, and it was scary!"

The protests resumed in 1974, when NOW converged upon the resort during Pageant week to conduct a "Wonder Woman Convention." Once again, the feminists marched along the Boardwalk chanting anti-Pageant sentiments and denouncing Miss America as a "degrading, mindless boob-girlie symbol." Ironically, the reigning titleholder at the time, Rebecca King, entered law school the next week with Pageant scholarships, and her successor, Shirley Cothran, earned a doctorate

Phyllis George, Miss America 1971, became the first prime-time female sports broadcaster (NFL Today) and the wife of Kentucky governor John Y. Brown. Here, Phyllis displays her good-luck charm, pet hermit crab "Moonshine," during her postcoronation press conference in 1970. MICHAEL KURTZ

with her scholarship award. NOW's attacks puzzled Marilyn Van Derbur, a former Miss America and educational film producer. "I never could understand why the feminists put down the Miss America Pageant, because they were talking about burning bras and [the Pageant] being just the worst usage of women—and I was talking about the most exciting and important scholarship program for women in America. I really never understood why they tried to bash it."

If critics weren't bashing the Pageant for exploiting women, they were busy calling it "lily white." As the civil rights movement gained momentum in the late sixties, the NAACP pressed for the Pageant to publicly voice its commitment to increasing minority participation. Albert Marks reiterated that, by charter, Miss America was open to women of all races and creeds, and that past national contestants had included American Indians, Hispanics and Orientals. While organizers would love to see a black woman make it to the national level, he said, they couldn't very well "conjure up" such a candidate.

Fortunately, they didn't have to. In 1970, lovely Cheryl Browne won the Miss Iowa title and became the first black to compete in the national contest—an important milestone in Pageant history that fostered an immediate increase in the visibility of ethnic minorities in the program and paved the way for the selection of the first black Miss America thirteen years later.

Although the harsh criticisms aimed at the Pageant during the era were disheartening to

In 1974, two of the Pageant's most accomplished winners shared the spotlight—as feminists protested the Pageant's "degradation" of women. Miss America 1974, Rebecca King, earned her law degree with Pageant scholarships, while her successor, Shirley Cothran, used her award to earn a doctoral degree. EARLE HAWKINS

Cheryl Browne, Miss Iowa 1970, was the first black woman to win a state title and compete in the national Pageant—an important milestone that paved the way for the first black Miss America thirteen years later.
MISS AMERICA PAGEANT

fans, a number of lively bloopers lightened the gloom. In 1967, Bert Parks suffered an embarrassing microphone fiasco during the victory walk of the newly crowned Miss America, Debra Dene Barnes. Albert Marks recalled, "Bert sometimes got carried away a bit when he would sing *There She is*," but in this particular instance, "Bert didn't realize that the technician had installed a short cable. As he backed up, singing away, he paid no attention to the cord on the mike, pulled it out, and ended up singing to a dead mike."

The chairman chuckled at the memory of Bert bellowing what appeared to be a mime rendition of the famous tune. "The audience in Convention Hall never saw it because they were in an uproar at that point—but it sure was a funny sight to see on camera!"

Later, Bert informed a *Chicago Tribune* reporter that his wife received an amusing call about the incident. "We got back to the hotel and Annette somehow got a phone call from this kid down South. He said, 'Miz Parks, how come your husband sang that song for the rest of the country and not for us folks down heah?'"

Then, according to Marks, there was the time the unsuspecting emcee was handed the wrong list of semifinalists. "Through no fault of Bert's, when he was announcing the top ten, they were the *last year's top ten!*" Somehow, during the frenetic moments before the broadcast, the Pageant's librarian had accidentally handed Mr. Parks's assistant the *practice* cards from rehearsals, which were simply copies from the previous year's show. As Bert began to rattle off the names, Marks realized to his horror that the wrong contestants were being announced on live television. "We had contact [with Bert] out of the wings and stopped him cold! I picked up the telephone so fast, I almost broke it! Fortunately," Marks recalled, "the word got to him to stop, and he was given the right cards, but that happened *on camera!*" While the foul-up must have been hair-raising for poor Mr. Parks, it was merely a sample of the occupational hazards inherent to live television. "We apologized," explained Marks, "but those things happen. I hope on a very seldom basis—but they will happen."

While there were both amusing moments and notable successes during the period from the late 1960s through the 1970s, the era, on the whole, was particularly difficult for the Pageant and its participants. Miss Rhode Island 1972, Michele Passarelli, comments on the sen-timents she observed. "They were almost like the wash years of the Pageant. It seemed to me that the times were very anti-Pageant. *Exceptionally* so!"

THE 1980S—AN ERA OF EXTREMES

The eighties proved to be an era of extremes. The Miss America Pageant basked in the glow of some of its greatest triumphs, but the program also suffered some of its most difficult and well-publicized challenges.

The decade started off on a bright note when, during the September 1980 competition, for the first time in Pageant history *two* black candidates placed in the top ten: Washington's Doris Hayes, a talent winner, and Arkansas's Lencola Sullivan, a swimsuit winner. Sullivan cracked another racial barrier as the first black to finish among the top five. Three years later, the scenario repeated itself, as once again, two black candidates made the semifinals. However, this time, as the judges' verdict was announced to the nation, the results were even more historic. Suzette Charles and Vanessa Williams had not only made the top five, but they had emerged as first runner-up and Miss America 1984. Their victories made headlines around the world and proved conclusively that a minority could win the coveted Miss America crown. "We were very proud of her," stated Adrian Phillips, "and it encouraged other girls because it proved to them that there were no barriers. If they have what it takes, they can make it."

Another victory for the Pageant was the impressive growth of its scholarship fund. In 1980, the program awarded just over $2 million in awards, with Miss America receiving a $20,000 scholarship. By 1989, those figures had been increased to over $5 million in available scholarships and a $35,000 award for the winner. In fact, according to Albert Marks, officials did a computation shortly before he retired in 1987 to determine how much financial assistance had been available to participants since the inception of the scholarship program in 1945. He reported proudly, "We estimate about _sixty million dollars!_"

Despite such noteworthy triumphs, the Pageant also experienced a number of somber moments. The first challenge occurred in 1980, when Bert Parks was replaced as master of ceremonies. Organizers felt that, while Parks had done a superb job for a quarter of a century, the television format required updating. However, in an unfortunate turn of events, before Mr. Parks had received a letter informing him of the change, a reporter broke the news to him. A media blitz ensued, with Johnny Carson initiating a "Bring back Bert" campaign, and fans bombarding the national headquarters with phone calls and letters. Despite the howls of protest, chairman Albert Marks held firm, maintaining that his decision was necessary for the Pageant's long-term success.

Fortunately for Mr. Parks, the flood of publicity generated lucrative offers, including hosting positions with other pageants and an appearance in the Marlon Brando film _The Freshman_. In 1990, Parks was invited back to co-host the Miss America Pageant in honor of its seventieth anniversary. His contributions to the program's history thus acknowledged, Parks is enthusiastic: "To have been associated all these years with the grandmother of pageants . . . well, the only feeling could be one of pride and joy, and I'm very happy about that association. But," he quips in mock disappointment, "I've never _won!_"

In 1980, actor Ron Ely replaced Parks as television host before being succeeded by Emmy Award–winning television personality Gary Collins. In retrospect, Collins admits he often "marveled" at Bert's charismatic presence—and the plum position Parks epitomized. "I used to think, 'What a grand job!' It

Emmy Award–winning television host and actor Gary Collins served as the Pageant's emcee from 1982 to 1990. Collins is married to former Miss America Mary Ann Mobley.
MISS AMERICA PAGEANT

never occurred to me that there might be a day when _I_ would be doing it."

Bert Parks was not the only familiar face missing during the 1980s. The celebrated coronation song _There She Is_ was banished in 1982 because of a contractual dispute. During its absence, Miss Americas Debbie Maffett, Vanessa Williams, and Sharlene Wells were serenaded by two other familiar Pageant tunes, _Miss America, You're Beautiful_ and a revamped version of _Look at Her_. However, the public's disappointment was undeniable when the national headquarters was besieged with requests that _There She Is_ be reinstated. Eventually, the dispute was resolved and the famous theme song once again graced the telecast.

The Pageant faced another flurry of publicity in 1982, when the _Dallas Morning News_

In 1983, Vanessa Williams became the first black woman to win the Miss America title. A popular winner, she ended her reign sadly after the publication of nude photos she had modeled for previously. Vanessa has since gone on to achieve success in music, television, and films. EARLE HAWKINS

tion, "you would have thought I'd had a *sex change!*"

When the 1983 Pageant finally rolled around, a weary Albert Marks quipped to UPI reporters, "So far, no problems, thank God. My hide has gotten as thick as a rhinoceros's in the last few years, but it still can be pierced." It soon would be. Six days later, Vanessa Williams was crowned Miss America. Until July of that year, she reigned as one of the most successful queens in Pageant history. Then, the shocking news surfaced that sometime prior to her participation in the Pageant, Vanessa had posed nude for sexually explicit photographs. *Penthouse* magazine, which had purchased the collection, announced that the photos would be strategically published to coincide with the conclusion of Vanessa's reign.

As a hurricane of damaging media coverage ensued, distraught officials were faced with an extremely difficult decision. While they sympathized with Vanessa's predicament, they also had grave concerns that the situation was potentially explosive. Because the long-term suc-

When Vanessa Williams resigned in the summer of 1984, she was succeeded by first runner-up Suzette Charles, who became the Pageant's second black Miss America. Here, Charles receives her crown from Pageant press representative Mary McGinnis. IRV KAAR

reported that the newly crowned Miss America, Debra Sue Maffett, had undergone cosmetic surgery prior to her victory. Despite Debbie's insistence that the supposed "nose job" was merely an operation to correct a deviated septum, the media doggedly pursued the issue throughout her reign. "By the time they were through," she recalls in exaspera-

cess of the Pageant's scholarship program hinged upon the public's perception of its figurehead, Miss America, a prolonged scandal could seriously damage, or destroy, the time-honored program. Regretfully, the board requested that Vanessa submit her resignation.

On July 24, 1984, during a mobbed press conference that was telecast live throughout much of the country, Vanessa Williams informed reporters that, in order to avoid further damaging the Miss America program, she was giving up the crown. Vanessa's first runner-up, New Jersey's Suzette Charles, succeeded her as the Pageant's second black Miss America, and served for fifty-four days before crowning the 1985 titleholder.

One of Vanessa's traveling companions, Midge Stevenson, remembers her as "one of the most admired and loved Miss Americas we ever had."

Yet, she agreed with the Pageant's decision—and with Vanessa's handling of the situation. "I agree with what was done at the time because this _is_ a role model. If anything, young women learned the lesson that if you're heading for a public life of any kind, you've got to be careful about what you do getting there.... The Pageant would have given anything to keep her as Miss America, but could they hold that up as a standard?" Midge points out that while Vanessa could have fought the decision, "she decided on her own that it wasn't worth destroying a tradition, the Pageant.... Had she fought it at that point in time, we would have lost our sponsors and there would have been no scholarships. She is a very bright young woman, and I think she was very aware of all those things. She did what I think was the honorable and graceful thing."

Not content with the damage he had inflicted upon both Vanessa Williams and the Miss America Pageant, Bob Guccione inflamed the situation by announcing that he had obtained slides of one of the 1984 state queens in the buff. If the young lady happened to win, Guccione gloated, _Penthouse_ would publish them. His rhinoceros hide toughened by this point, Albert Marks retorted, "It's a cheap shot on Guccione's part. I don't think he has them. If he does, I'm calling his bluff. Let him _produce_ them!" When the publisher refused to verify his claims with the evidence, Marks complained to reporters, "All he has to do to gain this publicity is when the winner is announced say, 'Oh, that wasn't the girl!' In the meantime, he's gotten the publicity—and we've gotten this grief!" As it turned out, Sharlene Wells, an impeccably wholesome Sunday-school teacher from Utah, became Miss America 1985—and Guccione never presented a single slide to substantiate his claims.

Guccione wasn't the only person to resort to shameless publicity gimmicks. During the live broadcast of the 1988 Miss California Pageant, as the winner was about to be announced, Michelle Anderson, Miss Santa Cruz, reached down into her gown bodice and yanked out a banner proclaiming the message "Pageants Hurt All Women." However, that evening it wasn't the pageant that hurt contestants. It was the revelation that Anderson had coolly plotted her protest for months as she feigned friendship with contestants and volunteers. Later, Anderson admitted in _People_ magazine that she felt a twinge of remorse about her calculating conduct. "People took me into their hearts, and I wasn't who I said I was. I have to ask myself who I was to do this to them."

The incident infuriated Miss California president Robert Arnhym, who explained, "While I respect their right to their point of view, I have a right to conduct this program and my contestants have the right to participate in this program. We do not interfere with their efforts to protest it and they have no right to interfere with our efforts to conduct it." Contrary to what the feminists had intended, the extensive media coverage actually benefited

Leonard C. Horn, a prominent Atlantic City attorney, was appointed the Pageant's chairman of the board, CEO, and executive producer in 1987 upon Albert Marks's retirement. Horn has made significant contributions to the program's development in the years since. MISS AMERICA PAGEANT

the Pageant. "In retrospect," Arnhym reports, "we owe them a great debt of gratitude because they afforded us an opportunity to tell our story from forums and podiums which we would never have had access to. It was a wonderful chance to tell our story."

The dramatic events of the 1980s made headlines time and time again, yet the Pageant managed not only to survive, but to thrive in spite of them. However, in 1987, Albert Marks, who had shouldered the ordeals of the Pageant's most turbulent era, retired from the Miss America Pageant after a quarter century as chairman of the board and chief executive officer. Marks continued his involvement with

the Pageant, serving as chairman emeritus until his death in September 1989. Leonard C. Horn, a prominent Atlantic City attorney, past Pageant president and chief operating officer, and the program's legal counsel since 1967, was appointed to succeed Marks in both capacities.

Horn's appointment was met with enthusiasm throughout the Pageant system. "I have great respect for Leonard Horn," says Eleanor Schaefer, mother of former Miss America Laurel Schaefer. "I think he's going to change things around and it's going to be for the best, because he is an intelligent man who sees things in a new perspective. He is putting the Pageant in context with today's society and today's woman."

THE PAGEANT APPROACHES A NEW CENTURY

As attorney Horn took over the helm of leadership and guided the Pageant into the 1990s, he reaffirmed the program's commitment to the advancement of American women and implemented a number of changes to continue the program's development and broaden its opportunities:

- The establishment of a parent Miss America "Organization" comprising three distinct divisions: the traditional Miss America "Pageant" and "Scholarship Fund," and a new Miss America "Foundation" to expand scholarship opportunities beyond contestants alone.
- A women's advisory committee, composed of prominent professional women, to advise officials on women's issues, program development, and Miss America's reign.
- A Fruit of the Loom "Quality of Life" program, which awards over $60,000 in scholarships annually to young women

whose volunteer efforts, ranging from battling cancer to working with the elderly, improve the quality of life in their communities.

- A $10,000 "Women's Achievement Award" grant to outstanding American women whose volunteer efforts benefit society. Award recipients include former First Ladies Betty Ford and Rosalynn Carter for their work with mental health, breast cancer, and chemical dependency recovery programs.
- A $10,000 contribution to the college attended by Miss America to financially as-

In 1990, Illinois's Marjorie Vincent succeeded Debbye Turner as Miss America 1991. The victories of two consecutive black winners, a historic milestone, occurred appropriately during the Pageant's seventieth-anniversary broadcast. TERRY CHENAILLE

Debbye Turner, the first Miss America to utilize an official issues platform during her reign, encouraged disadvantaged children to overcome economic handicaps by striving for personal excellence. GEORGE SORIE

sist female students, thereby expanding scholarship opportunities to include noncontestants.

- An official issues "platform" to allow Miss Americas to champion social causes during their reigns.
- The requirement that national contestants submit written essays on social issues of particular concern to them.
- An improved judging format that increases the weight of personal interviews while deemphasizing the swimsuit competition.
- The inclusion of an extemporaneous on-stage interview to showcase contestants' understanding of critical issues of the day.

The significant changes currently under way in the Miss America Organization are yet

Gary Collins and Phyllis George welcome back Bert Parks during the Pageant's seventieth-anniversary broadcast. PAUL ABEL, JR.

another link in the fascinating evolution of this great American tradition—a tradition that the late Pageant president Adrian Phillips observed during his seven decades of volunteer service. In 1990, as the Pageant entered a new decade and approached a new century, Phillips pondered the remarkable transformation the program had undergone since he viewed the first Pageant in 1921. "Things evolve," he remarked succinctly. "The press likes to refer to 'changes,' but most everything that has happened has been a precedent of something *evolving*. It *comes* by evolving and it *disappears* by evolving. And *that,*" said the man who had seen it all, "has been the history of the Miss America Pageant."

CHAPTER 3

The Women Who Would Be Miss America

As the Miss America Pageant has evolved since the first competition was staged seven decades ago, the young women who embody the program, their reasons for participating, and how the public views them have also evolved with the times. "As the years move on, things change," says former Miss America Rebecca King Dreman, who observes that each generation of contestants has been "a definite reflection of what's going on in our society," mirroring the contemporary attitudes and ambitions of the American heartland from which they emerged.

For instance, during the tumultuous twenties, when bootleggers and temperance groups battled over Prohibition, women won the right to vote, and uninhibited flappers scorned the constraints of domesticity, the young women who sought the crown reflected the social metamorphosis. Pageant organizers faced a potpourri of entrants ranging from innocent schoolgirls and farm-grown maidens to worldly fashion mannequins, motion picture players, and "professional mermaids." In an effort to sort through the curious mixture baf-

fled officials separated the young women into appropriate categories—"Amateur Beauties" and "Professional Beauties." Sometimes, the clash of styles sparked grumbling backstage—like the year contestants complained they could accept anyone but one of the glitzy New York contenders representing theatrical concerns as the winner. "It's the old antagonism of the outlands for little old New York," explained the *Atlantic City Press,* "and the other contestants can't quite see why any girl from New York can be the queen of typical American girls." As it turned out, homespun charm almost always won the day, with most Miss Americas of the era being of the all-American schoolgirl mold.

Indeed, the preference for a wholesome prototype to represent the "ideal" American beauty was so prevalent during the twenties that judge Joseph Cummings Chase publicly boasted about his panel's choice of Ohio's Mary Katherine Campbell as Miss America 1922. The winner was not only descended from ten generations of American-born ancestors, he pointed out, but she "is possessed of a great vivacity and an inherent shyness that constitute a wonderful combination. She is typically American and altogether an ideal type." The newly crowned "America's Queen of Beauty" was careful to confirm her virtue. "I don't use cosmetics," she assured reporters after her coronation. "I never have and I don't need them." Despite her proclamations of purity, Hollywood filmmakers clamored to glamorize the new queen on-screen. Instead, she spurned their lucrative film contract offers to care for her invalid mother.

Despite the innocence exhibited by most contestants, there was an undeniable undercurrent of craving for life in the spotlight—as illustrated by an informal poll, "Marriage Versus the Movies," conducted by the city paper. It seems that all seventy-four of the 1923 contestants admitted they would gladly pass up marriage for a chance to make good in the movies. Two years later, California's first Miss America, Fay Lanphier, managed to do *both*, appearing in *The American Venus* and in a Laurel and Hardy flick before abandoning Hollywood for matrimony.

By the mid-thirties, when the beauty tournament was reorganized with the cooperation of Variety Clubs showmen, the event had evolved to reflect the nation's growing infatuation with Tinsel Town. Even Pageant officials were smitten with the silver screen. "Once a winner makes good in pictures," Variety Clubs national president John Harris predicted, "the Pageant will assume great importance and attract the finer types of girls." In fact, cinematic ambitions became so prevalent that would-be movie stars emerged as the norm and winners were awarded Hollywood screen tests as grand prizes. Miss America 1936, Rose Coyle, epitomized the sentiments of the era during her postcoronation press conference. "I know I can make it in the movies," she gushed. "All I need is a chance."

In the decade that followed, talent scouts representing Howard Hughes and other Hollywood moguls converged upon the Pageant to search for potential screen stars. A number of winners did achieve recognition in the entertainment industry, thereby bringing the predicted surge of glamorous publicity for the Pageant. Miss Coyle went on to appear with celebrities such as Abbott and Costello and to wed a Warner Brothers executive, Patricia Donnelly appeared in the movie *Cover Girl* and on Broadway, Rosemary LaPlanche signed with RKO Pictures and appeared in eighty-four films, Jo-Carroll Dennison signed with 20th Century-Fox and married comedian Phil Silvers, Jean Bartel starred in several Broadway productions and hosted a TV series, Marilyn Buferd signed with MGM Studios, appeared in fifteen Italian motion pictures, and romanced Roberto Rossellini, and New York's Bess Myerson distinguished herself as a television personality on such programs as *The Big Payoff* and *I've Got a Secret.*

Despite the shift in favor of glamour girls, judges' verdicts reflected a lingering uncertainty about whether America's "Queen of Beauty" should be a sophisticated starlet or the wholesome girl-next-door. During the marriage-mad postwar era, a string of winners from the original motherhood-and-apple-pie mold nudged aside the aspiring screen goddesses. Miss America 1947, Sunday-school teacher Barbara Jo Walker, made it clear that Hollywood wasn't on her agenda when she informed reporters, "There's only one contract I'm interested in and that's the marriage contract." Lenora recalls that Barbara Jo arrived at the contest "with a great big diamond on her hand," and then proceeded to advise the judges "that she was engaged to be married—and *planned* to be married." Undeterred, the panel awarded her the crown. Months later, they met again at another resplendent ceremony—where Barbara Jo became the first Miss America to marry during her reign.

Following their honeymoon, *Mrs.* America

and her obstetrician husband returned to Atlantic City, where Barbara Jo crowned her successor. In keeping with the mood of the times, BeBe Shopp, a Minnesota marimba player, beat out future movie star Vera Ralston Miles for the 1948 crown. BeBe, a bona fide farm girl and daughter of a Quaker Oats executive, remained utterly unaffected during her reign, inviting reporters to the family farm for a demonstration of her prowess plowing fields!

Her successor, Jacque Mercer, managed to follow in *both* her predecessors' footsteps. A country girl who hailed from the X-Bar-X ranch in Arizona, she eloped with her high school sweetheart midway through her reign. Sadly, the marriage was short-lived, and Jacque asked officials to protect winners from such fiascos by prohibiting Miss Americas from marrying during their reigns.

By the 1950s, the public had managed to fuse the contrasting images—Miss America the movie queen, Miss America the bride, and Miss America the farm girl—into a fitting reflection of the golden era. "The fifties were the age of innocence," observes Evelyn Ay Sempier, Miss America 1954, "and that's what they expected Miss America to *be*. Be friendly, be bright, and have that Doris Day, fresh-scrubbed look." Like Day, the quintessential Miss America of the fifties was beautiful but not overtly sexy, unquenchably bubbly yet bright, ambitious but wholesome, interested in both college *and* Hollywood, and devoted to the hallowed institutions of marriage and family.

While the tradition of wholesome feminine beauty has continued unabated in the three decades since, the composition of the national pool of contestants has undergone a significant change in recent years. By the seventies and eighties, entrants had begun to represent an increasingly broad segment of the American populace, with participation by ethnic minorities sharply increased. An unprecedented example of the trend occurred during the 1989 national pageant, when the ten finalists included two Asian-Americans, an African-American, a hearing-impaired classical pianist, and an organ transplant recipient! The judges awarded the crown to Missouri's Debbye Turner, making her the third black Miss America. Yet, a year later, an even more momentous event occurred when Debbye was succeeded by a fourth black victor, Illinois's Marjorie Vincent, the daughter of Haitian immigrants. Turner was moved by the historic results. "The point is that we now are entering a time when no one has to be limited based on the color of their skin, their nationality, their ethnicity—and certainly not their gender."

THE IMPACT OF THE SCHOLARSHIP PROGRAM

Another notable change in recent years has been an increased emphasis on the program's scholarship fund. By the early seventies, spurred on by the success of the women's rights movement, the Pageant had determined to shed its image as a "beauty contest."

As always, contestants' aspirations quickly mirrored that change. "I think being Miss America used to be an end in itself," says Terry Meeuwsen, Miss America 1973, "but women began to enter the Pageant knowing what they wanted to *do* with it. Women wanted to be journalists, commercial artists, lawyers, whatever. They knew what they wanted to do and the Pageant helped them to accomplish that."

Two of Terry's successors, Shirley Cothran and Rebecca King, were perfectly timed examples of the Pageant's maturing image as an effective career springboard. Cothran used her scholarship as Miss America 1975 to earn a Ph.D. in educational guidance, while King became the first national winner to earn a law degree. Now an attorney with the firm Gottesfeld and Dreman, King created a stir in 1974 when, during her postcoronation press conference, she admitted she had entered the Pageant for—gasp!—the *money!* "When I told them that I had entered to get scholarship money so I could go to law school, it was pretty much a shocker! It was big news back in those days, but what I was saying was really supporting the Pageant because I was calling attention to it by saying, 'Hey, this is a *real* opportunity and let's take advantage of it!'"

Indeed, as the scholarship opportunities have received greater recognition, the program has attracted increasingly accomplished women who view their participation as a means to furthering lofty academic and career goals. Admirable examples of the new breed include: Dr. Charmaine Kowalski, a Phi Beta Kappa graduate of Penn State and Harvard Medical School; Debra Cleveland, a physics graduate and aerospace engineer; Dr. Katherine Karlsrud, a graduate of Albany Medical College and a clinical instructor at Cornell; Dr. Sandra Adamson Fryhofer, a magna cum laude chemical engineering major and Emory Medical School graduate; Sophia Symko, a cum laude graduate pursuing a master's in physics; Ligaya Stice, a summa cum laude graduate in chemistry; Janet Ward Black, a cum laude graduate in economics, state-level Rhodes scholarship nominee, and graduate of Duke Law School; Virginia Cha, a Fulbright Scholar and cum laude graduate of Princeton; and Kristin Huffman, a summa cum laude master's of music recipient.

Such outstanding women have become increasingly common in the Pageant over the years, according to Donna Axum, Miss America 1964. Donna, who earned a master's degree with Pageant scholarships, recently served on the national panel and was stunned by the impressive academic credentials today's candidates possess. "It was a real thrill for me to look down those biographical sheets and read the academic backgrounds of these young women," she exclaims. "Their scholastic records are outstanding, and I'm thrilled that the educational emphasis is coming to the forefront!"

A WOMAN OF THE TIMES— ADDRESSING CRITICAL SOCIAL ISSUES

One of the most recent and highly visible developments, the utilization of an issues "platform" for the reigning titleholder, has focused emphasis upon Miss America being a "thinking woman of the day"—a spokesperson for meaningful issues and causes. "I think that's the best thing that ever happened to us," says Dr. Leonard Hill, a consultant who prepares the national judges. "Getting Miss America out of the role that all she does is ride in parades and cut ribbons in car lots—that she can be a spokesperson to *issues* . . . If the current philosophy continues, I think we're going to see the era when Miss America is going to be viewed as a thinking, talented woman. . . . We want to foster the image that [Miss America] is a woman who can think—and we're not afraid for her to think."

As a result, recent winners have emerged as among the Pageant's most articulate and influential representatives by using their reigns to champion social issues of particular concern to them:

- Kaye Lani Rae Rafko (1988), an oncology-hematology nurse for the terminally ill, promoted the nursing profession, raised funds for medical research, visited hospitals and hospices around the nation, and addressed a congressional committee on the nursing shortage.
- Gretchen Carlson (1989), a classical musician and honors student at Stanford

University, promoted fine arts education among the nation's schoolchildren.

- Debbye Turner (1990), a graduate student in veterinary medicine, shared her message, "Motivating Youth to Excellence," with schools and youth groups around the nation, encouraging children to overcome social and economic disadvantages by striving for excellence.
- Marjorie Vincent (1991), a third-year law student at Duke University, spoke out against violence against women, addressing legal groups, lobbying legislatures, and visiting counseling centers and women's shelters.

Because of the new Miss America issues platform such exemplary titleholders will become the norm during the 1990s, according to chairman Leonard Horn. "We are looking forward to continuing this tradition of having Miss America become an activist in today's world, as we believe that a role model has to be." To cultivate that concept, the Pageant now requires national contestants to submit written essays on meaningful issues each would adopt as her platform if chosen Miss America. Essay subjects have ranged from feminism and the environment to gun control and child abuse. "These women have something to _say,_" Horn declares. "That is why we have adopted this program, in order to give them an opportunity to make a difference. . . . Some people in the press continue to misunderstand what we're trying to achieve here. . . . We're giving these young ladies an opportunity to demonstrate—to those few who still need convincing—that a woman can be attractive and intelligent. It's as simple as that."

After seven decades, the Pageant's message that Miss America is an articulate, purposeful, socially conscious woman finally appears to be getting across. A recent _Miami Herald_ article acknowledged that today's titleholders reflect the values and concerns of contemporary American women. HERE SHE IS, the paper's headline heralded, REAL AMERICA.

CHAPTER 4

The People and Powers Behind the Throne

In the public's mind, the words "Miss America" conjure up images of a teary-eyed beauty bearing a crown and roses, but there is another Miss America—the nonprofit Miss America *Organization*. Although a small paid staff works year-round to coordinate national activities, the system's vast nationwide program is operated by civic volunteers and is financially undergirded by American businesses. In fact, a glimpse behind the Convention Hall throne reveals a huge army of volunteers and corporate sponsors, fondly nicknamed the Miss America "family," who keep the shine on Miss America's crown.

THE NATIONWIDE NETWORK OF VOLUNTEERS

The pillars of the Miss America Pageant system are the 300,000 civic volunteers who lavish their dedication and energies upon the program and its contestants. Although volunteers seldom join their contestants in the spotlight, their efforts are the life's blood of the program. "Very few national organizations get volunteers to the degree that the Miss America grass-roots program does," chairman Leonard Horn points out proudly. "There are approximately three hundred thousand volunteers throughout this country who in effect *run* this program. It's a nonprofit corporation and we depend upon the volunteers. These people . . . do this because they love the program and they think it has great intrinsic value. There's no other reason to *do* it," Horn emphasizes, "because nobody is making any money."

Perhaps it *is* a financially thankless hobby, but according to Miss California president Robert Arnhym, who has been involved with the program for three decades, many volunteers are community leaders who enjoy having the opportunity to positively influence the lives of young women. "They are professional people who *give* to their communities, who work in constructive ways to do things for others, and who are proud that they have been able to make a contribution to young lives and to work with the largest women's scholarship program in the world."

While the joys of helping young people are often cited, friendships are an equally meaningful part of the volunteer experience. "We all become excellent friends," asserts

40

Nathan Zauber, executive director of the Miss New Jersey Pageant, and a Pageant volunteer for four decades. "That's another area of the program that is very important and which keeps many of us in it for so many years. We're sisters and brothers. It's amazing, but we *are!* That's why we call it the pageant 'family.' It's a term that was coined accidentally some years ago for the reason that no matter where you're from, no matter what your accent, you have this program in common."

Every September, thousands of members of the "family" pack their bags and make the pilgrimage to Atlantic City for the highlight of their year—Miss America week! For these Pageant devotees, it is more than an occasion to crown a new figurehead—it is an eagerly anticipated family gathering. "The gathering in Atlantic City is a reunion each year," says Karen Aarons, the Organization's executive vice president, "and people really do enjoy it. To see people who come from such disparate walks of life be drawn together by one project is really very rewarding."

Year after year, these devoted men and women work tirelessly to build the runways that launch thousands of starry-eyed ladies on the road to Miss America. Their efforts go largely unheralded, but as former Miss America Maria Fletcher points out, they are the undisputed backbone of the Pageant program. "It is their love, encouragement, and inspiration," she insists. "*That's* what Miss America is all about! The volunteers across the country who love Miss America, and who are very idealistic. That's what Miss America is. We Miss Americas are a part of that—but just a small part."

SEVENTY YEARS OF NATIONAL LEADERS AND VOLUNTEERS

Special recognition is also due the individuals whose vision, dedication, and years of service on the national level transformed Atlantic City's bathing beauty contest into a respected scholarship pageant system and a legendary American institution.

LENORA SLAUGHTER FRAPART

Often described as the "real Miss America," Lenora Slaughter Frapart joined the Pageant staff in 1935 when she was "borrowed" from the St. Petersburg Chamber of Commerce. Promoted to national executive director in 1941, Lenora is credited with transforming the Pageant's image. She built the program's civic volunteer base, achieved full state representation, added the talent competition, and developed the hostess committee and scholarship program. Lenora, who married Pageant business manager Bradford Frapart in 1947, retired in 1967 after three decades of service to the Miss America program.

ALBERT MARKS, JR.

Albert Marks, Jr., a stockbroker and former president of the Atlantic City Chamber of Commerce, became involved with the Pageant in 1952 and was invited to assist with the first live telecast in 1954. Distinguished by his expert contract negotiations with Philco and ABC, he was elected to the board of directors in 1955, as Pageant president in 1961, and as chairman of the board, chief executive officer, and executive producer in 1965. After three decades of unpaid volunteer service, the legendary Al Marks retired in 1987 and assumed the post of chairman emeritus until his death in September 1989.

LEONARD C. HORN

Appointed the Pageant's chief executive officer, chairman of the board, and executive producer in 1987, attorney Leonard C. Horn has already made significant contributions to the Miss America Organization—developing additional scholarship awards and an official issues platform for Miss America, appointing an advisory committee of women professionals, improving the judging format and television presentation, adding onstage interviews, and requiring contestants to submit written essays. His previous posts include serving on the board of directors since 1966, as general counsel since 1967, as president (1979–81) and chief operating officer (1982–87). Attorney Horn is a senior partner in the prestigious Atlantic City law firm Horn, Kaplan, Goldberg, Gorny and Daniels.

ADRIAN PHILLIPS

The Pageant's longest-serving volunteer, Adrian Phillips, worked with the Miss America program from 1922 to 1990, and served as Pageant president and on the board of directors and executive committee. Adrian, who observed the original contest in 1921 and personally knew every winner, remained an active volunteer until his death at age ninety-two in 1990. "He represented the very heritage and legend of the Miss America Pageant," remarks Debbye Turner, Miss America 1990, "and I think we've lost a little bit of that legend in losing him."

BERT PARKS

Bert Parks, a popular TV and radio host (whose CBS program, *Two in Love*, aired opposite the Pageant's first live telecast on ABC in 1954), was hired as emcee in 1955. He introduced the melody *There She Is—Miss America* during his debut, and reigned as television host for twenty-five years before being replaced in 1980 in an effort to modernize the show. In 1990, he was invited back to co-host the Miss America telecast in honor of the Pageant's seventieth anniversary.

GARY COLLINS

Emmy Award–winning television host Gary Collins replaced emcee Ron Ely in 1982 and served as the Pageant's master of ceremonies until 1990. Gary is married to former Miss America Mary Ann Mobley, with whom he has co-hosted previous Pageant telecasts. Host of *Hour Magazine* and *Home*, Collins has also appeared in over one hundred television and motion picture projects, including *Airport, Valley of the Dolls, Roots*, and *Born Free*.

ORIGINAL 1921 PAGEANT COMMITTEE

Thomas P. Endicott	A. J. Feyl
Harry Godshall	Harry Latz
William Fennan	Linton P. Arnold
Louis St. John	Charles Godfrey
Samuel P. Leeds	Willard Eldredge
David Braunstein	A. J. Purington
Fred Packer	William S. Emley

CHAIRMEN OF THE BOARD/CHIEF EXECUTIVE OFFICERS

John R. Hollinger,
  general chairman/chairman of board of governors (1935–39)
Joseph Wagenheim,
  honorary chairman (1958–65)
Albert Marks, Jr.,
  chairman of the board/CEO/executive producer (1965–87)
Leonard C. Horn,
  chairman of the board/CEO/executive producer (1987–present)

PAGEANT PRESIDENTS

John R. Hollinger (1934–39)
Bennett E. Tousley (1940–41)
J. Howard Buzby (1942)
Harry L. Godshall (1943–44)
Arthur S. Chenoweth (1945)
Park W. Haverstick (1946–50)
Arthur G. Broll (1951–53)
Hugh L. Wathen (1954–56)
Howard H. Melvin (1957–58)
Robert Nesbitt (1959–61)
Albert Marks, Jr. (1962–65)

John C. Rowe (1966–67)
Adrian Phillips (1968)
William S. Cowart (1969–71)
Samuel Butcher (1972)
Howard F. Haneman (1973–75)
Carl R. Fiore (1976–78)
Leonard C. Horn (1979–81)
Richard Cummins (1982–84)
Ellen Plum (1985–87)
James J. Lees (1988–90)

EXECUTIVE DIRECTORS
Thomas P. Endicott (1921–23)
Armand T. Nichols (1924–33)
Eddie Corcoran (1935)
George Tyson (1936–41)
Lenora Slaughter Frapart (1941–67)

PRODUCTION/STAGE/TELEVISION/BUSINESS
Adrian Phillips,
    board of directors/committee chairman (1922–90)
William Schoppy Trophies,
    Miss America's crown (1933–present)
J. Howard Buzby,
    producer (1941–53)
George Buzby,
    producer (1953–60)
George Cavalier,
    field director/producer (1961–86)
John Koushouris,
    producer/packager (1961–present)
Bill Muncrief,
    national field director (1962–75)
Bill Caligari,
    field director/production (1969–present)
Richard F. Mason,
    production supervisor (1966–present)
Glenn Osser,
    music director (1955–86)

Don Pippin,
    music director (1987–present)
Bernie Wayne,
    Pageant songwriter
Bob Russell,
    emcee (1940–54)
Bert Parks,
    television host (1955–79)
Ron Ely,
    television host (1980–81)
Gary Collins,
    television host (1982–1990)
Bradford H. Frapart,
    business manager (1949–67)
Robert Bryan,
    business manager (1979–present)
Ruth McCandliss,
    director of field operations (1947–86)
Karen Aarons,
    executive vice president (1985–present)

ATTENDING TO THE NATIONAL CONTESTANTS
Dr. David Allman,
    Pageant physician (1933–71), founder, Allman Medical Scholarships
Mrs. C. D. White,
    founder of Hostess Committee (1937–43)
Mrs. Malcolm Shermer,
    chairman of hostesses (1937–1954)
Elizabeth Alton,
    chairman of hostesses (1954–68)
Mildred Brick,
    chairman of hostesses (1969–78)
Ellen Plum,
    chairman of hostesses (1978–84)
Marilyn Feehan,
    chairman of hostesses (1984–present)
Margaret Taliaferro,
    head wardrobe mistress (1949–89)

PAST AND PRESENT TRAVELING
COMPANIONS TO MISS AMERICA

Harriet Allen	Peggy McMahon
Evelyn Baldwin	Margaret O'Neill
Irene Bryant	Anita Puhala
Jean Dishongh	Eleanor Ross
Carol English	Dorothy Schwager
Joan Grady	Betsy Sherman
June Graves	Betty Simpson
Mary Korey	Bonnie Sirgany
Christina Marks	Margaret Stevenson

THE CORPORATE SPONSORS

In 1945, when Lenora Slaughter pitched the unprecedented concept of a pageant scholarship program for college girls, five farsighted American business firms, Joseph Bancroft and Sons, Catalina, F. W. Fitch, Harvel Watch, and the Sandy Valley Grocery Company, contributed the original $1,000 checks that inaugurated the Miss America Scholarship Fund. In the years that followed, Joseph Bancroft and Sons virtually carried the scholarship program, first by raising its contribution to $10,000 in 1946, and then by actively supporting the program for two decades. Another prominent company, Philco, was responsible for sponsoring the first live broadcast of the Pageant in 1954. Special recognition is also due the Gillette Company, which joined the ranks of national sponsors in 1958 and has remained a pillar of the Pageant program for over three decades. All told, the unwavering support of the nation's finest corporations has been the financial backbone of the Miss America Pageant, enabling the program to make available over $5 million in scholarship opportunities annually on the local, state, and national levels.

1991 NATIONAL CORPORATE SPONSORS

The 1991 corporate sponsors that take pride in their affiliation with the Miss America Pageant program are:

The Gillette Company,
    Personal Care Division
Clairol
Crafted With Pride in the U.S.A.
    Council, Inc.
Chevrolet Motor Division
Fruit of the Loom, Inc.
Keebler Company
Revlon, Inc.
Chesebrough-Pond's USA
General Mills, Inc.
Nouvage Nail Enamel,
    Division of Quintessence
Du Pont

1991 MISS AMERICA SCHOLARSHIP AWARDS

Miss America 1990	$35,000
First Runner-up	$20,000
Second Runner-up	$14,000
Third Runner-up	$11,000
Fourth Runner-up	$ 8,000
Forty remaining contestants	$ 6,000 each
All talent preliminary winners	$ 1,500 each
All swimsuit preliminary winners	$ 500 each
Eight nonfinalist talent winners	$ 1,000 each
One nonfinalist interview winner	$ 1,000

National sponsors also provide a $1,000 scholarship grant to each of the fifty state pageants and a $1,000 fashion award to each of the fifty state winners.

National corporate sponsors support the Pageant in other ways as well. Fruit of the Loom provides additional educational funds through its "Quality of Life" program, which awards over $65,000 in scholarships annually. The firm gives $10,000, $2,000, and $1,000 national scholarship awards and fifty $1,000 state

Suzanne Lawrence, Miss Texas 1990, has a smile as she looks through the Fruit of the Loom Quality of Life Award granting her a $10,000 scholarship at the Miss America Pageant. Fruit of the Loom, a major sponsor of the Pageant, honors contestants for their community service activities. FRUIT OF THE LOOM

awards to young women whose outstanding volunteer efforts, ranging from battling child abuse to caring for the elderly, have improved the quality of life in their communities.

Sponsors also contribute their products and services to benefit contestants. For instance, Clairol cares for Miss America's hair whenever her schedule permits her to visit their New York City headquarters. They also support the hairdressers of the Miss America contestants by having an annual event the day before the Pageant—Clairol's way of saluting the hairdressers' efforts to keep America beautiful. Additionally, Clairol supplies all of the contestants with an array of hair care and styling products for their use during Pageant week.

Other sponsors provide refreshments during Pageant week and present contestants with gifts of their clothing and personal care products. In addition, "Crafted With Pride in the U.S.A." outfits the new Miss America with a four-season "Made in the U.S.A." wardrobe by American designers, and Chevrolet presents her with a new Corvette convertible.

While contestants benefit from the companies' public support, gifts, and educational funds, sponsoring businesses also find their association with Miss America beneficial. Because of the Pageant's unique demographics—an almost exclusively feminine audience of 55 million viewers—Miss America is an ideal ve-

Susan Calandro, manager of Clairol's Technical Training Department, and Marjorie Vincent, Miss America 1991, during a hair-color consultation. RON COHEN FOR CLAIROL, INC.

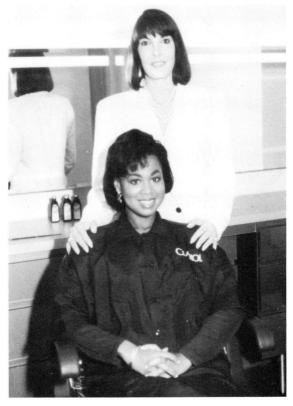

Robert E. Swift, executive director of the Crafted With Pride in the U.S.A. Council, and Miss America 1991, Marjorie Vincent, know it's "Made in the U.S.A." that matters when it comes to superior quality, style, and value in apparel and home fashions. The Crafted With Pride in the U.S.A. Council is a four-year Miss America Pageant sponsor. RANDY BROOKE

hicle for businesses to promote their products. It's smart business from both perspectives, and a partnership that furthers the education of American girls.

Because corporate sponsors play such a critical role, Pageant officials are selective in the type of firms with which they establish sponsor relationships. Their criteria are that sponsoring firms maintain a public posture of supporting education for women, that their executives become personally interested in the program, and that each firm be American-based. "One of the public service issues that we feel are particularly conducive to the Miss America Pageant program is the promotion of quality American-made products," states Leonard Horn. "We have consistently selected companies that are particularly rooted in America,

not foreign corporations. This is an *American* program—and our sponsors are as American as apple pie!"

THE TELEVISION NETWORKS

Television networks have also made significant contributions to the Pageant's development over the decades. Since ABC first broadcast the Miss America Pageant into the homes of 27 million Americans in 1954, network executives and technical teams have played a vital role in increasing the popularity of the program nationwide and overseas. ABC continued its Pageant broadcasts until 1957, when CBS televised the proceedings. CBS, which lengthened the telecast from ninety minutes to two hours in 1958, aired the Miss America finals until 1966, when NBC conducted the Pageant's first full-color broadcast. In the quarter of a century since, NBC's Pageant broadcasts have consistently garnered excellent ratings, with estimated annual audiences of 60 million viewers. In addition to its live coverage of the Pageant in the United States, NBC also transmits the event to Canada, Central and South America, Australia, New Zealand, parts of the Far East, and to U.S. naval fleets and military installations in seventeen nations.

NETWORK COVERAGE

1954—ABC	1967—NBC	1980—NBC
1955—ABC	1968—NBC	1981—NBC
1956—ABC	1969—NBC	1982—NBC
1957—CBS	1970—NBC[3]	1983—NBC
1958—CBS[1]	1971—NBC	1984—NBC
1959—CBS	1972—NBC[4]	1985—NBC
1960—CBS	1973—NBC	1986—NBC
1961—CBS	1974—NBC	1987—NBC
1962—CBS	1975—NBC	1988—NBC
1963—CBS	1976—NBC	1989—NBC
1964—CBS	1977—CBS	1990—NBC
1965—CBS	1978—NBC	
1966—NBC[2]	1979—NBC	

[1] Broadcast expanded from ninety minutes to two hours.
[2] First color broadcast.
[3] Highest-rated telecast—80 million viewers.
[4] TV anchor booth discontinued.

CHAPTER 5

The Miss America Pageant Judging System

Forty—30—15—15 . . . They are the most important "figures" at the Miss America Pageant—the judging percentages that determine which young lady will wear the crown. While Miss America's judicial "measurements" have shifted considerably over the years as officials have updated the judging format, the Pageant has always placed a priority on maintaining a quality judging system at all levels.

DEVELOPMENT OF THE JUDGING SYSTEM

The original judging format, utilized throughout the early twenties, was memorable for its amusing complexity. During a final "measurements check" conducted in a local school auditorium, perplexed judges found the deliberations so difficult that they resorted to measuring the size and shape of contestants' heads, fingers, and feet according to the following formula:

Construction of head—15 points
Eyes—10 points

Hair—5 points
Nose—5 points
Mouth—5 points
Facial expression—10 points
Torso—10 points
Legs—10 points
Arms—10 points
Hands—10 points
Grace of bearing—10 points

Throughout much of the decade, the judging format remained a strictly comparative system, with the reigning Miss America serving as the "ideal" standard against which the candidates were judged. In 1923, when judges admitted they were seeking a beauty exhibiting "carriage, form, health, features, simplicity, character, personality, training, adaptability and distinctiveness," no one could outdo the reigning queen, Mary Katherine Campbell, and she was awarded the crown a second time. The two-time Miss America, judges gushed, was "almost perfection." Several years later, after the retiring queen, Ruth Malcomson, had a spat with officials and refused to return to defend her title, judges were left without their key player and a new voting procedure was hastily devised.

By the mid-thirties, the system had begun to vaguely resemble today's format. Talent was added as an optional, and then mandatory, phase of competition, and the practice of dividing contestants into three alternating preliminary groups was incorporated. Soon after, the five-place ballot system was established, requiring judges to point only the five most outstanding candidates in each competition group:

First place—5 points
Second place—4 points
Third place—3 points
Fourth place—2 points
Fifth place—1 point

By the forties, scoring awarded 25 percent each to talent, evening gown, swimsuit, and personality, with a final ballot to determine the winner. Then, in 1960, talent was increased to 50 percent of preliminary balloting and one-third of balloting during the televised finals. That format remained relatively unchanged until 1986, when officials switched from comparative balloting to the modified Olympian scoring system currently used nationwide.

Talent	40 percent
Interview	30 percent
Swimsuit	15 percent
Evening gown and onstage question	15 percent

The new judging format requires judges to:

- Award a score to _every_ contestant, as opposed to only the top five contestants.
- Judge each candidate only against herself, rather than comparing her against other candidates.
- Award scores from 1 to 10, using whole numbers only.
- Score candidates immediately upon their completion of a segment of competition, rather than waiting until all contestants have finished and then assigning scores.
- Not allow impressions from a girl's performance in one category to influence their voting in a different category.

At the conclusion of the final competition, between one and three auditors, depending on the pageant, tabulate ballot scores and verify that information on the auditor's sheets and original ballots match. There is no final ballot to rerank the top five. The young lady who accumulates the highest number of points wins, the contestant who earns the second highest number of points becomes first runner-up, and so on. As the auditor determines the final standings, he places the list in a sealed envelope and hands it to the judges' chairman, who in turn presents it to the emcee for the official announcement. As the program concludes, the auditor's sheets and final ballots are placed in a sealed envelope, which is stored for safekeeping.

The meticulous attention to honest, effective judging has contributed to the program's record for integrity—a reputation officials work hard to ensure remains unblemished. "Integrity is the most important thing of all," explains Leonard Horn, "so, we spend a great deal of time and effort every year to see to it that the judging system is as fair and unbiased as it can possibly be."

HOW PRELIMINARY JUDGES ARE SELECTED

Because the decision of any judging panel can only be as reliable as the individuals who comprise that panel, the selection of a well-qualified team of judges is an important priority in the Miss America system, and organizers are rightfully finicky about whom they invite to serve.

Panelists traditionally are selected from lists of approved judges who have been authorized by the state organizations to judge local and state contests. These individuals are called "qualified Miss America preliminary judges." The majority of such judges are experienced officers with other local or state programs, but judges may also be celebrities or experts in related fields who, while not being involved with the Miss America system in an official capacity, have professional expertise that gives them valuable insight into various aspects of the competition. Whatever the particular backgrounds of the members of a judging panel, each individual has been selected because of outstanding accomplishments and expertise that equip them to contribute to a balanced, well-qualified panel—and a successful outcome.

It should be noted that, while judging on the local or state level is an exciting and much sought-after opportunity, it is an entirely *unpaid* one. While meals and lodging are provided by the host pageant, judges almost always pay their own travel expenses. (Although some state organizations such as Arkansas and Texas also provide air fare.)

EDUCATING JUDGES FOR THE ROLE

Because judging plays such a critical role in the program, the Pageant expends considerable effort to ensure that local- and state-level judges are knowledgeable and well equipped for their responsibilities.

First, the Pageant has produced an instructional video tape, *And the Winner Is: The Miss America System of Judging,* which Pageant CEO Leonard Horn feels should be mandatory viewing for every prospective judge, because it explains the philosophy of the program and the specific qualities that should be evaluated in each phase of competition.

Judges' training workshops are another popular means of preparing judges, and many state organizations conduct such clinics annually to prepare new judges and enhance the skills of veteran judges. Workshops offer updates on the judging format and instructive speeches by Pageant officials and experts in various competitive categories.

The purpose of judges' clinics and instructional tapes is to foster a unanimity of *quality;* judges who fully understand the philosophy of the program, its judging system, and their responsibilities as the individuals who determine which young ladies step from the runway to the throne.

THE VIEW FROM THE LOCAL/STATE JUDGES' BENCH

Serving as a judge in the Miss America system is both a privilege and a responsibility. The nature of the role necessitates making decisions that affect both the Pageant and the women who offer themselves for consideration. It is a responsibility judges do not take lightly. "They understand that they have the ability to change—*dramatically*—some young woman's life," Horn explains. "They have a major responsibility, and judges fully appreciate the impact their decision-making will have upon the candidates."

Because judges *do* understand the emotional impact their decisions will have upon youthful contestants, the responsibilities of judging can be heart-wrenching—even for veteran judges. "I *hate* judging!" confesses Nathan Zauber, who has judged over four hundred local and state pageants. "I've judged more than anybody in the country, but I hate judging. Because when there are fourteen girls on the stage, one wins and thirteen don't. Even after all these years, I just never get over that feeling of seeing the other thirteen." Why does he continue? "I don't turn down any judging position because I *do* have the experience and I wouldn't be worthy of being in the program if I would take away my experience when needed. But that doesn't mean that I enjoy judging."

Like Nathan Zauber, longtime judge Anne St. Pierre admits that the pressures of making decisions that matter so deeply to contestants often make her physically ill. "Very often I come home—especially if it's been a very close pageant—and I have a migraine for two or three days because I know I've made or broken a young lady."

While the pressures of making or breaking dreams can be intense, the rewards are gratifying. Watching a shaky adolescent blossom into an accomplished, confident young woman is one of the rewards of the judging experience. "It's a thrill for me," says John Moskal, a veteran of fourteen years of judging. "One of the reasons I enjoy it so much is because of the development. You'll see a girl who is awful. She'll tremble at the mike, sing off-key, and almost have cardiac arrest in the interview. Then you'll see her come back, at let's say the Miss California Pageant, and you see the progress! It's such a thrill to see their development!" He adds softly, "It's just like your own child."

JUDGING A FUTURE MISS AMERICA

Sometimes the young woman's pathway leads her directly to the national throne, and the preliminary judges who voted for her back in Starkville, Mississippi, or Elk City, Oklahoma, watch in delight as "their" girl walks the famous Convention Hall runway as Miss America. It's one of the reasons so many pageant "family" members travel to Atlantic City each September, according to North Carolina's "Miss Pattie" Ruffin, who has judged over three decades: "We all go to see the girls from the different states—and *you bet* I'm hoping that one I judged will be Miss America. Lord, that would be great! Something you dream about!"

For a handful of local and state judges each year, the dream *does* become reality when they find themselves looking into the eyes of a contestant they *know* is destined for the throne. Bob Wheeler, whose judging experience spans three decades, holds the distinction of having judged four Miss Americas on the state level. When Wheeler served on panels that sent Susan Powell, Terry Meeuwsen, Dorothy Benham, and Cheryl Prewitt on to Atlantic City, he instinctively sensed he was watching a Miss America–in–the–making. Terry Meeuwsen was so outstanding, he says, "that she raised the hair on my arms when she sang. I actually sat on my hands!" Likewise, Cheryl Prewitt left Wheeler with no doubt that he was looking at the young lady who would earn the crown in Atlantic City. "I remember sitting there thinking, 'Okaaay, I wonder who's going to be the *first runner-up?*' "

While veteran judges often recognize a future queen when they encounter one, the experience of serving on the panel that actually sends her on to the national pageant remains a thrilling—but rare—occurrence. According to B. Don Magness, past chairman of the Miss Texas Pageant, who has judged over six hundred pageants nationwide, "You get caught up in them, but whether or not you have a Miss America is just luck—being in the right place at the right time." When it *does* happen, however, the experience of having contributed to the making of a Miss America is an unforgettable thrill. The glory belongs to the champion, but it's sure nice to bask in the realization that you somehow contributed to the dream. "You like to sit back and think you played a part in it," says Magness, "no matter how small that part was."

THE PEOPLE WHO PICK MISS AMERICA

Each year, there is one group of people who play more than a small part in making the dream come true—the national judges who determine which young lady will wear the Miss America crown. Over the decades, some of our nation's most distinguished individuals have served on Pageant panels: Grace Kelly, Joan Crawford, Norman Rockwell, Merv Griffin, Eileen Ford, Elizabeth Arden, Deems Taylor, George Balanchine, Arthur Fiedler, Peggy Fleming, Sidney Sheldon, Ed McMahon, Brian Boitano, Lili Fini Zanuck, and Dr. Joyce Brothers.

Being a celebrity judge may appear to be a glamorous job, but it is never an *easy* one—as experience has illustrated. One early panel found the assignment so tough that they deliberated from late afternoon until midnight, forgoing meals in the process, only to emerge from their box to face jeers from the audience. Film star Grace Kelly, who served as a judge in 1954, reportedly snapped several pencils under the strain, and in 1960, Hollywood cosmetics king Bud Westmore suffered a heart attack on Pageant morning. Even the ever-so-stoic Joan Crawford described the effort of choosing among fifty "extraordinary" contestants as "a wrenching, harrowing" experience.

Today, as the program enters the 1990s, the job of selecting Miss America remains as arduous as ever. "I found judging very difficult," confesses recent national judge Phyllis George. "My heart was in my throat the entire time! I found it tremendously stressful because you really have to have total concentration. You can't waver your attention for a minute. And I knew, more than anyone on that panel, that we were going to change that young woman's life! You have to study and make such quick decisions—and those decisions will affect their lives. So, I took it very, very seriously!"

During the late Albert Marks's quarter century as Pageant chairman, he observed that the experience of serving on a national panel invariably left judges with a deepened appreciation for the program: "Some of them come here with a bit of disbelief, wondering, 'What am I doing here? I'm taking a week of my time and it's a bunch of fluff,' when they first arrive. But they don't *leave* here feeling that way. After they get a chance to talk to these women, they leave dedicated people. It very definitely changes their perspective."

SELECTING A NATIONAL PANEL OF JUDGES

How do Pageant officials select the judges who will choose Miss America? According to Leonard Horn, because of the importance of compiling a well-qualified panel, the Pageant "carefully monitors, to the greatest degree possible at the national level, the type of people who are asked to be judges." As officials consider various individuals for the job, they carefully evaluate and balance their areas of expertise to ensure that the panel has the knowledge and experience necessary to render accurate decisions. According to Horn, "We are looking for people who are intelligent, who have integrity, who bring good common sense into the judging panel, and who have some degree of experience with the various types of competitions that we run in the Pageant."

Recently, the chairman altered the national judging format in an effort to boost judges' credibility with viewers. Some of the biggest names in entertainment, athletics, business, and the arts were invited to serve on the national panel, but problems with their limited availability prompted another change. "Few people of this caliber are able to give us a full week of their time," Horn explains, "so, we went to the _two_ judging panels in an attempt to attract prominent judges for the finals on Saturday night."

The innovative system utilizes dual teams of judges with differing qualifications and purposes. The first panel, comprised of extremely qualified but lesser-known individuals, evaluates contestants in the private interviews and three evenings of preliminary competitions. Their overall scores determine the ten finalists, while their interview scores are carried over to Saturday evening's tabulations. The celebrity panel judges the top ten in talent, swimsuit, and evening gown during the televised finals, and their scores are added to the preliminary panel's interview scores to determine Miss America and her court.

Contestants embraced the change as an improvement on the dynamics of judging. "I think the new judging system is wonderful!" said Marlise Ricardos, Miss California 1988. "Having one panel choose the top ten and a separate panel on the final night is good because it prevents any individual from carrying on a favorite. The new panel comes in with an unbiased opinion, takes a look at the contestants as a brand-new group, and decides who they believe should be Miss America."

Leonard Horn has been pleased with the results, which he describes as a "high caliber" of judging panel with the ability to present the Pageant with "nothing but the best."

PREPARING THE NATIONAL PANEL

Once the official roster of judges has been determined, the process of preparing those individuals for their role begins. First, in order to acquaint them with the women they will be evaluating, members of the panel are sent copies of the contestants' résumés. Then, as the two teams of judges arrive separately in Atlantic City during Pageant week, they each undergo in-depth "orientation" sessions that explain the program's philosophy and judging format, and the general qualities being sought in the winner. According to Dr. Leonard Hill, a veteran official who supervises orientation, the emphasis is upon the _essence_ of the national titleholder. "During the very opening of orientation, we always discuss 'Who _is_ this woman we call Miss America?' "

Orientation sessions offer judges general guidelines to prevent the clashes of images that occurred in decades past, when, as Marilyn Van Derbur recalls, "judges would come in with their own perceptions." For instance, when Marilyn judged in 1964, she was "astonished" by how diverse judges' expectations for Miss America could be. While Marilyn envisioned Miss America as "a cheerleader type, girl-next-door," another judge, a male television executive, had a different image in mind. "His perception was more of what I'd call a beauty queen...This long-haired, kind of slinky [type] who wandered down and looked deeply into your eyes. We just had totally different ideas!" Today's improved method of preparing panelists eliminates such judicial guesswork. Dr. Hill impresses upon judges that the young woman they honor with the crown must be "a vital, thinking woman with opinions, values and ambitions—a woman of the day."

In addition, Albert Marks explained, judges are encouraged to consider whether a candidate possesses the maturity to handle the demands of her exhausting, and often unglamorous, reign. "We try to get into the judges' minds that this is a balanced human being who should do as well before the Rotary Club on a blizzardy night in January as she does under the television lights on that night in September."

By Saturday, the second panel of judges has emerged from orientation with a firm understanding of the criteria their choices for Miss America should meet. They have also reviewed previously taped interviews of the top ten candidates and attended a "monitored discussion" with the first panel. Finally, they are put through a practice run to work out any kinks *before* they enter the judges' booth that evening. "We have them practice scoring a few ballots," explains judges' co-chairman Ellen Plum, "so there are no surprises when they get in that box."

Hours later, with their preparations completed, judges are escorted into Convention Hall, where, as millions of critics look on, they cast the ballots that affect the lives of fifty anxious young women. However unnerving the task may be, panelists undertake it with the confidence that their decisions have the unwavering support of the national leadership. As two-time national judge Sam Haskell recalls,

"They told us, 'We have entrusted to you the responsibility of picking Miss America. We want you to pick the one girl who you feel best exemplifies what we stand for. We will honor your decision and support it one hundred percent.'"

At the conclusion of the evening, as television credits roll and a mob of well-wishers surrounds one ecstatic young woman, a weary group of individuals emerges from the judges' box with the thrilling memory of having transformed a starry-eyed young lady into American royalty. For Haskell, the experience—however challenging—was an unforgettable highlight of a lifetime. "It's quite a heavy responsibility," Haskell acknowledges, "but we judges know that we've done something very special that will become a part of history. I know that I am directly responsible for completely changing the lives of two girls in this country who became a part of the tradition of being Miss America—and that makes me feel *great!*"

In 1935, talent was introduced as an optional event. MISS AMERICA PAGEANT

PART II

COMPETING IN THE
MISS AMERICA PROGRAM

CHAPTER 6

The Private Interview

The first phase of competition in the Miss America Pageant is a series of private interviews conducted between judges and contestants prior to the three onstage competitions. Weighted at a hefty 30 percent of tabulations on the local, state, and national levels, the personal interviews are frequently likened to crucial career interviews. "Every contestant who enters the Miss America Pageant system is applying for a position as a local, state, or national titleholder," explains Karen Aarons, "and each time she has a judges' interview, she is essentially having a job interview for a job which may change the direction of her life." Furthermore, although it is a 1-in-80,000 long shot, there is the possibility that the "job interview" may promote the contestant to the ultimate plum position—Miss America. "That's all part of the stark realism of the interview," remarks Bill Wolfe, past chairman of the Miss Florida Pageant. "It's part of what I like to call the application for a two-hundred-thousand-dollar-a-year job. That little girl who comes in to interview is applying for the title of Miss America—and if she goes all the way, her life will be dramatically changed!"

Because the interviews are the first and most revealing phase of competition, they offer judges a crucial opportunity to assess which young woman is best equipped to undertake the responsibilities of the crown she seeks. As they meet with candidates, panelists consider many specific qualities: overall first impressions, personal appearance, personality, speech, vocabulary, grammar, interpersonal skills, intelligence, and general knowledge and understanding of the issues of the day.

The practice of arranging for judges to chat with the candidates has been an aspect of the Pageant since the early 1920s. However, over the years, the particular format for such meetings has varied considerably. For instance, in 1921, when beauty of face and form were the only qualities evaluated, judges were allowed to converse with the contestants, but the impressions of their personalities were not officially balloted.

As the program gradually expanded its format to include personality and intelligence, interviews emerged as a legitimate phase of competition. At first, these "interviews" were merely formal breakfasts, luncheons, or dinners where judges rotated tables every few

Rosemary LaPlanche, Miss America 1941.
MISS AMERICA PAGEANT

minutes throughout the meal in order to mingle with all fifty candidates. In 1946, national judge Earl Wilson described the experience to *Atlantic City Press* readers: "I'd just sat down at one table with six girls when one of the officials rang a bell and said, 'Time's up. Move to the next table.' I kept moving so much I didn't get anything to eat. It was the most wonderful breakfast I ever *didn't* have."

Not surprisingly, from the contestants' perspective, the atmosphere resembled an odd cross between an ever-so-proper social affair and a verbal hockey match. "Oh, to me that was the *worst!*" groans Marian McKnight Conway, Miss America 1957. As Pageant officials rang their bells, judges gamely swapped tables and jittery contestants vied to outshine each other. "You're sitting there trying to eat breakfast and at the same time trying to appear alert and tuned in to what's happening," she recalls. "It seemed that the minute you'd pick up a fork of anything and put it in your mouth *that's* when the judge would ask you a question!" And what questions! Judges "tested" contestants' wit and intelligence by asking them to answer questions, solve riddles, and occasionally to perform brief pantomimes. "It was *grueling,*" Evelyn Ay Sempier, Miss America 1954, recalls with laughter, "because the judges were free to create any kind of conversation that they wished." Inevitably, the fast-talking contestants managed to steal the spotlight. "The people who were really the most glib could pick up on anything and run," remembers Marian McKnight. "There was a lot of interrupting. It was really funny!"

The most humorous part of the situation, according to Evelyn, was the evening menu. "You wouldn't believe it," she reminisces with a laugh, "but on the final night, I guess they were going to give us the greatest treat of our entire lives—so they gave us *lobster tail!*" And *not* neatly removed from the shell, she points out. "Here's this meat inside of this thick crust.

We all giggled and laughed about it because we didn't know what we were going to *do* with it! Needless to say, few of us had any of it. As I look back on it, it was really comical that they even *thought* of trying to serve meals at those occasions . . . because nobody really ate!"

What Marian found bewildering about such "interviews" was how the judges could retain accurate mental observations about fifty women without benefit of written remarks. "It boggled my mind that none of the judges were taking any notes at all," she recalls in amazement. "I thought, 'Oh boy, they must be smart to remember everything that everybody said today.'" She speculates, "Maybe between tables they wrote very fast when nobody was watching, but I never saw any pencils. They must have committed everything to *memory*." Has her experience serving as a national judge changed her perspective on the task? "*Uhhhg!*" she admits with a shudder. "I start shaking just at the thought!"

Eventually, the meals with judges were discontinued and private interview sessions introduced. "I think somewhere along the line," Marian suggests with a giggle, "one of the judges must have said to an official, 'I think there's a better way to do the interview portion of this contest,' so I'm sure that's when they started the organized interviews."

During the 1960s, interviews were conducted on the afternoon of the candidates' appearance in the evening gown competition, with contestants being interviewed in groups of three. While the format was altered in 1970 to allow the young women to meet individually with the panel, their interview scores were not considered during the televised finals. Then, after a fast-talking future lawyer named Rebecca King won the 1974 Miss America crown and dazzled the press throughout her reign, interview scores were officially retabulated during the final competition. "I think it became very apparent that Miss America talks more than she does anything else," remarks King, "and the young woman needs to be able to represent herself and the Miss America Pageant. If she can't do that, she's in big trouble!" Becky chuckles. "I talked myself blue in the face and that next year the interviews did count as points toward the title."

The new format, which retabulated interview scores during the evening gown competition, appropriately produced a number of outstanding winners: Shirley Cothran (1975), who held a master's degree at age twenty-one and obtained a doctoral degree after her reign; Tawny Godin (1976), who had a 4.0 GPA at Skidmore College and was conversant in six languages; and Susan Perkins (1978), who held a degree in biology and worked as a speech writer for the Ohio State Senate.

According to Dr. Leonard Hill, who prepares the national judges, as the image of Miss America has continued to develop as the "well-balanced, thinking woman of the day," the interview segment has taken on even greater significance in the voting process. For instance, in 1987, when Kaye Lani Rafko earned the Miss America crown, the value for interview scores had been increased to twenty-five percent of the final evening's balloting. "I was told that it was my interview that really made the difference," Kaye Lani says, "because I was first overall in interview. They said I was several, several points higher than anyone else, and that was what pulled me through."

By the close of the decade, the value of the personal interviews had been further increased to a record 30 percent of balloting—a format change that resulted in the most academically impressive top five in Pageant history. Miss America 1990, Debbye Turner, was a veterinary student just months short of becoming "Doctor" Turner, and her court of honor included summa cum laude graduates, National Merit Scholars, a Fulbright Scholar, and two recipients of master's degrees. Because of

the growing emphasis on intelligence and articulateness, Hill explains, the approach to judging the interview competition will evolve accordingly during the next decade. "I think you'll see the system refine itself and be more exacting."

FROM THE JUDGES' PERSPECTIVE

As the image of the Miss America program has evolved and refined itself, interviews have taken on increasing importance. Because a local, state, or national titleholder is in constant contact with the press and public, judges consider a contestant's ability to communicate in an intelligent, competent manner to be of crucial importance—and the interviews provide an ideal opportunity for them to evaluate whether the ladies possess the qualities necessary to serve successfully as the titleholder. "Miss America will spend most of her time as a public relations person, speaking to groups, to issues, to causes," Dr. Hill explains. As such, "I think the interview gives [judges] the first glimpse of whether the girl can handle the job."

Former Miss Americas who serve as judges are particularly inclined to stress strong communication skills because they appreciate from personal experience how critical such qualities are to women who are constantly under public scrutiny. "I happen to _know_ what is expected of a young woman as she travels this country," says Evelyn Ay Sempier, "I know that she has to have the ability to answer well and to be morally grounded to make that opinion. She has to have a depth in her thought process. She cannot be just all fluff and frill." She jokes, "I mean that will get you a long way, but, finally, when you're out in the rain, you'd better know how to put up the umbrella—and quickly!"

That desire for a winner who displays

more than physical beauty has been a recurrent theme in the remarks of many recent national judges.

Blair Underwood: "They're all beautiful. We know that. But what's important is what's *beyond* that."

Dr. Joyce Brothers: "Because it's such a large scholarship, I think all of us are looking for the entire woman, the well-rounded woman with a *mind* behind the pretty eyes."

Donna Axum: "I think it's terribly important that the young woman, as Miss America, have excellent communication skills, that she be intelligent and have an in-depth grasp of what's going on in the world around her and have opinions on those issues."

Rick Lester: "I think we wanted to find someone who was articulate.... Whoever is chosen Miss America is going to spend a year representing this country ... and she had better be able to attach a noun and a verb together in a way that's not going to embarrass either herself or the Pageant."

In order to allow judges to evaluate carefully such intellectual qualities, the method of interviewing has been subtly altered to "get to the *depth* of the individual." Dr. Hill points out that until recently, the interviews tended to be "a lot of one-way directed questions, which a lot of times was playing back their résumés or demonstrating that they had read the latest issue of *Time*." Now, judges are instructed to ask "high gain" questions, "to phrase questions in such a way that she extends the dimension of herself."

For instance, rather than inquiring what a contestant thinks of surrogate motherhood, an approach that would allow the young lady to deliver a "canned" answer, Hill suggests probing deeper by rephrasing the question: "If your sister asked you to be a surrogate mother because she was childless, what things would you consider in answering your sister?" That, he

explains, would allow judges to determine "if she understands the whole issue of surrogate motherhood, and, two, to learn a little bit more about her value system and what kind of thinking woman she is." Hill is pleased with the results of the new approach. "By changing the complexion of the interview, I think we are going to break the illusion that you can program girls for this."

As expected, contestants who had assumed judges would inquire about their "positions" on the top issues of the day were startled to find panelists probing in earnest for the young women's thought processes and personal values. "Obviously, the judges were using a certain technique of interviewing that none of the contestants were used to or had been prepared for," remarks Maya Walker, first runner-up to Miss America 1989. "I think maybe they did that on purpose to really see what our reactions to particular issues or subjects were so that they would *know* that our answers and feelings were true—and not something we'd thought out for the last three months getting ready for the interview."

It should be pointed out that judges do not weigh the opinions of each contestant per se, but rather the *thinking* process evidenced in arriving at her convictions. "I stress very strongly," Hill explains, "that as a judge, it is never their place to agree or disagree with that girl. The judges' opinions are irrelevant. Their concern is: Does she have a position that she can express well and defend? Does it make sense? Is it logical? Was she able to express it to you in a way that you understood it? Did you learn something new about her and her values as a result of her answer?"

The benefit of such an approach, Leonard Horn observes, is that judges have a valuable opportunity to view the young women as *individuals,* with unique attitudes, values, beliefs, and outlooks on life. "Therefore, it gives an insight into the depth of the woman's character which I don't think the other competitions are able to achieve."

As crucial as intellectual skills are, they are not the only qualities scrutinized during interviews. Panelists also consider a number of other intangible personal traits during their scoring. "The judges are looking for that unique individual," says Karen Aarons. "They are looking for a young lady who has something special about her that makes her stand out from the rest of the contestants."

Former Miss America and national judge Rebecca King Dreman agrees that winners almost always possess a certain timeless charm that sets them apart. She puns, "There is an attraction—I hope it isn't *fatal* attraction—but an attraction. You can put a Miss America in a room with a group of other attractive women and you'll find you will know exactly who she is. It's almost like a magnet. There is an inner beauty, an inner glow—that intangible [quality] that you can't describe, but you know it when you come across it."

Bill Wolfe cites an example of a former Miss America who radiated that rare, but unforgettable, quality. "Every once in a while in life you meet people who, when they walk into a cocktail party, you know *somebody* has arrived. . . . I was sitting in a suite in Little Rock, Arkansas, where I was going to judge the Miss Arkansas Pageant, and Cheryl Prewitt walked into the room. Sitting here eight years later, I get chill bumps. When this lady walked into the room, you knew that *somebody* was in that room!" He recalls the warmth of her response to his respectful handshake. "She looked at my badge and said, 'Hey, Florida! Gimme a hug!' "

Cheryl's warmhearted gesture illustrates the quality 1988 national judge Deborah Norville believes is critical to Miss America's role. "I think all of us [judges] are looking for a woman who is someone you'd want to have over at your house if you had the opportunity to do that. . . . Someone who has the ability to

make people feel comfortable because that is what Miss America is. She is an ambassador for this program, and it is going to be her job to make people feel at home wherever she is."

Not surprisingly, the private interviews are where that special magnetism becomes most evident. "There is an aura that comes across in the interviews that I'm sorry to say you don't see onstage," affirms Marian McKnight Conway. "Once in a while, somebody will walk into the room as you're doing interviews and you just say, 'If that's not *her,* she's really close up there!' "

As a case in point, Laurie Schaefer shares a revealing conversation she had with two of her national judges shortly after her victory in 1971. "I can remember Art Fleming, and I think it was Edward Lobe, who said that I had so impressed them in the interview that they had gone back to their hotel after the interviews were over, marked my name on a piece of blank paper, put it in a sealed envelope, and put it in their desk." Days later, when Schaefer won, the perceptive judges produced their sealed predictions and informed their spouses, "That was after the interviews. I picked her *then* as Miss America." From experience judging two recent Miss America Pageants, talent agent Sam Haskell agrees with Fleming's observation that the biggest battle for the crown really *is* waged offstage. "I feel that Miss America is *won* in the interview."

PREPARATIONS FOR THE PERSONAL INTERVIEW COMPETITION

Like their counterparts on the national level, local and state judges also stress the significance of personal interviews—and the importance of contestants being at their best in that competition. "We tell them that they are interviewing for a job that will be worth about one hundred thousand dollars plus a year if they become Miss America," says Miss Arkansas executive director Bob Wheeler. "They've got to do their best in interview—because they're only going to get *one* chance at it!"

Because the interview is perceived as critical to victory, the prospect of facing a table full of eagle-eyed judges with pens and ballots poised in hand can be the most intimidating aspect of competition. However, according to Tom Hensley, president of the Miss Tennessee Pageant, *preparation* can transform interview jitters into relaxed self-confidence. "The only way they can relax is to be confident, know what to do when they go in there, and to be knowledgeable. Because when you're *prepared,* you're relaxed." Hensley explains that such preparation simply involves the contestant's becoming informed about the major issues facing society, exploring how she feels about those issues, and learning to articulate her opinions. "They cannot go through life—or be Miss America—if they're completely oblivious to what is going on in the world around them. They have to be knowledgeable to formulate opinions and be able to articulate them. Your Kellye Cashes, your Kaye Lani Rafkos, and your Gretchen Carlsons are prime examples. They are people who are knowledgeable about what is going on in the world."

Cultivating a knowledge of social and political issues is not as difficult as contestants might expect, says Joseph Sanders, president of South Carolina's program. "The things that we ask our girl to do are these: 'Make sure you read the newspaper every day, make sure you watch the evening news every day, and read at least one news magazine every week. Make sure that you know what the issues are today and answer the questions the way you feel. You need to be aware of what's happening in the world, and if you do that you'll do fine.' It's just not that hard."

Once the young lady has familiarized herself with the issues of the day, the interview

becomes an enjoyable challenge. "When I've worked with girls to prepare them for national-level interviews," says Vernon DeSear, a past Miss Florida Pageant vice president, who boasts a decade of experience preparing state winners for Atlantic City, "I always tell them that if they have initially done their homework, if they have prepared themselves in the right manner, then they will *enjoy* the interview. The girls who do well in Atlantic City usually *adore* interview, and they come out saying, 'Oh, it was just wonderful! I had the best time, and they were so nice!' "

Consider the case of Carla Haag, Miss Mississippi 1988. When Carla emerged from her private interview, she insisted her conversation with the judges had been one of the most enjoyable aspects of her experience at the Miss America Pageant. "You know, people think the interviews are like a firing squad!" she jokes. "But I was glad to be there. I just walked in and we had a conversation. It wasn't really like judges and contestant. It was more personal: 'Well, how do you really *feel* about this?,' which gave me an opportunity to express some views I had. It was every bit as relaxed and fun as I wanted it to be—and it was exciting!"

BENEFITS OF THE INTERVIEWING PROCESS

While the interview competition provides contestants with opportunities to impress judges and gain points toward a local, state, or national pageant title, the process of *preparing* for pageant interviews offers contestants several important lifelong benefits.

First, pageants provide an environment for college girls to develop the strong communication skills they will need to excel in career interviews. "We try to help our girls develop the composure, calmness, and inner confidence to be able to interview well for a job or to talk with the press," explains Adair Brown, executive director of the Miss Colorado program. "It's no secret that in order to be good in interview, contestants have to work at it—but once they _become_ good in interview, it's a quality that will benefit them for their entire lives."

Former Miss Arkansas Christi Taunton affirms that the experience of preparing for Pageant interviews was critical in helping her beat tough competition for a position with a major pharmaceutical firm. "There is no doubt in my mind that I would not have been hired if I didn't have the experience I gained in the Pageant," Christi reports. "But because of the confidence I gained ... I walked into that job interview and I _handled_ it! There is no doubt in my mind that if it hadn't been for the Miss America Pageant, I would not have this job. That makes it worthwhile for me—to know that I used the experience I gained from that year to go on with my life."

Preparations for Pageant interviews serve another purpose. During an era when the Times Mirror Center for the People and the Press issued its findings that today's youth are less knowledgeable and more apathetic than previous generations, preparing for interviews encourages contestants to expand their intellectual horizons and learn more about the world and their place in it. Lee Beaman, Miss North Carolina 1988, elaborates: "Through the teen years, so many of us are trying to find out who we are and what we stand for. In our teen years, we're usually not very interested in current events and political issues. The Pageant has really helped me with that, because to form opinions on those things, you have to find out what your basic beliefs and values are and develop an awareness of what's going on in the world today."

That emphasis on political awareness and personal development is applauded by Deborah Norville, who believes that it is one of the program's most valuable contributions to participants. "To walk into that room and sit in front of those judges and spew your ideas about the world, your community, your role as a woman, and the United States's role in the world requires an awful lot of inward evaluation," she remarks. "That, in and of itself—whether these girls ever make it down the runway—is a positive thing because when you know yourself, you are going to be able to be in tune with what it is that you want to accomplish in life." In fact, Norville says, "_That_ is where I think the greatest value for this program comes."

CHAPTER 7

The Swimsuit Competition

The first onstage competitive event in the Miss America Pageant is the swimsuit competition, where each candidate individually models a swimsuit of her own choice before the audience and judges. The segment is currently valued at 15 percent of tabulations on the local, state, and national levels, making it one of the less significant phases of competition. Nevertheless, officials insist that swimsuit is a justifiable event that affords judges an opportunity to assess whether the contestant has the following qualities:

- The perseverance and discipline to maintain a physically fit and healthy physique.
- A proportioned physique with muscular development and weight appropriate for her height and bone structure.
- Attractiveness of face and figure.
- Poise, good posture, and grace of carriage.
- Composure and confidence onstage.

As the oldest event in the Pageant, the swimsuit competition dates back to the origi-

nal National Beauty Tournament in 1921, when newspaper editors invited young ladies to compete for the title of "the most beautiful bathing beauty in America." "It got started as a publicity gimmick, by somebody saying, 'Let's have a Miss America, and let's put her on the beach!' " explains Leonard Horn. "And if you're going to be on the beach in the summertime," he adds with a shrug, "you might as well put on a swimsuit!" Since that first contest, the swimsuit competition has become a deeply entrenched American tradition—and one that has reflected accurately society's ever-changing standards for women's figures, fashions, and exercise.

THE SEARCH FOR THE PERFECT SWIMSUIT

The competition has been particularly reflective of preferences for swimwear fashions. During the Pageant's early years, contestants pranced along Atlantic City's beaches attired in knee-length bathing ensembles—baggy wool tunics jauntily sashed at the hip and coordinated with bloomers or heavy leggings. Then, at the height of the Roaring Twenties, daring flappers created a stir when they donned fitted garments and—gasp—rolled down their stockings to reveal naked knees!

Following the Depression, the advent of elasticized fabrics revolutionized the swimwear industry and the comparatively primitive styles of the twenties were replaced by improved, figure-hugging designs that vaguely resembled today's shorts. During World War II, Betty Grable's legendary pinup made curvaceous gams a fashion statement, and a more revealing design featuring a high-cut leg and taut skirt or "modesty panel" across the abdominal area became the rage.

When Catalina, a bathing suit manufacturer, came on board as a national sponsor during World War II, the firm provided contestants with identical competition suits that launched several memorable incidents. In 1945, Miss Slaughter deemed Bess Myerson's white Catalina too snug in the derriere and reissued Bess a larger pea-green suit. Realizing the baggy green number was a sure loser, Myerson's larger sister, Sylvia, slept in the white suit to stretch it, let the shoulder straps out fully to lengthen the seat, and then *sewed* Bess into the garment for the preliminary and final competitions. Undaunted, Bess simply wore the Catalina under her talent costume

In 1921, when contestants competed for the banner of "The Most Beautiful Bathing Beauty in America," spectators gasped at the display of feminine charms. Margaret Gorman, voted Miss America 1921, is third from the left. MISS AMERICA PAGEANT

During the mid-twenties, swimwear began its evolution toward the "paneled" suits that dominated the Pageant scene for the following four decades. ATLANTIC FOTO SERVICE

and evening gown until Sylvia cut her loose.

Then, in the late forties, in an apparent surge of creativity, Catalina furnished several startlingly different designs. In 1947, shortly after the shocking "bikini" was introduced to the world, contestants were outfitted with regulation *two-piece* swimsuits for the first and only time in Pageant history. Apparently, bare bellies didn't go over well, and in 1948, Catalina switched to an unforgettable black-and-white-striped maillot it touted as the height of fashion. Garment manufacturers had been experimenting with a new cable-knit fabric and

decided to apply it to swimwear. Unfortunately, the resulting suit had the disastrous effect of riveting attention to girth of the hip and upper thigh area while flattening the bustline.

"Oh, they were terrible! Terrible!" BeBe Shopp, that year's winner, laughs. "Because we weren't allowed to add anything or subtract anything in the suits, they were flat unless you really *had* something!" BeBe, at an ample 140 pounds, 37-27-36, clearly *did*. Recently, she pulled the distinctive suit out of mothballs to display at a Pageant reunion. "No one could *believe* that's what we had to wear," she reports with a giggle. "We felt like a bunch of zebras onstage!"

By coincidence, the year of the zebra suit was the first occasion since the twenties that Miss America was crowned in an evening gown

During the 1930s, elasticized fabrics revolutionized swimwear and baggy bathing dresses were abandoned for the improved, figure-hugging design modeled by Miss America 1938, Marilyn Meseke. MISS AMERICA PAGEANT

After Lenora deemed Bess Myerson's Catalina too short in the derriere, Bess's sister let the straps out fully and sewed Bess into the garment. Despite wearing the swimsuit beneath her stage wardrobe, Myerson easily captured the 1945 title. MISS AMERICA PAGEANT

rather than a swimsuit. Despite a threatened boycott by the press, the coronation was staged with BeBe in a modest evening gown. There was a small compromise for the press, however. At Shopp's side were four runners-up—each clad in an eye-catching zebra-print swimsuit.

Striped swimsuits disappeared from use in Atlantic City, but the well-constructed,

In 1947, for the first and only time, contestants wore identical two-piece swimsuits. The winner, Barbara Jo Walker, Miss Memphis, is near the center. CENTRAL STUDIOS

boned swimsuits that had dominated the competition since the thirties continued as the suit-of-choice for another two decades. Finally, in 1970, Phyllis George won both a swimsuit trophy and the Miss America crown after competing in an officially "approved" panelless swimsuit, thereby popularizing the updated style.

Then, the 1980s ushered in a revolution in Pageant swimwear. First, the famous white "supersuit" surged onto the Pageant scene, drowning the competition in its wake, as wearers captured a string of swimsuit trophies and Miss America crowns. "I think the reason my suit does well," explains Ada Duckett, its de-

signer, "is because it is elegant, not sexy. I call it a 'physical fitness suit' more than a 'swim' suit, because that's what the girl represents."

In turn, the huge success of the supersuit spawned the development of a new generation of high-tech competition swimwear: figure-flattering designs featuring patented construction secrets and custom-designed, light-absorbing colors and fabrics. "Let's just say they make the very most out of the figure," swimwear designer Laurel Schaefer intimates with a knowing smile.

Today's carefully engineered swimsuits undoubtedly offer a stark contrast to that first swimsuit competition, when Margaret Gorman's baggy knee-length swimming dress helped her win the crown. Despite the radical changes, however, one aspect of the competition has remained unchanged over the past seventy years. As the *New York Times* suggested back in 1922, "The art of the costumer may have as much to do as Mother Nature with the results."

THE EVER-CHANGING "IDEAL" AMERICAN PHYSIQUE

Bathing suit fashions are not the only aspect of the competition that has evolved over the decades. Society's ideas about what constitutes an "ideal" feminine physique have also changed radically. For instance, in the Roaring Twenties, Miss Americas were frequently petite beauties with small-busted boyish figures—as evidenced by the first winner, Margaret Gorman, whose 5-foot 1-inch frame measured 30-25-32! By contrast, contestants during the war years were larger, more-buxom women whose ample curves reflected the physiques of the major screen stars who established fashion trends. "Bodies looked different," Evelyn Ay Sempier reports. "It was a time when the norm was set by movie stars and their shapes. They had broad shoulders, bosoms, and bottoms.

In 1948, BeBe Shopp was crowned in an evening gown rather than the customary swimsuit. Her runners-up, however, appeared in that year's distinctive striped swimsuits. "We felt like a bunch of zebras onstage!" BeBe laughs. (Film star Vera Miles, Miss Kansas, is second from left.) ATLANTIC CITY PRESS

In the 1980s, resourceful contestants discovered high-tech swimwear such as Ada Duckett's famous "supersuit." Cheryl Prewitt, the first winner to wear Duckett's creation, later developed a pageant swimwear company, Cheryl's Winners. IRV KAAR

Thin was not something the world was striving for. Women were more . . . well . . . *womanly*."

For shapely candidates—and those who weren't so well endowed—the era's emphasis on voluptuous silhouettes led to comical situations. For instance, Neva Langley, Miss America 1953, apparently was so abundantly blessed that some of the mothers charged her with illegal padding during the competition. "We had a few jealous parent-chaperons who accused me of stuffing the top of my swimsuit,"

she recalls in disbelief, explaining, "No padding was allowed or anything like that." Fortunately, Neva was spared a frisking when her official hostess rushed to her defense. "My chaperon from Atlantic City actually had to vouch that I had *not* been padding!" she says laughingly, with a hint of indignation.

Two of Neva's fellow queens, however, had the opposite problem. Despite winning the 1955 Miss America title and a swimsuit trophy, Lee Meriwether insists she was flat-chested, scrawny, knock-kneed, *and* bow-legged! In fact, she reveals, her figure was so flawed that out of twenty-two girls at her state pageant, Lee placed a dismal *twentieth* in swimsuit. Her director fretted, "Oh, Lee, we've really got to do something," and then ordered a custom swimsuit that "wouldn't pinch in any skin around the tushy area, and had tons of ruffles across the bustline. It hid a multitude of sins!" she quips. They also taught Lee to force her legs together to disguise their unique shape. Months later, when the national judges selected Lee as a preliminary swimsuit winner, she was flabbergasted. "It was so bizarre I couldn't believe it," she admits with a laugh. Apparently equally surprised by the award, her sorority wired Lee its reaction. "Thought they checked you for falsies!" their message teased, "Love, Delta Phi."

Another less-than-buxom queen, Marilyn Van Derbur, remembers the afternoon she took her measurements for the Pageant program book. "My best friend and I sat down and rolled on the floor with laughter over my measurements," she confesses. "We were hysterical laughing! Fortunately, nobody checked you because I *couldn't* have written down what I really was!" Apparently, the results were so bottom-heavy that her mother joked, "*Back* in and maybe you'll win!" Marilyn explains with a laugh, "I just did not have what you would call a 'Miss America figure.'" In fact, when Marilyn won the 1958 Miss America title a few weeks later, her sister couldn't resist sending her a reminder of that fact. Her telegram read:

> Roses are red.
> Violets are blue.
> Flat-chested girls,
> can be beauty queens too!

By the Vietnam era, despite the influence of scrawny fashion trend-setters such as Twiggy, most contestants still displayed shapelier physiques. "Hourglass figures with the soft curves," explains Judith Ford, Miss America 1969, "the Marilyn Monroe type." As a result, when Judi, a muscular champion gymnast, won the swimsuit award she was stunned. "Winning swimsuit really *said* something," she exclaims, "because I was an athlete and had an athletic body." Two years later, Phyllis George, who

had admitted she thought her muscular cheerleader legs were "unfeminine," also won her swimsuit preliminary. Their victories were among the first indications that the traditional ideals of feminine attractiveness that had dominated the competition for years would soon be revolutionized by society's burgeoning interest in physical fitness training.

THE IMPACT OF THE PHYSICAL FITNESS MOVEMENT

During the late sixties, however, today's emphasis upon athletic training had not yet become widely accepted among American women and, according to Judi, most contestants had no idea how to "prepare" for swimsuit competition. "Girls who weren't athletic,"

In 1957, when voluptuous figures ruled, Marilyn Van Derbur (third from right) *won the Miss America crown despite her less-than-buxom physique. Her sister's congratulatory telegram teased: "Roses are red, violets are blue, flat-chested girls can be beauty queens too!"*
FRED HESS & SON

she says, "would just depend on what they had. Girls didn't go out running, they didn't go to the health spa back then. I mean, you just didn't *think* of lifting weights!" She confesses with a laugh, "Back then, if you needed to lose weight, instead of exercising, you would go to a *steam room!*"

However, during the seventies, the nation's emerging interest in physical fitness training began to transform the swimsuit competition. Young women suddenly realized that formerly male-dominated training procedures such as weight-lifting could also prove beneficial for pageant contestants attempting to achieve optimal physical condition. "One of the things about the Miss America program that a lot of people miss," says Debra Maffett, Miss America 1983, "is that women in the Pageant were into training like an athlete years before it was ever in style for a woman to do that."

By the 1980s, contestants had expanded their training routines to include sprinting, fast walking, hydroaerobic training, high-intensity aerobic classes, and computerized cardiovascular and weight-training programs—a trend that has encouraged young women who have failed to achieve a high level of physical fitness in the past to hone their bodies into the healthiest condition of their lives. "That's the difference between back then and now," Judi Ford observes. "Because of the physical fitness movement, girls are thinking more in terms of body-building and weight-lifting to hide figure flaws. People realize that, boy, you *can* resculpt your body and help your body function better by taking care of it through exercise."

In the past two decades, as the swimsuit competition has evolved to mirror the nation's growing physical fitness mania, the benefits of preparing for swimsuit have received greater recognition. "At first, I couldn't understand why, if it was a scholarship pageant, they would have a swimsuit competition," Kaye Lani Rafko acknowledges, "but now, after years of nurse's

training, I *do* understand the importance of swimsuit competition. This program has helped me to keep physically healthy and to eat the right foods. And I can tell you it feels good when you're healthy and physically fit. And *that's* really what the swimsuit competition is about."

THE ONGOING CONTROVERSY

While the swimsuit competition has evolved with the times to emphasize physical fitness, the competition continues to be denounced by a small but vocal group of critics who would like to see the event dumped. Still, it remains an integral part of the Pageant's public identity. "This is a tradition, and our research indicates that the swimsuit competition is so identified with our competition that it would be very difficult to find something to replace that," explains Leonard Horn. The chairman admits that while there may be alternatives, officials have yet to find one that "would be as successful and popular as the swimsuit competition and accomplish the same purpose." And, he adds with a hesitant grin, even if they *did* manage to come up with an alternative, they would introduce it "with a good deal of trepidation." From past experience, such trepidation would not be unwarranted.

Albert Marks recalled the uproar that ensued back in 1970, when after years of complaints from feminists, he wearily announced he was considering replacing the swimsuits with "play clothes." "I tossed out a trial balloon during Pageant week," he explained. "Well, you might have thought I'd desecrated the Constitution! The deluge of mail and telephone calls I got was almost unbelievable!" He added with a chuckle, "So, I said to myself, 'Oh, the hell with this!'—and the swimsuits stayed."

The tug of war between the public's in-

*Kaye Lani Rafko, an oncology nurse, defends the swimsuit event. "After years of nurse's training, I do **understand the importance of swimsuit competition. This program has helped me to keep physically healthy and to eat the right foods . . . and** that's **really what the swimsuit competition is about."***
© *PRO PHOTOGRAPHICS, JOE PROFETTO*

sistence that the swimsuit competition be continued and feminists' demands that it be eliminated has resulted in a highly publicized impasse. Kaye Lani Rafko cites an example of the polarized opinions on the issue. During a press conference, when a critic snarled, "Why do you even *need* a swimsuit competition? No one even enjoys it!," another reporter challenged, "Wait a minute—*I* do!" "The point is," Kaye Lani asks, "who are we going to satisfy? There is no way that everyone in America can be satisfied. There are lots of people who enjoy watching the swimsuit competition, along with the talents and evening gowns, and we receive many of our ratings from those viewers. It's almost like a cycle. If we were to delete the swimsuit competition, we might lose some of our viewers, and therefore drop in our ratings. If we lose ratings, we lose sponsors and we lose the scholarships and the essence of what the program is all about. I do not see anything wrong with the swimsuit competition," she insists. "It is a vital and important phase of competition that we cannot delete."

JUDGING THE SWIMSUIT COMPETITION

While the swimsuit segment has been retained as a competition, emphasis on the event has steadily decreased over the decades. "One has to realize," national judge Bernard Dobroski explains, "that the scoring criterion in swimsuit is only fifteen percent. It still recognizes the attractiveness and physical fitness of the young lady, but in terms of scoring, in terms of weight, it's not very much." In fact, when compared with the 40 percent value for talent and 30 percent value for interviews, swimsuit is clearly one of the least important factors in balloting for Miss America.

In recent years, the specific judging format has been updated to modernize the event. First, when comparative judging was eliminated in the late eighties, the practice of evaluating contestants in group form during swimsuit fell by the wayside. Instead, the new format presents each young lady onstage individually, shortens the time she poses before the panel, and eliminates the heels-together stance. "Everybody is pleased, I think, with the new swimsuit format," says national production manager Bill Caligari, "with not having to, shall we say, 'ankle-up.' I feel it really helped to de-emphasize the swimsuit competition because it's a pleasing picture we're after—not the perfect body."

If judges aren't seeking a perfect body, what qualities *are* they considering judicially? First, because the concept of physical fitness has emerged as such an integral aspect of the competition in recent years, it is now the first quality discussed with the national panel during judges' orientation. "This is her expression of physical fitness," Dr. Leonard Hill informs the panelists, and, as such, judges should ask themselves, "Is she demonstrating that she legitimately cares about her body and is physically active? Is her weight under control? Is she well toned?" In essence, "Does she project a sense of physical fitness and good health across the footlights?"

Specifically, judges are instructed to consider a number of qualities *relating* to physical fitness: muscular development and tone, an appropriate weight for the young woman's bone structure and height, and a balanced, well-proportioned physique. But they also evaluate a variety of other attributes such as grace, poise, posture, composure, and self-confidence under pressure. "This is one of the more stressful phases of competition," Hill acknowledges. As such, "Does she exhibit control over that stress? In swimsuit, she should be able to wear that swimsuit with a sense of *confidence*."

In the past decade, the value of the swimsuit competition has steadily decreased. During the 1990 Pageant, when swimsuit was valued at only 15 percent of scoring, Duke law student Marjorie Vincent won the crown.
GEORGE SORIE

Similarly, a contestant should also be able to model her swimwear before the panel with grace and elegance. "The swimsuit competition gives judges the best opportunity in all the phases of competition to see how graceful she really is with her walk," explains Jeffrey Quin, Pennsylvania's executive director. When a candidate appears before him onstage, he observes, "Does she have good posture? Is her carriage right? Does she *glide* across that stage or does she *walk* across that stage?"

Marian McKnight Conway, who has experienced the event from the perspective of both contestant and judge, agrees that swimsuit provides an ideal opportunity for young women to gain points for graceful carriage. "In an evening gown, they can disguise from the waist down and you can't see if a person is loping or has these garish strides or whatever," she observes with a chuckle, "but swimsuit really shows me how a girl walks and what her posture is." So rather than pointing ideal physical features, such as "the most beautiful legs or the tiniest waist," McKnight prefers to focus upon contestants' "overall stature."

As judges' observations reveal, today's swimsuit competition has evolved substantially since 1921, when entrants in Atlantic City's bathing beauty contest wiggled in their bloomers to attract the judges' eyes. Today's competition challenges contestants to achieve and maintain physical fitness and health, and to present themselves with a confidence, grace, and wholesomeness befitting the title of Miss America.

MISS AMERICA PRELIMINARY SWIMSUIT WINNERS

1940 Frances Burke
1941 Rosemary LaPlanche
1942 Jo-Carroll Dennison
1943 Jean Bartel
1944 Venus Ramey
1945 Bess Myerson
1946 Marilyn Buferd
1948 BeBe Shopp
1949 Jacque Mercer
1951 Yolande Betbeze
1953 Neva Langley
1954 Evelyn Ay
1955 Lee Meriwether
1961 Nancy Fleming
1962 Maria Fletcher
1964 Donna Axum
1966 Deborah Bryant
1968 Debra Barnes
1969 Judith Ford
1970 Pamela Eldred
1971 Phyllis George
1972 Laurel Schaefer
1973 Terry Meeuwsen
1975 Shirley Cothran
1977 Dorothy Benham
1980 Cheryl Prewitt
1982 Elizabeth Ward
1983 Debra Maffett
1984 Vanessa Williams
1985 Sharlene Wells
1986 Susan Akin
1987 Kellye Cash
1988 Kaye Lani Rae Rafko
1990 Debbye Turner

CHAPTER 8

The Talent Competition

The talent competition is one of the unique features that distinguish the Miss America program from so-called beauty contests. Weighted at 40 percent of balloting from the local to national levels, it is unquestionably the most important phase of competition. It is also one of the most revealing, allowing judges to gain insight into the contestant's appreciation of the fine arts, her willingness to discipline herself to achieve excellence in her chosen field, and her ability to successfully communicate that talent to the audience. "The talent competition is merely a vehicle to establish her effectiveness in the presentation of that talent," Leonard Horn explains. "Talent, in and of itself, is not a criterion for who should or should not be Miss America, because once she is selected, she rarely performs her talent, unless she's a singer or something like that. It's merely a vehicle. It's one more way to try to get at who this woman is and whether she would be a good ambassador and role model for our program."

"Talent," first introduced as an optional event in the 1935 Showmen's Variety Jubilee, was upgraded to a mandatory phase of competition in 1938. In the decades since, the event

has produced some of the most memorable moments in Pageant history—with both breathtaking world-class performances and charming *attempts* at showing talent. Kenn Berry, who has attended the national contest since 1947, observes that the competition has undergone dramatic changes over the years. "The talents today are *dynamite*," he acknowledges, "but don't forget that they weren't always. If you go back into the history of the Miss America Pageant, it's *hilarious* what they've done!" In fact, during the past half century, audiences have been treated to a wide spectrum of talents, ranging from a contestant who disappeared during her magic act, to others who performed the Mexican hat dance, danced on giant drums, and hauled homemade furniture onstage.

Dancers have whirled through fast taps, military taps, and taps with fire batons. Other dancers have performed flamenco, rock-umba, Siamese, cha-cha, cancan, samba, Afro, Tahitian, modern, Charleston, and Egyptian dances—not to mention moonwalking *en pointe,* hula dancing while strumming the electric guitar, and tap dancing upside down!

In the dramatic realm, contestants have

offered talks on raising cows, the Air Corps, surgery, industrial arts, nuclear fallout, the dangers of smoking, the art of packing a suitcase, and Abraham Lincoln's funeral train. Two hopefuls delivered the Sermon on the Mount, while a third portrayed a psychopathic bomber! Comedically inclined contestants have impersonated Marilyn Monroe, Bette Davis, Victor Borge, Ed Sullivan, Carol Channing, and Tiny Tim; while more dramatic actresses have portrayed the demises of Romeo and Juliet, Joan of Arc, and Mary Queen of Scots.

Musicians have conducted the Pageant orchestra, played the Convention Hall pipe organ, plucked *Ol' Man Mose* on the bass fiddle and *Old Black Joe* on the autoharp. They have beaten out *Stars and Stripes* on the drum, twanged zithers and ukuleles, blown trumpets, trombones, bassoons, and harmonicas, and performed with dulcimers, marimbaphones, and vibraharps.

More physically oriented queens have galloped horses down the runway, fenced with an assistant, stomped on broken glass with their bare feet, flipped on trampolines, ice-skated on tiny rinks, and shown home movies of assorted aquatic sports. One particularly creative contestant won a judges' trophy after she maneuvered a tractor around the stage and then jumped off to display her clothing designs!

As Pageant history richly—and sometimes humorously—illustrates, a mind-boggling array of talents has entertained Atlantic City audiences for generations.

THE EARLY YEARS

The talent competition has evolved considerably since its infancy. Back in the 1930s, when effective procedures had not been implemented to guarantee the slick productions we see today, sitting through an evening of talent offerings could be risky business—especially when contestants subjected weary onlookers to identical performances. For instance, in 1938, three girls performed *A-Tisket, A-Tasket*—two of them back-to-back. The unfortunate local reporter assigned to cover the Pageant sarcastically informed morning readers that the next contestant "did *not* sing *A-Tisket, A-Tasket.*"

By the 1940s, although regulations had been tightened considerably, contestants' offerings remained quite colorful, with future celebrities producing two of the most delightfully offbeat performances of the era. During the 1946 program, eventual Academy Award–winning actress Cloris Leachman entertained the crowd with a parody of a one-man radio program, spiced with comical characterizations and a piano interlude. Two years later, future film star (*Psycho*) Vera Ralston Miles mesmerized the Convention Hall audience with a speech about her plans to combine a career in acting with raising a close-knit family of *twelve children!*

NEW TALENT RULES INTRODUCED

During the dawning of the television era, a number of unforgettable incidents triggered increasingly stringent regulations. For instance, after three contestants repeated the *A-Tisket, A-Tasket* fiasco and dragged the audience through identical scenes from *Joan of Arc,* officials ruled that only one candidate could perform a given selection. Then there were problems with memorable animal blunders. "There's one talent that always sticks in my mind," Albert Marks once reported. "Before we instituted rules barring such things, a contestant had twelve trained pigeons as a prop. Well, there is heavy lighting on our stage and when one of the larger lights blew with a rather loud report, it scared the devil out of the pigeons and broke up her act!" To make matters worse, he recalled with a laugh, "The pigeons flew all over Convention Hall leaving their 'calling cards' on the audience!"

However, the antics of the contestant's feathered friends were tame by comparison to the unforgettable demonstration of equestrian skills exhibited by a champion horsewoman during the 1949 contest. As Miss Montana, Carol Fraser, strutted her palomino onstage, the animal suddenly slipped near the edge of the stage, reared up in fright, and teetered dangerously over the orchestra pit for several hair-raising seconds. "I don't know how she did it," Lenora Slaughter marvels, "but she turned that horse and moved right on and never missed a step! It was the most breathtaking thrilling thing you've ever seen!" Nevertheless, the Pageant board, "petrified" over what *could* have happened had the horse plunged into the orchestra, promptly banned animals from the stage. Sadly, the new ruling impinged upon the plans of Miss Nevada, a farm girl who raised thoroughbred cattle. "You mean I won't be able to have my *cow* perform?" she lamented to officials. "Sorry," Lenora replied apologetically, "nobody will ever bring an animal onstage again." "And they haven't!" she declares.

Another dilemma developed when contestants began performing with "weapons"— bows and arrows, swords, fire batons, and the like. One year, a contestant dressed as Robin Hood leaped onstage and shot arrows down the runway toward her target. Another archer speared balloons out of her father's hand. While the ladies managed to hit their bull's-eyes rather admirably, their exhibitions were somewhat hair-raising for the audience. However, it was the *judges* whose hair stood on end the year Miss Nebraska accidentally tossed a flaming baton into the judges' booth. Finally, after another fire baton twirler scorched her eyelashes off, officials gave the thumbs down to talents with the capacity to inflict injury.

MEMORABLE TALENT PERFORMANCES

To the relief of organizers, the quality of talent performances steadily improved as the Pageant matured, with many Miss Americas being unquestionably accomplished performers. Still, other winners managed to earn their crowns after whipping together so-called talents at the last minute. In fact, according to former Miss America Neva Langley, "Several of the most popular and successful Miss Americas

Lynda Lee Mead, Miss America 1960, performs her winning monologue, Schizophrenia. *EARLE HAWKINS*

Marjorie Vincent, Miss America 1991, greets the crowd (previous page)*, receives the crown from Debbye Turner* (right)*, accepts her Corvette from Chevrolet* (left)*, and poses with her family* (below)*. ©CP NEWS*

*Kaye Lani Rae Rafko, Miss America
1988, performs her Tahitian dance
(right) and crowns her successor,
Gretchen Carlson (left). Contestants
go tropical during the 1988 broadcast (below).* ©CP NEWS

Contestants sightseeing on the Boardwalk (right) *and posing for photographers during the Miss America Parade* (below). *GEORGE SORIE; A.M. BIVANS*

Gretchen Carlson performs a classical violin solo (left). Gary Collins and Bert Parks chat during the 1990 broadcast (below). Contestants take a break from rehearsals (bottom). GEORGE SORIE; TERRY CHENAILLE

*Kaye Lani Rae Rafko's dream led her from Monroe, Michigan, to the 1988
Miss America crown.* ©*CP NEWS*

In 1961, Michigan's Nancy Fleming won a talent trophy and the Miss America crown for her original fashion design exhibition.
EARLE HAWKINS

did not have that much talent, but they went on to do some wonderful things!"

Evelyn Ay Sempier is a quintessential example. Ay's victory in Atlantic City was a masterful accomplishment in light of her featherweight talent—"a pretty poem about Hawaii and hibiscus. I really had a lot of nerve to do it as I look back!" she admits with a chuckle. What took even more gumption was Evelyn's decision to perform her talent before twenty-five thousand people without practicing a word of it beforehand. In fact, Evelyn hadn't bothered to even _memorize_ the poem until midway through Pageant week! After persuading the producer not to bother with her rehearsal, Miss Pennsylvania strolled onstage and confidently recited a poem called _Leaves From My Grass-House,_ from Don Blanding's _Vagabond's House._ "It was the first time I had

ever said it out loud," she confesses with a grin. So it was that the most unrehearsed contestant in Pageant history became Miss America. During Evelyn's reign, she and Miss Slaughter often joked about her winning performance. "I used to kid her, 'Lenora, those judges probably looked up there and said, "My God, if that little kid can do _that_ she could do _anything!_" ' And she'd say, 'Evelyn, I think you're right!' "

Lenora undoubtedly could have repeated the conversation with Evelyn's successor, Lee Meriwether. Although Lee would later be nominated for an Emmy Award, her acting debut in the Miss San Francisco Pageant was farcical. Lee's sorority was involved in an inter-sorority-fraternity group, and it seems Lee's fraternity brothers entered her in the contest but forgot to inform her. When a classmate broke the news on the day of the pageant's talent audi-

Soon-to-be Miss America 1966 Debbie Bryant performed triple roles (damsel in distress, villain, and hero). EARLE HAWKINS

tions, Lee raced over, only to discover she was up against serious classical performers. She hastily revised her plans to perform a comical ditty about a girl's prom dance-partner disasters. "Obviously, this is real high-class stuff," she scolded herself. "They're gonna laugh me right outta here!" She switched to Synge's *Riders to the Sea*—but as she struggled to recall her lines, officials beckoned her onstage. Luckily, a pronounced gift for ad-lib saved the day. Lee remembers feigning a heavy Irish brogue, "doing a lot of moaning and wailing 'Lord, Lord!,' and crossing myself any number of times—just to get myself *through* it!" Glad to have survived the ordeal, she assumed that was the end of her pageant career.

To her shock, she not only made the finals, but also repeated her performance successfully enough to win both the local and state titles. Months later, she performed the Synge piece again in Atlantic City under intense pressure. Still shaken by the sudden death of her father, and whirling from a state official's admonition, "Every Miss California from the year one has made it to the top ten—and you're *going* to!," Lee then learned that she would be performing during the Pageant's first live television broadcast with future Oscar winner Grace Kelly as a judge! "I tried not to think about it, to tell you the truth!" Lee admits with a laugh. Even so, she recalls being so nervous that she forgot her lines and ad-libbed liberally. After comparing her daughter's performance with the stiff competition, Mrs. Meriwether offered her daughter a well-intentioned—but ill-fated—wager. "Honey," she predicted diplomatically, "I *don't* think you're going to win." Fortunately for Lee, Grace Kelly was more impressed.

A few years later, a severe case of laryngitis prompted Miss America–to–be Marian McKnight to bring *two* talents to Atlantic City. If her laryngitis cleared up, Marian would show off her soprano voice. If not, she would imper-sonate Marilyn Monroe. "I didn't know which one I was going to do until the day before," she admits. "That was really scary! To wake up in the morning and know you have to do your talent that night!" As it turned out, her laryngitis lingered and she opted to perform her stand-up comedy routine, *The Monroe Doctrine*. Marian slinked onstage squeezed into a Marilynesque gown with a plunging neckline. "It was very low-cut," she divulges coyly, "as much cleavage as we could show then—or that we *dared* show then. And I just sort of fluffed my hair up the way Marilyn did, exaggerated the makeup, lowered the eyes, did the pout and the whispery voice. It really didn't matter if it was soft and a little raspy. I guess it might have even *added* to it a little bit." At any rate, she says, shrugging, "I muddled through."

Ironically, Marian's performance proved of special interest to one celebrity spectator—Monroe's legendary ex-husband, Joe DiMaggio. "I was just glad I didn't *see* him!" Marian gasps. After her coronation, a reporter asked DiMaggio for his reaction to Miss America's performance, to which he responded enigmatically, "Well, nothing beats youth!" Ironically, Marian later met DiMaggio at a public relations firm, where she says the pair "had a lot of laughs over that. But," she admits with a bemused expression, "I'm still trying to figure out what he *meant!*"

The era concluded, appropriately enough, with two performances that would become Pageant lore—an organist with a one-medley repertoire and a church choir member who pretended to strip. Although Marilyn Van Derbur's and Mary Ann Mobley's talents were clearly fly-by-the-seat-of-your-pants propositions, that fact only endeared them more to the public and the ladies emerged as two of the Pageant's most popular queens.

Van Derbur had nearly panicked months earlier when her sorority drafted her into the Miss University of Colorado contest. After she reluctantly agreed to go through with it, the girls inquired what Marilyn intended to do for her talent. "Talent!?" Marilyn gasped. "What in the world would I do for talent?!" "You'll think of something!" Her sorority sisters giggled as they rushed off. Van Derbur mulled it over and decided that an organ recital would spare her unflattering comparisons with more usual talents. Although she had never played the instrument before, she asked a friend to whip up a medley of *Tea for Two* and *Tenderly* that "*sounded* hard, but wasn't that difficult to do." Marilyn practiced the arrangement feverishly, and by the time she had survived local and state competition to perform before the Miss America judges, she had mastered the arrangement. "It was the only piece I knew by heart—but I could do it backwards and forwards." Onlookers, while noting that she seemed to play with two or three fingers, praised her incredible composure.

Marilyn might have *appeared* to be the picture of control, but the pressure took its toll. "I was not at all eager to play the organ in front of twenty-five thousand people," she admits. "I was so grateful when that was over that I went back to my hotel room and just sobbed. My family came into the room, and they were wondering what I was crying about, but I was so relieved that it was over. Then," she recollects with a groan, "I found out I was one of the final ten and that I'd have to go through it again—with eighty-five million people watching me on television!"

Marilyn's self-discipline paid off when she managed her recital flawlessly. *Too* flawlessly, she discovered the next evening, when, as the new Miss America, she was whisked to New York City to appear on *The Steve Allen Show.* As she was rushed backstage at the studio moments before the live broadcast, Marilyn collided with the famous television host. "Hellooo there, little lady!" Allen welcomed in his trademark voice. "Now there's no time for rehearsal,

but all we're going to do is play *Night and Day.*" Gulp. "Oh, Mr. Allen," Marilyn nervously pleaded, "could we play *Tea for Two* instead?" Sorry, he explained. The tune had already been cleared. "Besides," he added, "I saw you last night and you were *terrific!*" Marilyn turned to her mother in desperation. "But," she recalls with a laugh, "she looked away because she *knew* what I was thinking." Then she gasped to Lenora Slaughter, "You know, I'm not sure I can *do* this!" The director responded with vehement confidence, "*Of course* you can, honey!"

Mary Ann Mobley performed a memorable mock striptease. From the aria Un bel dì, *she suddenly switched to* There'll Be Some Changes Made *and yanked off her gown and slip to reveal skimpy shorts. EARLE HAWKINS*

You're *Miss America!*" For the second time in twenty-four hours, Marilyn faced a huge live television audience with sheer pluck. "I *acted* as if I was in complete control," she explains, "and you know, people weren't really listening to who was doing what. He played and played and I just did the best I could." Fortunately, Marilyn says, "Lenora Slaughter had such a strong presence that she really carried me through that."

When Van Derbur's successor, effervescent Mary Ann Mobley, stepped onto the Convention Hall stage the following year, she created two minor, but memorable, ruckuses. For starters, the petite southern belle arrived without a proper musical score. "I won the Miss Mississippi contest two weeks prior to leaving for Atlantic City," Mary Ann explains, "so I didn't even have an orchestration. My church organist wrote down my music in pencil on a lead sheet. When [producer] Glenn Osser said, 'Okay, Miss Mississippi—it's time to rehearse. Where's your orchestration?,' I said, '*Orchestration?*' and handed him this one sheet of paper." When Osser inquired in astonishment, "Honey, this is it?," Mary Ann weakly nodded in the affirmative. "To his credit," she reports, "he looked over at the orchestra and said, 'Ladies and gentleman of the orchestra—this little girl needs some help, so bring out your pencils, and if you know a note, put it in.'"

That was the first bombshell. The second went off that night when Mobley performed her talent, a delightful song-and-dance routine spiced with a mock striptease. Mary Ann began her performance wearing a demure white gown and sweetly singing the aria *Un Bel Dì*. Suddenly, the orchestra stopped and, with a lick of the drumsticks, launched into the sultry jazz tune *There'll Be Some Changes Made*. Mobley flashed a mischievous smile at the audience and then yanked off her ball gown and slip, leaving her clad in a skimpy bodice and shorts. Needless to say, her saucy performance cap-

In 1964, Vonda Kay Van Dyke and "Curly-Q" belted out Together *to earn the crown. Vonda had practiced so relentlessly that she had to remind herself to* move *her lips during Pageant week.* EARLE HAWKINS

tured the attention of the judges— and the Pageant's director. "I was shocked!" Slaughter recalls, adding with a grin, "But it *was* terrific!" Even so, she reports, "After that we wouldn't let 'em strip anymore!"

While a number of popular queens earned their crowns with only middling demonstrations of talent, other winners dazzled judges with superb professional-quality performances. One of the most memorable, Yolande Betbeze, Miss America 1951, was one of the most extraordinary performers ever to grace the Convention Hall stage. "Oh, she had a voice!" exclaims Lenora. "A glorious voice! She had been trained by a retired Italian opera star, and her life's ambition was to sing at the Metropolitan Opera—and she had the voice to do it!" Ironically, Betbeze failed to win her talent preliminary when, during her performance of *Sempre Libera,* an overzealous member of the orchestra drowned out one of her spine-tingling high notes. Agitated, she turned to glare at the trumpeter and snapped that she would finish alone. The incident so irritated Yolande that she switched musical selections and dashed off to Philadelphia to locate a pianist to accompany her during the Saturday

Shirley Cothran, who won the 1975 title with a spirited flute medley, later remarked as a national judge, "Showmanship, selection of material, and how a contestant portrays her talent are just as important as the level of difficulty." EARLE HAWKINS

finals. The resulting performance from *Rigoletto, Caro Nome,* was so breathtaking the audience chanted for an encore.

Two years later, another brilliant talent ascended to the national throne, after a Wesleyan Conservatory administrator drafted a gifted piano pedagogy student into the school's new pageant. His appointee, Neva Jane Langley, was such a proficient pianist that during the local contest, when the electricity failed midway through her classical talent performance, she calmly completed the difficult composition in the dark. Later, in Atlantic City, Miss Georgia's flawless rendition of *Toccata* bowled the judges over and earned her both a talent award and the Miss America title. Respected composer Deems Taylor, who served as a judge that year, was so impressed by Neva's skill that he took her father aside after the Pageant and gushed that the new Miss America "threw a mean left hand on the piano."

By the seventies, professional entertainers had begun to view the Pageant as an effective career launchpad. One of the first of these veteran performers was Wisconsin's Terry Meeuwsen, a gospel singer and former New Christy Minstrel who hoped to finance advanced musical studies with Pageant scholarships. Meeuwsen's unforgettable rendition of the tune *He Touched Me* was easily one of the most spectacular performances in Pageant history. Yet, unbeknownst to the audience, Terry had nearly been overcome with stage fright moments before her performance. "I remember I was so terrified on Saturday night that I was sick to my stomach." A television technician she had met during an appearance on *The Tonight Show* noticed her expression and reassured her, "You are going to be great! This is no problem. You've done this before!" Terry, who admits his words seemed like a heaven-sent dose of confidence, calmly took her place in the spotlight. When the strains of music began, she became engrossin the music. "I just went

Well-known singer/actress Susan Anton performs Put on a Happy Face *during the 1969 talent competition. She tied for second runner-up.* MISS AMERICA PAGEANT

into another world! The sound was perfect. The music was perfect. I just said, 'Tonight, for this moment, I am just going to sing this song for *me,* to the max, the best I've ever sung, and I'm going to enjoy this moment in case it never comes again.'"

By all accounts, Miss Wisconsin's performance was breathtaking. Fellow contestant Michele Passarelli remembers the sensation it created in the wings. "We were all standing backstage listening to her over the loudspeaker system, and everybody was just hugging each other and almost crying because she was so

wonderful." As Terry bowed to the judges and dashed into the wings, the technician directed her attention back to the audience, which was saluting her performance with a rare standing ovation. "That's for *you!*" he exclaimed, as Terry gaped at the sight. "It was really a special time for me," she states modestly, "and it's neat that a moment that was so special for me personally touched somebody else."

BARRIER-BREAKING TALENTS

Although such superbly executed traditional talents have become common at the Pag-

When Kaye Lani Rafko gyrated through her Hawaiian-Tahitian dance, a veteran state judge informed his wife that Rafko would win. "You may not think it's something that belongs on the Miss America stage, but that was *perfect* talent.*" "You're the judge,"* shrugged his skeptical spouse.*
© PRO PHOTOGRAPHICS/JOE PROFETTO

In 1988, Gretchen Carlson left the audience spellbound with her performance of Gypsy Airs _and became the first violinist to capture the Miss America title._ © _PRO PHOTOGRAPHICS/JOE PROFETTO_

eant, there has also been a perceptible trend toward acceptance of nontraditional talents. "There was a time when [the winner] was either the pianist, the singer, the musician, or the dancer," observes Nathan Zauber, a veteran of three decades of judging, "but I think we're much past that. That's one of the changes that I've noticed over a period of years. There's a greater variety of talents and the uniqueness of them. It doesn't matter what they do because the most basic concept is—if they're good at what they're doing, _who cares?_ If she presents it well and sells it and she's the best one in the Pageant, she gets the top vote."

The most famous case in point is Judith Ford, Miss America 1969, who holds the distinction of having succeeded with one of the most innovative talents of all. Ford, a national junior trampoline champion, created a memorable stir in Atlantic City—and won a talent award—with her daring thirty-foot flips and spins on the trampoline. "It was extraordinary!" exclaimed Adrian Phillips. "It took a lot of courage to interject that as a talent in a Miss America contest, but she was so extremely good at it that it was amazing!" Judi fully appreciated the fact that such a unique talent was a risk, after her state directors warned her that her performance "could go either way—they could love it or they could hate it." Fortunately for Ford, the judges were spellbound. In retrospect, she says, "I'm not egotistical enough to think that anybody in the world would have picked me. Another set of judges might have said, 'This is a circus thing. We don't want something like that for Miss America.' It just

Debbye Turner won the crown with a lively performance of Flight of the Bumble Bee *and* Can Can. *"I was on!" she exclaims. "I knew that I was being carried by the wings of God . . . and I was having fun!"*
© *PRO PHOTOGRAPHICS/JOE PROFETTO*

Rafko," admits Pennsylvania director Jeffrey Quin. "There's no question that so many people who watched it in person or on TV said, 'I can't believe this! I can't believe she's even in the top ten!' But when she finished her talent, I turned to my wife and said, 'There's the winner,' and she said, 'Whyyyyy!?' So I told her, 'Well, you may not like Tahitian belly dancers or think that it is something that belongs on the stage at Miss America, but she did it *perfectly*. I mean, she got the crowd going and she didn't miss a beat. That was *perfect* talent. That was probably a nine or a ten.'" His wife looked at him skeptically and replied, "Well, you're the judge, I guess." Quin laughs. "Obviously, an hour later I was smiling."

Jane Jayroe won a talent trophy and the 1967 Miss America crown after she conducted the Pageant orchestra to the tune One, Two, Three. *EARLE HAWKINS*

turned out that with the judges I had, it went well for me." Was there any flak about "the queen of femininity" being a bona-fide *jock?* "Oh sure!" she exclaims, pointing out that her strenuous performance bucked the tradition that "Miss Americas aren't supposed to sweat."

Two decades later, another young woman bucked tradition to win the crown. The judges' selection of a bare-bellied, hip-gyrating Hawaiian-Tahitian dancer as Miss America 1988 initially left astonished fans locked in debate. "The talent my wife and I are probably going to go to our graves debating is Kaye Lani Rae

Kaye Lani's victory fueled the trend toward a wider spectrum of talents being used successfully at the national level. She was followed by Gretchen Carlson, an award-winning violinist, Debbye Turner, a marimba player, and Marjorie Vincent, a classical pianist. Indeed, since talent was introduced a half century ago, traditional performances have blended with less-conventional talents to create a fascinating, ever-changing competition. And while today's contestants have reached a level of technical sophistication unheard of when the talent competition was in its infancy, the comparative innocence of bygone eras embellished the tapestry of Miss America history with performances that were noteworthy—if not for impressive technique, then certainly for endearing warmth, creativity, and humor.

JUDGING THE TALENT COMPETITION

While watching the talent competition is entertaining, _judging_ the event is most definitely not. In many instances, evaluating the vast array of contestants' performances is an exercise in snap decision-making that requires nerves of steel, the judicial instincts of Solomon, and Ed Sullivan's eye for talent. The fact that talent is valued at 40 percent of balloting dramatically increases the importance of accurate judging, and panelists fully appreciate that every score they award in talent will have a significant impact on the eventual standing of the contestants.

To ensure that the national panel evaluates contestants' talents as effectively and impartially as possible, Dr. Leonard Hill instructs judges to focus on three key qualities that must be evident in any strong performance. First, he says, judges are instructed to "acknowledge the _quality_ of the talent being presented. I don't care whether it's a violin, a hula, or a belly

Miss America 1984, Vanessa Williams, brought the house down and earned a talent trophy for her stirring rendition of Happy Days Are Here Again. _IRV KAAR_

dance; there is a dimension of quality that you can standardize. As long as judges apply the standard consistently, the consensus process will even out with that many judges."

The second major quality judges are instructed to consider is the _technical_ proficiency with which each young woman presents her talent. "We do some training about technical skills—how they can detect poor breathing, improper extensions in dance, or missed keys on the piano."

Third, he notes, the panel considers "the 'feeling' with which they bring that talent

A trained classical pianist, Marjorie Vincent won the talent competition and the 1991 Miss America title with her flawless rendition of Chopin's Fantasie Impromptu. PAUL ABEL, JR.

across. What was the entertainment value? With the performing arts, the bottom line is *feeling*." Ideally, Hill summarizes, judges should balance the three basic qualities. "You marry the standard of quality with an awareness of the technical skills and the feeling that is joined with that technical dimension."

In addition to these three broad categories, there are numerous specific qualities that judges consider: the degree of discipline required to develop the talent, the level of achievement and difficulty, execution, technique, stage presence, synchronization, voice, use of body, costuming, choreography, confidence, projection, originality, facial expressions, and showmanship. When these qualities merge, they result in an effective balance between the contestant's technical proficiency and her ability to reach out and touch the judges emotionally.

Creating that emotional impact requires the ability to "project personality across the footlights," according to Tom Hensley, who has judged for three decades. "It's being able to

sell it! I can name two Miss Americas right off who couldn't play the piano or sing, but they're Miss America because they had the ability to project beyond the footlights and sell it." That quality is communicated by eye contact, confidence, and personality, Hensley explains—but primarily in "not being afraid of the stage and spotlight. With the two Miss Americas I have in mind, they could stand there in rehearsal and be just plain and dull but when that spotlight would hit them they'd absolutely come alive!"

Former Miss America and national judge Shirley Cothran-Barret agrees that during a close race in which many candidates demonstrate impressive technical proficiency, a contestant who displays that extra dose of magnetism onstage can pique the judges' interest. "Yes, there has to be a basic talent," she acknowledges, "but her showmanship, selection of material, and how she portrays and performs her talent are just as important as the level of difficulty."

It seems that in the final analysis, the success of a contestant's talent presentation hinges, not merely upon a well-crafted, superbly executed performance, but also upon her ability to transcend the barriers of the stage to rouse the judges' emotions. "Technical is one thing," asserts national production manager Bill Caligari, "but to me," he emphasizes with a thump toward the heart, "it's what I feel _here_. What gives me goose bumps and stands the hair up on the back of my neck. That's what counts—and that's what's going to make her Miss State and Miss America."

MISS AMERICA TALENT PERFORMANCES

1921 to 1933
No talent competition
1935 Leaver
Song/dance, _Living in a Great Big Way_
1936 Coyle
*Song/dance, _I Can't Escape from You/ Truckin'_
1937 Cooper
Vocal, _When the Poppies Bloom Again_
1938 Meseke
Dance, _The World Is Waiting for the Sunrise_
1939 Donnelly
Vocal/bass fiddle, _Ol' Man Mose_
1940 Burke
Vocal/dance, _I Can't Love You Anymore_
1941 LaPlanche
Ballet tap
1942 Dennison
*Vocal, _Deep in the Heart of Texas_
1943 Bartel
*Vocal, _Night and Day_
1944 Ramey
Vocal/dance, _Take It Easy_
1945 Myerson
*Piano/flute, _Summertime/Concerto in A-Minor_
1946 Buferd
Drama, _Accent on Youth_

1947 Walker
*Piano/vocal/painting exhibit
1948 Shopp
Vibraharp, _Caprice Viennese_
1949 Mercer
*Drama, _Romeo and Juliet_
1951 Betbeze
Classical vocal, _Sempre Libera/Caro Nome_
1952 Hutchins
*Drama, _Elizabeth the Queen_
1953 Langley
*Classical piano, _Toccata_
1954 Ay
Poem recital, _Leaves from My Grass-House_
1955 Meriwether
Drama, _Riders to the Sea_
1956 Ritchie
Drama, _The Murder of Lidice_
1957 McKnight
Comedy routine, _The Monroe Doctrine_
1958 Van Derbur
Organ, _Tea for Two/Tenderly_
1959 Mobley
*Vocal, _Un Bel Dì Vedremo/There'll Be Some Changes Made_
1960 Mead
Monologue, _Schizophrenia_
1961 Fleming
*Fashion design display
1962 Fletcher
Pantomime tap dance
1963 Mayer
Vocal/Broadway vignette, _Wishing Upon a Star_
1964 Axum
Vocal, _Quando Me'n Vo/I Love Paris_
1965 Van Dyke
Ventriloquism/vocal, _Together_
1966 Bryant
Drama, _Miserable Miserliness of Midas Moneybags_
1967 Jayroe
*Vocal/dance/conduct orchestra, _One, Two, Three_

* Preliminary talent award winners.

1968 Barnes
Piano, four variations of *Born Free*
1969 Ford
*Trampoline/gymnastics
1970 Eldred
Ballet, *Love Theme from Romeo and Juliet*
1971 George
Piano, *Raindrops Keep Fallin' on My Head/Promises, Promises*
1972 Schaefer
Vocal, *This Is My Beloved*
1973 Meeuwsen
*Vocal, *He Touched Me*
1974 King
Vocal, *If I Ruled the World*
1975 Cothran
Flute, *Bumble Boogie/Swingin' Shepherd Blues*
1976 Godin
Original piano composition, *Images in Pastels*
1977 Benham
*Classical vocal, *Adele's Laughing Song*
1978 Perkins
*Blues vocal, *Good Morning Heartache*
1979 Barker
Gymnastics, *Rocky/Feelin' So Good*
1980 Prewitt
Vocal/piano, *Don't Cry Out Loud*

1981 Powell
*Classical vocal, *Lucie's Aria*
1982 Ward
Vocal, *There'll Come a Time*
1983 Maffett
*Vocal, *Come in from the Rain*
1984 Williams
*Vocal, *Happy Days Are Here Again*
1984 Charles
*Vocal, *Kiss Me in the Rain*
1985 Wells
Vocal/Paraguayan harp, *Mis Noches Sin T*
1986 Akin
Vocal, *You're My World*
1987 Cash
*Vocal/piano, *I'll Be Home*
1988 Rafko
Hawaiian/Tahitian dance
1989 Carlson
*Classical violin, *Gypsy Airs*
1990 Turner
Marimba, *Can Can/Flight of the Bumble Bee/Czardas*
1991 Vincent
*Piano, *Fantasie Impromptu Op. 66* (Chopin)

CHAPTER 9

The Evening Gown Competition

The final phase of competition in the Miss America Pageant, the evening gown competition, is a multifaceted event designed to celebrate beauty of the individual. Although deceptively simple in appearance, the competition actually entails much more than just beautiful young ladies and spectacular gowns. It provides an opportunity for each contestant to gain points by projecting her individuality, personality, poise, intelligence, and physical beauty across the stage footlights.

Today's evening gown competition, which currently is valued at 15 percent of scoring on the local, state, and national levels, is divided into two distinct segments—a modeling phase and an onstage question/answer exercise. When combined, the dual phases provide judges with the opportunity to assess numerous qualities:

- The intelligence, perception, confidence, personality, warmth, and communication skills displayed verbally.
- The gracefulness of her modeling movements and her ability to carry herself with poise and dignity.

- The appropriateness of her choice of evening wear as a statement of individuality.

When all facets of a contestant's appearance in evening gown blend effectively, the result is a lovely, polished presentation becoming a candidate for the Miss America crown.

Introduced during the Roaring Twenties to broaden the scope of the developing National Beauty Tournament beyond that of a mere bathing beauty contest, the evening gown competition was originally limited to a simple fashion parade onstage. Although it has become more multidimensional in the decades since, the competition's format has remained relatively unchanged, with each new generation of contestants gracefully modeling their formal attire before judges and audiences. In the process, the event has provided a fascinating reflection of ever-changing standards of beauty and fashion in twentieth-century America.

The first evening gown award recipient, Thelma Blossom, Miss Indianapolis, was named "The Most Attractive Contestant in Evening Dress" in 1922, outshining an array of glamorous candidates attired in the very latest

Christian Dior introduced his opulent, wasp-waisted "New Look" and women quickly abandoned the comparatively bland styles of the previous era. Pageant sponsor Joseph Bancroft & Sons popularized the look among contestants when the firm began outfitting Miss Americas with custom-designed formal wardrobes to promote their newly developed "Everglaze" fabrics. The Bancroft designs—magnificent ball gowns with strapless bodices, huge hoopskirts, and tightly cinched waistlines—were quickly

Fashion trendsetter Jacqueline Kennedy popularized crisply tailored designs during the early sixties. Donna Axum, Miss America 1964, notes that many contestants sewed their own gowns during the "wholesome" era. EARLE HAWKINS

During the Roaring Twenties, the evening gown competition was added to broaden the scope of the beauty tournament. Norma Smallwood, Miss America 1926, models fashionable flapper attire of the era. MISS AMERICA PAGEANT

in flapper fashions—unfitted knee-length evening dresses jauntily sashed at the hip to accent the popular dropped waistlines.

During the 1930s and 1940s, the Great Depression and World War II imposed austerity upon consumers, and practical, unadorned floor-length styles dominated pageant fashions. Then, as the mid-century mark approached,

Miss America 1960, Lynda Mead (fifth from left) *and her fellow semifinalists model the traditional ball gown silhouette popular during the fifties.* FRED HESS & SON

embraced as the blueprint for Pageant attire for the fifties.

Interestingly, as contestants gravitated toward these extravagant creations, with their luscious faille, tulle, lace, and net fabrics, they softened the overwhelming impact of the look by retreating from the use of bold colors. Virginal white emerged as the undeniable favorite of contestants—and apparently judges—with the majority of participants and every Miss America from 1950 to 1966 attired in various hues of white.

During the sixties, under the influence of fashion trend-setters such as First Lady Jacqueline Kennedy, the huge ball gowns evolved into immaculately tailored, softly draped designs in heavy satins, taffetas, and brocades. Donna Axum, Miss America 1964, admired the flattering styles of her era, which, she observes, "didn't overpower" young women. "I loved the elegance of the gowns with a beautiful cut and a beautiful kick-train in the back—just simple el-

egance." At the time, she explains, contestants "either bought a gown off the rack or it was homemade, instead of custom-made. You'd just get a pattern out of *Vogue Pattern Book* or *McCall's,* or whatever." She chuckles at the comparison between yesteryear's economical gowns and today's pricey designer creations. "We certainly were *wholesome!*"

As the seventies approached, formal fashions shifted gears again when distinctive chiffon gowns with heavily ornamented bodices emerged as the basic design for competition wear. The new ultrafeminine profile, introduced by Miss Americas Jane Jayroe and Pamela Eldred, ushered back into popularity delicate, flowing fabrics in a rainbow of pastels. The look, which remained popular well into the late 1970s, was frequently praised for its exceptional beauty and fluidity onstage.

However, during the eighties the lavishly materialistic influence of the Reagan/*Dynasty*/*Dallas* era brought sweeping changes to the

By the late sixties, the tailored silhouette had softened into flowing chiffon designs in a rainbow of colors. Debra Barnes, Miss America 1968, is fourth from left. MISS AMERICA PAGEANT

event, as softly feminine designs were abandoned for spectacular, heavily beaded, figure-hugging gowns that one judge aptly nicknamed "walking chandeliers." While the stunning gowns have been understandably popular with contestants, their considerable expense has caused concern among Pageant officials. National production manager Bill Caligari, who has observed the trend during his visits to local and state pageants around the country, points out that it is *contestants*—not the Pageant— who are encouraging the use of exorbitantly priced evening gowns. "I think it's ridiculous!" he gripes. "I'd like to see us get back to the less flashy gowns. . . . It gets to the point where a five-thousand-dollar gown is crazy—especially for what they're competing for—the scholarships. I'd like to see if there's some way we can limit the gowns they would wear. We just don't know how to put a stop to it," he asserts, "but we're trying." For instance, in order to decrease wardrobe costs, the Pageant now provides national contestants with opening production-number dresses by American designers and limits the number of gowns that contestants are permitted to bring into the dressing room.

Ironically, while the trend of the last decade has been toward the use of more expensive designs, a number of recent winners have refused to participate in that trend and have competed successfully in reasonably priced or homemade gowns. For example, Elizabeth Ward's original lace-and-rhinestone design, which helped to popularize the form-fitting, jewel-encrusted look, was actually fashioned from a lace tablecloth, hand-sewn, and punched with rhinestones by her grandmother! Past Pageant president Ellen Plum admits that Ward's gown stands out in her memory for more than its exceptional beauty. "When we got her to her hotel that night after she was crowned," she recalls with a chuckle, "all the prongs on the rhinestones stuck to the upholstery of the car seat and we had to *peel* her out!" Anecdotes aside, Plum asserts that from her vantage point as judges co-chairman, she is convinced the expense of a candidate's wardrobe has nothing to do with who wins the crown. "Clothes do *not* make a Miss America," she intones. "She makes herself!"

During the Reagan/Dynasty/Dallas era, *heavily beaded gowns, aptly termed "walking chandeliers" by one judge, emerged as the design of choice.* EARLE HAWKINS

Some recent winners have bucked the trend toward more expensive gowns, and competed successfully in moderately priced, or hand-sewn, garments. Elizabeth Ward, Miss America 1982, wore a gown her grandmother fashioned from a lace tablecloth. EARLE HAWKINS

Kaye Lani Rae Rafko is another example of a candidate who won the Miss America crown without spending a fortune. The beautiful white lace creation Kaye Lani wore during the 1987 national Pageant was actually a donated wedding gown that had been altered and decorated with iridescent sequins. "I never spent a cent going to Atlantic City," she explains. "Everything was donated. You *don't* have to spend a lot of money on beaded evening gowns to win a pageant!"

The sensible competitive philosophy Kaye Lani promoted during her reign pleased Pageant officials, who realize how strongly Miss America's actions and values influence the young women who hope to follow in her footsteps one day. Bill Caligari reiterates what winners like Elizabeth Ward and Kaye Lani Rae Rafko have proven. "It isn't the gown that makes the girl. It's the girl that makes the gown."

JUDGING THE EVENING GOWN COMPETITION

The evening gown competition often appears to be the easiest portion of the Miss America Pageant to judge. In reality, it is considerably more challenging than one would suspect. Judges must consider not only the on-stage interview (which will be discussed in the second half of this chapter), but numerous nonverbal qualities such as contestants' physical beauty, poise and grace of bearing, fluidity of movement, composure, and choice of gown. "I think there are many more dimensions to the whole person in that competition than in any other one," observes Evelyn Ay Sempier, who judged the 1985 national Pageant. "There is so much to see in the evening gown segment, and the judges have the opportunity to judge many more facets."

Because the evening gown competition

Similarly, Kaye Lani Rae Rafko won the 1988 Miss America title wearing a donated bridal gown she altered and enhanced with sequins. "You don't *have to spend a lot of money on beaded evening gowns to win a pageant," she stresses.* MISS AMERICA PAGEANT

focuses upon the celebration of individual beauty, one of the first and most revealing qualities judges observe is each contestant's choice of an evening dress. Specific criteria the panel may consider include: what personal statement a contestant's gown makes, whether the dress and its wearer complement each other, if the gown is in good taste, if she attempts to clone a previous titleholder or expresses individuality, and if the total picture created is lovely and harmonious.

It should be noted, however, that while the choice of gown is scrutinized, the gown itself is *not* the criterion being scored. Rather, according to Karen Aarons, the panel is instructed to evaluate qualities relating to the young woman's *choice* of a gown. "What we always say to the judges is, 'You are not judging the gown. You are judging the appropriateness of the girl with the gown. The two should complement each other.' "

In order for a contestant and her evening gown to create a complementary picture, the young woman's attire should make an accurate "statement" about who she is as an individual—her unique personality, style, and image. "Your gown should look like *you,*" advises Melissa Aggeles, Miss Florida 1988. "You're creating an image, and it should fit your style and your look." Sometimes a clash of images may occur, as when an innocent ingenue-type walks onstage squeezed into a low-cut red sequined gown trailing boa feathers. It's a matter of the gown failing to complement the image of the young lady, says Joe Dickens, a past Miss Georgia director. "You can see a girl come out in the most gorgeous gown you've ever seen, but the girl and the gown just don't *go together.*"

Another pitfall inexperienced candidates fall into is assuming that they must imitate the gown style worn by a previous winner in order to compete successfully. "Every year, whatever Miss America wears, I see *thousands* of those dresses for the next year!" says veteran judge Vernon DeSear. Unfortunately, the tactic doesn't work because that particular titleholder's gown was the right choice for *her.* Wearing a gown that clones the reigning queen will not assure a repeat of her success. Each young woman should wear the evening dress that is most flattering to her unique height, bone structure, weight, skin tone, and hair coloring. "Be original," advises DeSear. "Don't copy somebody. Come up with what is right for *you.*"

Sometimes, contestants choose overly ornamental gowns that tend to detract from a young woman's natural beauty by drawing judges' attention away from the girl—and onto the gown. "That is what I mean when I say, 'That dress is walking,'" Evelyn Ay Sempier explains with a laugh. "When you are in something that is so overpowering in color and detail, there is no room for the *person!* You're just walking this dress around. *It* does the turns and *it* walks down the runway!" Fortunately, she sighs, the domination of "sequin sausages" appears to be giving way to a renewed appreciation for simple elegance. "Every year in the judges' circuit, we hope for the phase-out of the sparkles. We're ready for nylon netting again, or a little tulle. Let's stop the glitz!"

Apparently, Evelyn's view is shared by others. During one recent Miss America Pageant, Miss South Carolina's appearance onstage in an unadorned black gown drew gasps from the Convention Hall audience—and several perfect scores from judges. "It was just a simple black velvet gown," recalls Joseph Sanders, the contestant's state director, "but it was so elegant it was unreal! It was the first time I've ever heard people gasp! People were standing up as she walked down the runway, giving her a standing ovation. It was amazing to me." He adds, "I think simple elegance is the name of the game. I think that's the key."

The simple gown created such a stir because it perfectly illustrated the true essence of the evening gown competition—the celebration of individual beauty. Rather than depending upon gobs of bugle beads and sequins, the designer, Gail Sanders, deliberately crafted the gown to allow the unique beauty of that particular young woman to shine through. Bill Caligari was impressed with the results. "It was definitely perfect for *that* girl," he notes, "because the gown could hang on somebody else and be just another dress, but on *her* it was stunning!"

In fact, individuality is such a paramount aspect of the competition that, according to Vernon DeSear, the crucial test of any gown's effectiveness is whether the girl has worn the gown—or the gown has worn the girl. "I don't like to see something overwhelm a person," he cautions. "To me, if the gown is so decorated that you don't even notice the girl, she has *defeated the purpose.*"

While the statement a contestant's gown makes about her as an individual is critical, DeSear reports that there is one key quality that transcends all others and makes the winning difference onstage—poised self-assurance. "There's a certain glow," he explains, "an aura, which comes from being confident enough to say, 'I am proud of who I am. I have done what I needed to do and now I am ready to stand in front of you and tell you that I want to win.'"

THE EVENING GOWN COMPETITION "INTERVIEW"

The second portion of the evening gown competition, the brief extemporaneous onstage "interview," has been an element of the Miss America Pageant for over a half century. Depending upon the particular format of a given decade, live interviews have been conducted either as part of the evening gown competition or during the final balloting of the top five. However, because the onstage interviews are currently conducted during evening gown, the subject will be discussed in this chapter.

Often likened to an extension of the private interviews, the onstage interviews give judges an opportunity to assess each contestant's ability to think and speak clearly under pressure, and to observe the warmth, intelligence, and poise she projects before a large audience. Specific qualities being scrutinized as the emcee interviews each candidate include her personality, sincerity, voice, vocabulary, composure, intelligence, confidence, and understanding of issues of the day.

During the history of the Pageant, the format for onstage interviews has evolved considerably. During the late 1930s, finalists were not questioned onstage. Instead, they took turns descending into the judges' box to be interviewed privately—while the curious audience strained to catch glimpses of how each young woman seemed to impress the judges. While these private conversations took place offstage, the show continued with the emcee gamely leading onlookers in sing-alongs. Unfortunately, the interview process prolonged the

By the 1940s, finalists were "interviewed" onstage by the emcee to test their personality and intelligence. Here, Bert Parks reads Miss Texas 1962 her big question. EARLE HAWKINS

program considerably, with the last contestant sometimes emerging from the judges' booth well past midnight.

For obvious reasons, the format was revamped in the early 1940s to allow the audience to hear contestants' responses as well. Master of ceremonies Bob Russell would ask the finalists questions to reveal their personalities and speaking skills. Miss Americas of the era remember the exercise as the most nerve-racking part of the contest. "I think every girl who has ever had to be interviewed onstage in an impromptu situation like that would tell you it is a great amount of pressure," confesses Neva Jane Langley, Miss America 1953, "a great amount of pressure! And I think you always walk offstage thinking, 'I could have done better.'"

In fact, as Neva relates it, her question almost became her Waterloo. "The thing I remember distinctly is that it was the September before the election between Truman and Eisenhower, and one of my questions was 'Who do you consider the most outstanding man in the world?' Off the cuff, my answer was 'Well, certainly the president of the United States has to be one of the most outstanding men in the world.' With that there was a 'Boooo!' all over the audience because Truman was very much out of favor at the time. I knew I had to overcome that in a hurry—and I can remember thinking if I could only show them the logic, that just the office had to be respected."

She managed to redeem herself with artful handling of the next question: "Where would you like to spend your honeymoon?" "Fortunately," she says, giggling, "my old mind was working and I said, 'Atlantic City!' So that's the way it went," she sighs in a tone that reveals she won't be forgetting the experience any time soon.

The following year, Neva's successor, Evelyn Ay, found her onstage interview equally memorable. In Evelyn's case, when she was

Sometimes the format varied, as in the 1963 Pageant, when contestants were asked to select and expound upon a character trait. Here an eventual runner-up ponders the options.
EARLE HAWKINS

asked, "What profession are you studying and where do you wish to practice that profession?," she drew a complete mental blank. Fortunately, her subconscious mind raced to the rescue by regurgitating a *National Geographic* article on India's medical crisis she had read years earlier. "Suddenly there was total recall..." Evelyn explains. "*That's* where the answer came from! I immediately went around the world to India! I took my medical technology and I talked about the starvation, I described the people, the conditions, and Gandhi—all of that. And I said, 'This is what I am going to do and this is where I feel needed.'"

Her heartwarming concern for the people of India stunned the judges, but Evelyn insists her answer wasn't calculated to gain points. "Although I had never given it a thought until that question was asked, it wasn't something that I just thought, 'Oh, this is gonna knock 'em dead when I give 'em this India story!' I said it very sincerely. Evidently, I had cared when I read that article and it just came out at that point." Evelyn giggles at her mind's cool handling of the predicament. "I never cease to be amazed at what the mind will do under pressure—and what mine *did!*"

A few years later the onstage interviews sported two new features that Neva and Evelyn hadn't faced: Bert Parks and a fishbowl filled with question slips. Marilyn Van Derbur laughs in recollection of the scene. "Each one of us in the final ten came up and pulled our questions out of a fishbowl and Bert stood there and asked us those questions—in front of eighty-five million people! We had to think on our feet!" Marilyn's two questions were whether a woman should propose to a man and what she felt was the greatest invention in history. In retrospect, she admits that while she was composed enough to answer proficiently, the exercise was nevertheless a numbing experience. "Just try to stand there in front of eighty-five million people and think of your name—much less answer those questions in an articulate way!"

Over the years, the onstage interviews have produced some amusing moments, most notably the 1958 Pageant, when two of the five finalists announced on live television that they had discovered during rehearsals that they shared a common bond—a two-timing Air Force cadet boyfriend! The exposure of the cadet's meandering ways made for interesting banter during the broadcast, especially when the two miffed contestants informed the audience that the cadet now had two ex-girlfriends. Bert Parks raised his eyebrows in mock horror—and millions of Americans convulsed with laughter at the predicament of the red-faced cadet, who at that very moment was probably quietly slipping away from his barrack's television set.

Such lively developments delighted television viewers, who tuned in in record numbers. Clearly, millions of armchair judges enjoyed observing how cleverly contestants could handle the sometimes inane questions. Often the girls' verbal agility didn't let their fans down—like the time Bert Parks asked North Carolina's Maria Fletcher, "As Miss America, you have just been introduced at a women's club luncheon. You discover the speech you brought with you is for the Cattlemen's Association meeting next week. What would you do?" Without a moment's hesitation, the future Miss America quipped, "I think I would just go ahead and deliver the speech I had planned and hope they would think it was a comedy routine!" During another prefeminist era broadcast, Bert inquired how eventual winner Lynda Mead would handle the following dilemma: "You're proficient at tennis or golf. You know you can beat your date. Would you? Should you?" "Ah wouldn't and Ah shouldn't," the southern belle answered drolly, "because Ah did once and Ah never saw him again!"

As engaging as some of the conversations were, the overall impression created by the segment was considered to be unflattering to the contestants, according to Bill Caligari. "Back in the old days, when they had the questions they were really kind of stupid, and they made them look like a bunch of airheads, which they are definitely *not*." In 1972, officials decided to try a new approach by replacing the live onstage interviews with brief memorized "speeches" during the evening gown compe-

In 1988, chairman Leonard Horn introduced a revised onstage question-answer segment during the evening gown competition. Marjorie Vincent, Miss Illinois, capably addressed the subject of violence against women. PAUL ABEL, JR.

tition. The prepared statements were used successfully on the local, state, and national levels from 1972 until 1987.

ASSESSING CONTESTANTS' VERBAL ABILITIES

In 1988, Leonard Horn reinstated a revamped onstage interview during the evening gown competition. The move was met with overwhelming approval from judges, who find the exercise provides a valuable window into the young women's thinking processes under the pressures of live television. The new format utilizes penetrating questions related to an issue the contestant has previously stated she has a vital interest in, ranging from the AIDS crisis to gun control. According to Dr. Leonard Hill, each question is designed to reveal whether the candidate is able to "extend her personality, express her beliefs, and defend them well and logically."

While expressing one's views on U.S. and world affairs as television cameras record every stutter may be nerve-racking for the young women, the exercise effectively spotlights each contestant's ability to handle the considerable pressures of Miss America's reign. "I realize that it is a really high-tension moment," acknowledges former Miss America Terry Meeuwsen. "But, nonetheless, she's under that all year long, so she'd better be able to handle it."

THE KEY TO UNDERSTANDING THE JUDGES' CHOICE

Over the years, the live questions have been a traditional favorite of both Convention Hall audiences and television viewers because they offer a glimpse of what the judges have observed in the privacy of the interview sessions—which, in turn, helps observers to better appreciate the eventual decision of the panel. "I think when the interviews are done onstage, it gives the audience such an insight into the personality of the girls," explains Marian McKnight Conway, who judged the national Pageant in 1985. "Once in a while you say, 'Oh, why did _she_ win? I liked so and so's talent better.' But, if you had only seen the interviews, you would know that the girl who won could think very fast on her feet, nothing threw her,

she was charming, and had a lovely personality. It allows you to see qualities that you just don't see in talent and swimsuit."

Conversely, the selection of Kaye Lani Rae Rafko is often cited as an example of what happens when audiences _don't_ have an opportunity to assess contestants' verbal skills. In 1987, when Kaye Lani earned the Miss America title, contestants merely recited brief memorized statements rather than speaking extemporaneously. Ironically, while Rafko, an oncology nurse, had touched the judges during the private interviews with her concern for terminally ill cancer patients, the lack of an onstage conversation prevented the audience from understanding that her warmth and sincerity had clinched the crown for her. "All of a sudden, their question was 'How can a girl in a grass skirt become Miss America?,'" Dr. Hill recalls. "Our answer was—'her _interview!_' Kaye Lani was one of the greatest interviews that have ever walked the Boardwalk. But they had no idea she could speak, that she was articulate, direct, and emphatic. They never _saw_ that!"

Hill explains that the reinstated live question phase is going to eliminate viewer surprise by allowing the audience to see the candidates in a fuller dimension. "Until this year, the viewer had only one perspective—what they literally saw onstage. And, basically, the only things they saw were the girls perform and walk the runway in their swimsuits and gowns. Now, it's different. They have to open their mouths and _say_ something. I think the surprises will start being less and less as we begin to showcase the girls more onstage and give them something to say. Then people are not going to be as shocked."

Indeed, the reintroduction of live questions has proven effective in helping viewers to understand and agree with recent judges' decisions. For instance, Bill Caligari reports that the selections of Gretchen Carlson, an honors student at Stanford, Debbye Turner, a graduate student in veterinary medicine, and Marjorie Vincent, a third-year law student at Duke, were met with a refreshing degree of public acceptance. "I didn't hear a word from anyone that the wrong girls became Miss America. I think everyone was happy with them." He chuckles. "There's been none of the 'How did *that* happen!?' or 'Where did *she* come from?' that we've had in the past."

Consequently, considering how important strong communication skills are to Miss America's reign, it is not surprising that Pageant-watchers have remarked for years that there is a close correlation between the ability to dazzle judges with a well-crafted answer and the ability to capture the crown.

Marian Bergeron, Miss America 1933.
MISS AMERICA PAGEANT

PART III

THE ROAD TO
MISS AMERICA

CHAPTER 10

Taking the First Step: The Local Pageant

Every September, millions of viewers tune in for the telecast of the Miss America Pageant, watching as one lucky young lady is crowned America's sweetheart. As the glittering tiara is placed upon her head and she begins her victorious walk down the Convention Hall runway, thousands of young women's hearts flutter. Evidently, there is something about that magical moment that is irresistible to legions of red-blooded American girls. When Bernie Wayne penned the Pageant's famous theme song, *There She Is—Miss America,* he must have been clairvoyant, for the fantasy has indeed become "the dream of a million girls."

"I think every little girl dreams about being Miss America," affirms Kaye Lani Rafko. "Everyone I've ever talked to has said that when they were growing up they would watch the Pageant, and when Miss America was crowned they'd run down the hall, get their silk flowers, and pretend to take their runway walk. I think it's every little girl's dream to become Miss America." Besides, Kaye Lani notes from experience, "there's nothing wrong with dreaming!"

While the dream of taking that thrilling walk in Cinderella's glass slippers is common, it is usually accompanied by the assumption: "Sure, it's a wonderful fantasy—but it could never happen to *me*!" But, then, the tantalizing possibility arises: "Or *could* it?" Like many girls, Shirley Cothran once assumed that "being Miss America is something that happens to someone else, but it never happens to you. But," she points out, "when you're there in Atlantic City experiencing it, you realize, 'This could happen to me. I *could* be the winner of this Pageant.'" Therein lies the key to young women's fascination with Miss America. It is a dream with a difference. It is *attainable.*

And the Pageant makes no bones about the accessibility of the crown. As Albert Marks once remarked to *USA Today,* "Our contestants are no different from other women . . . we're not trying to present Miss America as someone unattainable, on top of Mt. Olympus, but as someone within the reach of anyone—a goal anyone can aspire to."

Kaye Lani believes her victory illustrates Marks's point. "No one expected Kaye Lani Rafko, a nurse and a Hawaiian dancer from Monroe, Michigan, to win the title of Miss America. I was a long shot and I think that's why every-

Marilyn Van Derbur, Miss America 1958.
FRED HESS & SON

one was so happy for me." She shrugs. "I was just the girl next door, just like everyone dreams about. I wanted to have people realize that it can happen to *anyone*—and I am an example that it *does* happen to anyone."

Each year, thousands of contestants from around the country enter preliminary pageants in hopes of following in Kaye Lani's footsteps—and every year one young woman emerges from their midst to achieve that dream. "Once they start in the program, somebody who wins a local pageant is going to be Miss America," affirms Miss Tennessee president Tom Hensley. "One of them—*somewhere!* It's just a sifting, shaking-out process." However, before a young woman can manage to achieve that "dream of a million girls," she must first enter a local pageant.

LOCAL COMPETITIONS

As the first step along the road to Miss America, the nation's approximately two thousand local competitions are the important building blocks of the Miss America program. Nonprofit franchises are awarded by each state to carefully screened civic organizations, authorizing them to conduct official preliminary competitions in their respective communities. In order to ensure a uniform standard of quality, every local franchise is required to conduct its operations in accordance with Pageant regulations. Scholarship awards are held in bank trust or escrow accounts to guarantee protection of the funds, and are dispersed according to Scholarship Foundation regulations.

Once a young lady has decided to compete in the Miss America program, her thoughts focus on the question, "How do I begin?"

Prospective contestants can locate local competitions in their area by writing or calling the Pageant's national office (open year round)

for assistance. The staff will direct inquiries to state pageant officials, who will in turn put young ladies in touch with a regional or local director in their community. The address and phone number:

Miss America Scholarship Pageant
P.O. Box 119
Atlantic City, NJ 08404
(609) 345-7571

After a contestant has located a preliminary contest in her area and contacted pageant organizers, she begins the application process. She receives an information packet containing the official rules and regulations and an application form. If a prospective contestant meets the eligibility requirements, she then completes the entry form and returns it with any photographs that have been requested.

Because the application forms ("fact sheets") submitted by contestants are usually reproduced in the judges' workbooks, they offer judges their first glimpse of the candidates for the crown. As such, fact sheets should be carefully completed with attention to neatness, grammar, and spelling.

If an unexpectedly large number of girls apply to compete, the pageant may conduct a preliminary screening to pare the entrants down to a manageable number.

Contestants should also be aware that, unlike many other pageants, the Miss America system does *not* charge entry fees. The Pageant is a nonprofit corporation run by volunteers, so operating expenses and scholarship funds are raised through contributions from community businesses and ticket and program advertising sales—not from contestants' wallets.

THE LOCAL PAGEANT SCHEDULE

Once a young lady has been accepted as a contestant, she is issued a schedule detailing the various pageant events planned. The kick-off is traditionally a "get-acquainted" party and orientation meeting where entrants meet the pageant volunteers they will be working with over the next few weeks. Soon after, the young ladies begin practicing for the upcoming contest. Rehearsals are usually held weekly in a local school auditorium, with a dress rehearsal staged the night before the pageant to give contestants an opportunity to run through the entire production.

The following morning the first competitive event, the private interviews, is conducted at a suitable location such as a college or hotel conference room. These private conversations between judges and contestants are seven minutes long and are scheduled a few minutes apart to allow panelists time to thoughtfully award scores and reorganize their notes in preparation for the next candidate. Following the interviews, contestants return home to prepare for the evening's competition.

When pageant night finally arrives, it is inevitably a thrilling but nerve-tingling experience for the young women. The program begins with an opening production number, followed by an introduction of the judges and an acknowledgment of the sponsors. The reigning titleholder is presented to the audience, and then the actual competition begins. Between the three phases of onstage competition, entertainers are scheduled to give contestants sufficient time for costume changes.

At the conclusion of the last event, the evening gown competition, contestants remain in their gowns and are escorted onstage to await the panel's verdict. As the auditors complete their tabulations, the reigning queen delivers her farewell speech and concludes her reign with a tearful final walk. Then it's the moment they've all been waiting for—the announcement of which candidate will wear the local crown and represent her community in the state finals that summer.

As the master of ceremonies is handed the auditor's envelope, a hush settles over the audience. The contestants nervously hold hands as four runners-up are called forward to accept their trophies. At last, the emcee turns toward the remaining hopefuls and dramatically announces the name of the new local titleholder. All eyes focus on her as she gasps in delight. It is a magical moment, not only for the emotional winner, but for the audience, which wonders if the woman they are applauding will become their state titleholder—and perhaps the next Miss America!

During the dreamlike moments that follow, the sparkling crown is placed upon her head, her proud parents rush onstage to embrace her, her fellow contestants surge forward to offer their congratulations, and a crowd of photographers surrounds her. Soon after, officials whisk their winner away for a brief orientation, a moment to catch her breath, and possibly a judges' "critique."

JUDGES' CRITIQUES

The critique is a private meeting in which judges offer their winner feedback on her performance and suggestions for the upcoming state pageant. Critiques are conducted either with the winner present or with her director taping judges' remarks for later review. Whichever procedure is followed, new titleholders are eager to receive expert advice from the panel. "The majority of girls I have judged have appreciated the critique," says North Carolina judge "Miss Pattie" Ruffin. "I always tell them, 'You can improve on criticism, but you can't improve on praises! So you better listen and start writing.' And believe me," she reports with a grin, "they take notes!"

Other contestants are welcome to request written critiques from panelists, but they should be aware that judges who choose to respond are instructed not to reveal their scores, and to limit their comments to observations and suggestions for improvement. Young ladies who are interested in writing to judges should contact their pageant director for more information.

REACTIONS TO THE OUTCOME

Following the photo session and critique, the new queen, her alternates, and the remaining contestants appear at a postcoronation reception where they visit with family and friends. For the young ladies who have not won the crown, emotions are mixed. Some are disappointed because they had hoped to win or place higher, while others are thrilled merely to have summoned the courage to stand onstage as a contestant! Although the girls may not have won the crown that evening, they most definitely have not "lost." There are no losers in pageant competition because every woman who competes gains *something* through the experience. Perhaps it is increased self-confidence, sharpened performance and interviewing skills, or scholarship money. There may be only one crown to award, but there are innumerable benefits available for all.

For the contestants, it has been a long and exciting day, even if tinged with disappointment—but for one lucky young lady it is the beginning of a yearlong journey she will never forget!

NOW THAT YOU'RE A LOCAL TITLEHOLDER

It is an honor to hold a local pageant title—but it is also a responsibility. Each local queen should bear in mind that her actions will enhance or detract from the reputation of her community, her local pageant, and the Miss America program. Jeff Bell, a veteran local pageant official, advises entrants to "realize that if they are the winner, they have a big responsibility ahead of them and they have got to make sure that they uphold the values and morals of that particular crown." An official pageant/contestant contract explains the responsibilities of both the titleholder and the pageant organization she represents.

The months leading up to the state competition are a busy, exciting time, filled with public appearances: parades, style shows, social and business gatherings, and charity fund-raisers. Local queens also attend other preliminaries to meet some of the girls they will compete with at the state level, and in order to boost their confidence, they are encouraged to speak and perform their talents in public as often as possible. Whatever the particular appearance, a titleholder is always accompanied by a responsible woman chaperon and/or official to ensure her safety and well-being. Public appearances often involve a modest appearance fee for the young lady, and her travel expenses, hotel accommodations, and meals are paid by the organizations that request her presence or by her pageant franchise.

PREPARATIONS FOR THE STATE COMPETITION

With the state pageant only a few months away, preparations are a priority for the contestant and her director. Flattering photographs must be taken for the judges' workbooks and the program book, an updated fact sheet must be submitted, talent clearances must be obtained, her competition wardrobe must be chosen and packed, and the young lady must be prepared for every phase of competition.

With so much involved, the key to approaching the state competition with confidence is to prepare thoroughly in every area _before_ taking off for pageant week. Louisiana official Mike McMahan cautions, "You don't wait until you come to the state pageant to practice your talent or to work on your swimsuit. You work on that ahead of time on the local level, and then you come to the pageant, relax, do your best, and have a good time while you're there. Of course, that's hard for them to do, but if they _will,_ they'll be much more relaxed."

Effective preparation on the local level can really pay off, according to Shirley Cothran-Barret. After she won the Miss Haltom-Richland Area title, local officials worked tirelessly to prepare Shirley for the Miss Texas Pageant, replacing the flute she had been playing since the fifth grade, providing her first private flute lessons, improving her musical arrangement, and ordering several gowns made for her, including the spectacular white chiffon design she later wore in Atlantic City. "They really did a lot to prepare me, and that helped me tremendously," she recalls. "I was so prepared—I don't mean _molded_—I mean everything had been done for me to enhance _me_ as Miss Haltom-Richland Area. They did wonderful things for me!" In fact, they prepared Shirley so well that by the time she won the Miss Texas title, there was little left for state officials to improve on. With the exception of a haircut and some wardrobe additions, Shirley Cothran was already impeccably prepared when she arrived at her state pageant.

Shirley gives her local pageant's generous efforts much of the credit for her victory at the Miss America Pageant, and points out that a local pageant "family" should do everything possible to enhance the individual qualities of their representative. The end result should be a contestant who is practiced, polished, and self-assured in the knowledge that she is at _her_ very best.

CHAPTER 11

The State Pageant

Across the country, approximately two thousand local titleholders have been training, grooming, and practicing in anticipation of the upcoming state competitions—where fifty lucky young women will take an important step forward along the road to Miss America.

The state pageants, which are traditionally conducted in late spring and early summer, differ from region to region depending upon the size of the state and the number of participants. Smaller state programs, like those in New England, may have a dozen or so contestants, while larger programs like the Miss Utah and Texas pageants, have sixty or more participants. Because of such differences, state pageant schedules vary from one-day contests to week-long competitions.

For example, in tiny Rhode Island, where candidates live within short driving distances, it isn't necessary to house contestants for a week-long pageant. Instead, the girls drive in once a week for six weeks to rehearse production numbers. During the final week, they practice every evening, followed by a dress rehearsal the night before the pageant. Then,

on Saturday, contestants come in for afternoon judges' interviews, followed by the onstage competition that evening.

Those state programs with large numbers of entrants usually conduct week-long pageants. For instance, in Ohio, where forty contestants compete, officials conduct a week-long competition held in conjunction with the Miss Ohio Festival. "It's been heartwarming to see the tremendous number of people," says Robert Zettler, executive director of the Miss Ohio Pageant. "All of our hotels are filled and everybody's happy. If you do the kind of figuring that Chambers of Commerce often do ... this pageant probably has a minimum of a ten-million-dollar economic impact on the community of Mansfield."

State competitions are particularly popular affairs in the South, like the state of Arkansas, where over two hundred volunteers stage the state pageant. "We bring so many people in that it's like the Fourth of July weekend in Hot Springs!" reports Miss Arkansas director Bob Wheeler. "The restaurants stay open for us, hotels are full. Over a three- to four-night period, we'll bring in over thirteen thousand people."

Because of their large volunteer staffs and extensive community support, the larger programs have the resources to turn their competition schedules into whirlwind adventures. "We try to make all of our contestants feel like they're superstars!" Zettler explains. "They're always in the public eye during the first few days they're there ... and they really start to feel like they're something because *they're* the show! We try to take them out to various restaurants and public places to keep them in the public eye ... so it's a tough week, but it's a fun week."

In many states, the schedule is purposely designed to duplicate the national Pageant schedule in order to prepare the eventual winner for the demands of national competition. "We use the same system here that is used in Atlantic City," says Wheeler, "so when Miss Arkansas goes to Miss America, the schedule is the very same thing she experienced here in Arkansas. It's just on a bigger scale."

As the candidates arrive at the state pageant, they are introduced to their hostesses and escorted to their accommodations. Housing arrangements differ from state to state, ranging from placing contestants in private homes, to pairing girls in hotel suites, to lodging girls together in a local college dorm. After the young ladies check in, drop off their luggage, and freshen up, they gather at pageant headquarters for the welcoming ceremony and group photo.

In the days that follow, the girls are kept busy from early morning until evening with rehearsals, receptions, photo and autograph sessions, public appearances at local tourist attractions, television tapings, and meals at area restaurants. Later in the week, the actual competitive events take place, with the private interviews with judges preceding the onstage competitions. Contestants usually are divided into two or three preliminary groups that alternate phases of competition.

By Saturday, the preliminary events have concluded and the curtain is drawn for the long-awaited final competition. In many areas of the nation, pageants are telecast live statewide. Whether or not the production is broadcast, the evening is a great thrill for the contestants who anxiously await the announcement of the ten finalists and the young woman who will wear the coveted state crown and compete in the Miss America Pageant.

PARENTS AND PAGEANT WEEK

Contestants are not the only people who experience the excitement of competition. Family and friends who are present to cheer on the young ladies share in the hopes, dreams—and nervous jitters—of "their" candidate for the crown.

Recently, former Miss America Kylene Barker drew chuckles from a local pageant audience when she shared a personal example of *parents'* perspective on state-level competition. When Kylene described how, as she competed for the Miss Virginia title, her father "paced the floor more than he did when my mother went into labor when I was born," dozens of parents in the audience vigorously nodded their heads in appreciation. Apparently, there are few experiences as nerve-tingling as waiting helplessly to find out if your daughter is that lucky young woman who will move on to the Miss America Pageant.

Not surprisingly, parents don't necessarily have to be present in the auditorium to experience the joy. Debbie Maffett's parents, who live in rural Texas, couldn't attend the Miss California Pageant the night she won the crown. On the evening of the finals, they went to bed wondering how their daughter was faring. Hours later, as Nonnie Maffett slept, she suddenly experienced a flood of "warm good feelings, like someone had just told me extremely good news." She jolted awake with a smile plastered on her face, turned to her startled husband, and exclaimed, "The strangest feeling just came over me. They just crowned Debbie Miss California!" The couple had just managed to get back to sleep when the telephone rang and the caller asked, "Would you like to speak to the new Miss California?" Nonnie explains excitedly that because of the time zone differences, "the time they were crowning Debbie Miss California was the exact time I sat up in bed and told my husband that she had won. We didn't know what time the telecast was, or what time it would be ending, so it was kind of eerie!"

Because parents have such a deep emotional involvement with their daughters' ambitions to win the crown, officials strive to keep parents informed about their offspring's activities and responsibilities. "During the pageant, we have meetings with the parents," says past Miss Louisiana director Mike McMahan. "We go over the contract with them so they're not shocked or surprised." Then, the morning after Miss Louisiana is selected, officials have a "contract meeting" with the winner and her parents. "We sit down with the girl and her parents and go over all the phases of the contract, what we expect from her, and what she can expect from us. We let her parents meet all the people who will be involved with their daughter, such as her grooming committee and business manager." Keeping parents informed helps them to appreciate that their daughter is in the care of capable individuals who will work to make her reign a safe and rewarding experience.

WINNING THE STATE CROWN

As the week of competition concludes and the contestants stand onstage awaiting the verdict of the judges, each young woman yearns to hear *her* name shouted out as her state's representative to the Miss America Pageant. "You're hoping," admits Sophia Symko, Miss Utah 1988. "You're thinking, 'Just call my name, *pleeease!*' And if you're lucky, you do hear your name." When the moment becomes reality, the emotions defy description. "You can't really explain it," Sophia says. "It's wonderful, but something that you have to experience to understand."

It's even more spine-tingling when the contestant has lost before and is accustomed to watching other girls walk off with the laurels. "Every year, I had still been standing there when Miss Ohio was being named," says Sarah Evans, Miss Ohio 1988, "and she'd be going down the runway as I was still standing there applauding for her. But this year," she says, giggling, "when they announced the four runners-up and my name still hadn't been called, I sort of looked out of the corner of my eye at the other finalists around me, and I thought, 'Uh oh! I might really be . . . it might just really be . . . '" Seconds later, when her name was announced as the winner, she was overcome with emotion and trembled so badly that her predecessor had trouble positioning the crown and banner. "I was really just overwhelmed!" she exclaims. "It was the most incredible feeling in the whole world!"

The moment of victory traditionally arouses a flood of sentiments—pride at having reached a difficult goal, delight for one's parents, and excitement that the national Pageant lies just a few months down the road. "I knew vaguely in my mind that I was going to the Miss America Pageant," says former Miss Rhode Island Michele Passarelli. "And I was very excited and very confident—with the kind of confidence that only an eighteen-year-old can have—that I could actually go on and win the national thing."

But Michele also remembers her thoughts being focused upon the impact her success would have upon her future. "It was that optimistic wide-eyed feeling that I was wonderful!" she quips. "I didn't know where I was going from there, but I knew that everything in my life was going to take an upswing." She affirms with a wide smile, "And it *did!*"

POSTCORONATION EVENTS

The moments following the crowning of a new state queen are highly emotional, as contestants embrace and congratulate the winner. "It's a big release," explains Miss Florida official Roger Knight, "because those girls get to be very, very close. Some of them develop friendships that last, and at that moment, there's a lot of hugging and kissing and a release of tension that it's *over.*" While security men guard the stage area, the new titleholder's family and reporters are allowed onstage for photographs. The winner is then escorted offstage to attend several functions. While states differ, the schedule usually includes a short rest period for the young lady to freshen her makeup and collect her thoughts, followed by a brief press conference and possibly a critique.

The state judges' critique, like those conducted on the local level, allows the panel to offer their winner feedback on her performance. Conducted either with the new titleholder present or with her director taping judges' suggestions for later discussion, the critique's purpose is always to supply the young lady with constructive advice for improving for the national competition. "When our judges give Miss Arkansas a critique," Bob Wheeler explains, "I tell them never to tell her what to change, but tell her that she might want to look at something else.... We don't criticize her. We do not, at *any* time, do anything to tear down the confidence of the girl," he stresses. "We believe that our purpose in this is to instill confidence."

Following the critique and press conference, the winner, her court, and the remaining contestants attend a coronation reception where they are officially presented to guests. The Miss Texas program also uses this opportunity to award additional scholarships to the ten highest-scoring nonfinalists, and the best interviewee, most talented dancer, singer, musician, actress, etc. Girls are then free to visit with their families, friends, and local delegates until sometime after midnight, when the hostesses return contestants to their rooms.

The following morning, when contestants depart for their respective communities, they appreciate that while they won't be taking the state crown along with them, they will take home memories of an exciting—albeit fatiguing—week in the spotlight. "It's just an unbelievable experience for these girls," remarks Roger Knight. "It's a very hectic week, and when it's over, they've got to be exhausted! But it is one of the most enjoyable, memorable experiences they will ever have. They will *never* forget that week!"

1989 MISS FLORIDA PAGEANT SCHEDULE

Sunday

1:00–3:00	Hotel registration and check-in
4:00–5:30	Orientation
6:00–7:00	Picnic
8:00–10:00	Three groups, production number rehearsals

Monday

8:30	Breakfast at Sea World
9:30–1:00	Sea World publicity photos/ lunch
2:30–4:00	All contestants practice
4:00–5:00	Change for dinner
5:45	Dinner at country club
8:00–10:00	Patrons' reception

Tuesday

9:30–12:00	Breakfast at mall/autographs/ photos
12:00	Lunch in hospitality room or tea room
1:30–3:00	Group B interviews
2:00–3:00	Groups A and C practice
3:00–3:30	Group A and C rest
3:30–3:45	Three groups, rehearsals
3:45	Leave for dinner—restaurant
5:00–10:30	All contestants, rehearsals/ steam dresses

Wednesday

7:30–8:00	Breakfast in hospitality rooms
9:00–11:00	Group C interviews Groups A and B talent rehearsals
11:00–11:30	Swimsuit rehearsals
11:30–12:30	All contestants, production rehearsals
12:30	Lunch
1:30–4:00	Group A interviews
1:30–2:00	Groups B and C evening gown/talent rehearsals
4:30	Dinner at seafood restaurant
7:00	Arrive at auditorium
8:00	Curtain
After show	Visitation

Thursday

7:30–8:00	Breakfast
9:00–12:30	Talent rehearsals
12:30–1:00	Swimsuit rehearsals
1:00–2:00	Lunch
2:00–3:00	Production rehearsals
4:00	Dinner at steak restaurant
7:00	Arrive at auditorium
8:00	Curtain
After show	Visitation

Friday

7:30–8:00	Breakfast
9:00–12:30	Talent rehearsals
1:00–2:00	Lunch
2:00–3:00	Production/evening gown rehearsals
4:10	Dinner at Italian restaurant
7:00	Arrive at auditorium
8:00	Curtain
After show	Visitation

Saturday

9:30–11:00	Closed TV rehearsal onstage
11:00	Lunch
12:00–5:00	Continue TV rehearsal
5:00–6:00	Dinner
6:00	Call for final performance Voting for Miss Congeniality
6:30–6:50	Preshow
7:00–9:00	Show—statewide television coverage
9:30	Reception in ballroom

Sunday

8:00	Check-out and depart for home
8:00–2:00	Pageant photos
10:00–10:20	USO and Miss Florida photos
10:20	USO troupe orientation
11:00	Miss Florida press conference

YOU'RE A STATE TITLEHOLDER NOW!

The morning after the state pageant, one lucky young woman wakes, gazes across the room at a glittering crown and trophy, and realizes that the delightful experience wasn't a dream. The waking sentiments of one newly crowned winner, Florida's Melissa Aggeles, echoed the thoughts of multitudes of state queens who had gone before her. "This morning I woke up thinking to myself, 'After watching it for so many years, I am finally going to *be* at the Miss America Pageant!'"

Indeed, the entire focus of the first few months of a state queen's reign is directed toward preparing her for the upcoming Miss America Pageant. First, the new titleholder is introduced to her business manager and the team of volunteers that will help her prepare for the national competition. Her immediate schedule involves a morning press conference, faxing her talent request form to the national office, reviewing her contract with her parents and pageant director, updating her fact sheet for the national judges, and sitting for photographs for the national program book.

While the majority of state representatives work full-time during the summer months to prepare for the national Pageant (discussed in the next chapter), their schedules vary thereafter. In about a third of the states, the year-round demand for appearances by the titleholder is sufficient to warrant her taking a year off from college to take advantage of those opportunities. However, the remaining two-thirds of state titleholders have somewhat less demanding appearance schedules that they are encouraged to balance with light academic course loads. During personal appearances, state representatives are always accompanied by a woman traveling companion who oversees travel arrangements, drives the young lady to and from bookings, and assists her if uncomfortable situations arise.

The opportunity to serve as a state titleholder is a rewarding one in many respects. Depending upon the public interest in a titleholder's area and her success in the national pageant, a state queen's schedule can generate personal appearance income ranging from a few thousand dollars in New England or the western regions, to $5,000 to $10,000 in some midwestern states, to the mid-twenties in the South, and as high as $45,000 in Texas. Winners also receive impressive prizes. For instance, in addition to a $4,000 scholarship and $15,000 in personal appearance fees, Miss New Jersey 1988 received a fur coat, the use of a new automobile with insurance paid and special license tags "NJ-1," a jewelry wardrobe including a $2,000 custom pendant, a $5,000 competition evening gown donated by a New York designer, a $1,000 J. C. Penney shopping spree, and a $2,000 cruise on the *QE II* (with a stateroom suite). "The year is worth about thirty-five thousand to her," explains executive director Nathan Zauber. "We work on getting these perks fifty-two weeks a year, and if you add them up, it's not a bad year for the young lady!"

Other perks include expense-paid nationwide and international travel (like Misses California and Washington, who visit the Far East on promotional expeditions) and the opportunity to hobnob with celebrities and dignitaries. Her year is also filled with widely varying public appearances: radio and television talk shows, parades, style shows, banquets, receptions, conventions, festivals, sports tournaments, business promotions, and charity fundraisers.

While the reign affords a young woman unparalleled opportunities and makes a significant change in her lifestyle, her position as a state titleholder is more than a privilege. It is an important responsibility. "The first thing I would tell them is that it is not all glamour," says Miss New York field director Kenn Berry. "It takes a lot for a young lady to carry that crown the whole year. For the first few weeks, it may be great. You're Miss Whatever, people are lauding you, looking up to you, and you're the center of attention. But once that wears off, the crown can become heavy. You have to really *work* to be the best Miss Whatever that you can be!"

Although the responsibilities can be demanding, most young ladies cherish the opportunity to serve as their state's representative. As Lori Lee Kelley, Miss Oklahoma 1988, put it, "It's very glamorous, but there's a lot of responsibility that goes along with being Miss Oklahoma. Yes, there are times when you have struggles with it, but you just have to remember the reason why you were pursuing the crown in the first place. If I ever had a frustrating moment, I would just remember that there are so many girls who would love to have this crown on their heads right now."

Some of the demands of a titleholder's reign include the necessity of always looking her best despite a hectic schedule, living out of suitcases while traveling, preparing and delivering speeches, smiling for hours on end, signing thousands of autographs, working when she's not feeling up to par, and dealing with public expectations. "The public somehow doesn't think about the fact that you've been in a car for three hours," explains Sarah Evans, "that you had a late appointment the night before, and now you're here at six in the morning for them. You always have to be *up*. You need to be fresh, alert, and personable at every appearance. The public doesn't see the behind the scenes and you have to meet their expectations."

Sometimes, those expectations can be amusing, like the time Regina Hopper, Miss Arkansas 1983, arrived at her hotel after a particularly grueling day of travel. As she checked in at the front desk, she stated, "I'm Regina Hopper. I'm supposed to have a reservation here. It may be under the Miss Fayetteville Pageant." The clerk glanced up and asked, "Oh? Well, what are *you* here for?" When Regina replied, "I'm Miss Arkansas," the clerk did a double-take, gasped, "Are you kidding!" and then stammered in embarrassment, "Gosh . . . uh . . . we always thought she'd be like . . . you know, dressed up with a crown on!" Regina guffaws at the memory. "It was like they didn't want to give me a room 'cause they thought I was an *impostor!*"

Despite such humbling experiences, titleholders soon discover that even the most unlikely fans are intrigued by their position. For instance, Regina recalls that state troopers routinely found excuses to stop her car when they spotted its "Miss Arkansas" emblem. "Just to see what I looked like," she suggests with a laugh, "or to get an autograph for their 'little kid.' It was adorable because they'd say, 'Uhm . . . can I have an autograph for my son Tim?' "—to which Regina would inquire with an amused grin, "What's his daddy's name? *Tim?*"

Other queens who have attempted to travel quietly unobserved have experienced similar examples of the public's fascination. B. Don Magness recalls the time he and Cathy Castro, Miss Texas 1988, were returning from a shopping trip to New York City. As they changed planes in Atlanta, a grade-school soccer player returning home from a match recognized Castro as the new Miss Texas. He soon had his teammates and fellow passengers buzzing with excitement. "Well, they all decided that they had to have autographs!" Magness recalls. "Unfortunately, nobody had any paper to write on, so one of 'em came up with the bright idea that she could sign his airplane 'barf bag.' Well, she must have signed fifty barf bags!" He laughs at the reverence one of the little boys displayed when he warned his fellow passengers, "I'll tell y'all one thing. If I have to throw up, I ain't using *this* bag, so y'all better get ready over there!"

Even fellow contestants sometimes succumb to such reverence. "It's funny," admits former Miss New York Mia Seminoff, "but, suddenly, even people that I had been with all [state pageant] week were holding me in such reverence!" She imitates their awed expressions. "Ahhh! Miss New York!" Mia recalls, chuckling to herself. "Wait a minute! We've been together all week joking around. What's the deal? But," she reports, "all of a sudden, with that crown . . ."

While the crown brings opportunities to travel extensively, hobnob with celebrities, and bask in the glow of public admiration, the year seems to end as quickly as it began. A year later, in the same auditorium, on the same stage, in front of many of the same people, the wonderful year in the spotlight abruptly comes to an end. In those last few moments before the crown is bestowed upon another teary-eyed Miss America aspirant, the reigning title-holder takes her final walk before her home-state audience. Former Miss Mississippi Mary Donnelly recalls those final moments when she was lauded by those who had made her reign so meaningful. "You're walking the run-way, listening to your speech, and saying good-bye. It's a very emotional moment, because in your mind's eye you can see yourself as you were when you were crowned: the changes, the growth that you have experienced that year. And you feel that you're going to be losing that closeness and contact with the people who were responsible for that year being so wonderful."

Former Miss Florida Kim Boyce reflects upon the similar thoughts she experienced as she concluded her reign—thoughts that echo the emotions so many of her fellow titlehold-ers have experienced. "The pageant had become such a big part of my life, and the pageant people were my second family that cared for me. It was like the end of an era in my life," she says softly, "and it was really sad."

For the retiring queen, the evening she bestows the crown upon another young woman _is_ tinged with sadness because it marks the end of what has been a thrilling chapter in her life. However, for the ecstatic young woman who has just captured the state title, it is a night of possibilities—a night when the breathtaking realization dawns that, within a matter of weeks, during a magical evening in Atlantic City, she may become the lucky young woman who walks away with a $35,000 scholarship—and the Miss America crown!

CHAPTER 12

Preparing for a Dream

The final countdown to the coronation of a new Miss America has begun, and fifty young women have earned the right to compete in the Super Bowl of pageants. By mid-September, the field of national finalists will be narrowed again—this time to ten semifinalists, five runners-up, and a new Miss America. With so much at stake, and with the state representatives granted only one shot at the title, each candidate is eager to be at her personal best—and hopefully to be judged *the* best. It is a once-in-a-lifetime opportunity and a challenge contestants accept enthusiastically.

Despite the glamour and excitement, the last leg on the road to the crown is not an easy one. It is often an arduous test of determination, endurance, and *confidence*. "It's interesting because eighty thousand people strive every year to become Miss America," muses Miss Ohio director Robert Zettler. "And it *takes* that kind of elimination process to get the few women who can stand the pressure of a national competition and telecast and perform anywhere close to their ability in Atlantic City. Can they *take* that pressure? The Olympic con-

testants don't have any more pressure on them than our ladies," he insists. "They really don't. These young women are putting it all on the line. It's tough because they have one shot and they had better do it correctly!"

Aspiring Miss Americas recognize that dreaming about dazzling the judges in Atlantic City isn't going to put that crown within reach. A victory at the national level is earned through dedication to developing excellence, a willingness to invest countless hours in preparation, and the persistence to keep working when the going gets tough. "It takes that kind of effort," Zettler continues, "because there's the realization that all their hopes and dreams could come true for them there."

THE "ACCIDENTAL" MISS AMERICAS

There is no question that the quality of participants has improved and the intensity of competition increased dramatically since 1921, when Margaret Gorman trounced fewer than a dozen contestants to win the first Miss America title. At that time, a young woman could enter a regional contest on a lark, move on to Atlantic City without a thought of winning, and find to her astonishment that she had been voted Miss America. That's been a traditional part of the charm, according to national judge Sam Haskell. "It's the fun and excitement of seeing the Mississippi belle and the Kansas farm girl made into a star overnight. That's what it's all about." In fact, since that first coronation, many winners have been "accidental" Miss Americas who were "drafted" into the Pageant by sorority sisters and classmates, automatically dubbed local titleholder by new franchises, or persuaded to enter by family doctors, local businessmen, and parents. Lee Meriwether (1955) was entered into the Miss San Francisco Pageant by a fraternity president when she skipped an inter-fraternity-sorority meeting; Marian McKnight (1957) was simply appointed Miss Manning after the Chamber of Commerce started a new franchise; and Marilyn Van Derbur (1958) was literally drafted into the Miss University of Colorado Pageant by her sorority when she was called out of a meeting for a long-distance phone call.

Like many queens of the era, Evelyn Ay, Miss America 1954, entered and won the Miss America Pageant on a lark. Her family dentist, "an avid fan" of the Pageant, talked her into entering the local contest, which she managed to win despite her homespun recital of *The Spider and the Fly*. "It was really just serendipity!" she admits, giggling. Her "preparations" for the national contest were negligible compared with today's sophisticated candidates. "There wasn't the tremendous concentration on training," Evelyn explains, "taking this person and *creating* something out of this person. We just went as we were. Yes, we worked with the basics we each had, and we polished and developed them to the best of our ability—but it wasn't creating something out of clay. There's a professionalism today that we perhaps didn't feel we needed then."

Months later, Evelyn found herself representing Pennsylvania at the Miss America Pageant, an experience that she admits overwhelmed her. "I came from a small town. It was barely the age of television. The majority of us were dazzled. The stage. The lights. The runway. It was all so sophisticated! We had never seen such a big production!" Not surprisingly, Evelyn was dumbfounded to hear her name announced as Miss America. "I just couldn't believe it! It had never crossed my mind that I would be the winner." She adds with a laugh, "I couldn't even believe that I made the *top ten!*"

Another notable "draftee," Judith Ford, Miss America 1969, recalls she "just fell into it by accident." When organizers of a new local franchise asked Judi to represent them in the state contest, she accepted, was dubbed their queen and promptly dispatched to the Miss Illinois contest. She recalls doing virtually nothing to prepare for the event, and figuring that her college trampoline routine would have to suffice as her "talent."

To her surprise, she won and was ushered into preparations for the upcoming national contest—efforts she admits were rather comical by today's standards. "They took me to a modeling school in Chicago for a day and the instructor said I walked like an athlete. When I said, 'Thank you,' she said, 'No no no no no—that's *not* a compliment!'" Then state officials cautioned her, "Keep in mind not to get your hopes up because you have three strikes against you before you even walk onstage." It seems Ford was too young (eighteen) and too blond (after ten brunette Miss Americas), and sported an offbeat talent. "Thanks," she muttered under her breath. "I'm sure not going to be overconfident here."

When Judi and her fellow contestants arrived in Atlantic City that September, they were awestruck. "All of us were overwhelmed just that we were *there!*" In fact, she recalls the girls giggling backstage: "Wow! This is great! We watch this on TV!" Although Ford had hoped to make the top ten so she could perform on television, she was astonished to make the final cut. "I remember sitting there in the top five thinking, 'Oh my gosh! One of us is actually going to *win* this thing!'" Moments later, when Bert shouted her name as Miss America, Judi silently gasped, "You're kidding!" and nearly passed out. Like many of her predecessors, she admits, "The thought of winning the Pageant had never entered my mind."

MODERN MISS AMERICAS— WORKING TO EARN THE CROWN

While many Miss Americas have been accidental queens, other winners have been glowing examples of the great American philosophy that with enough elbow grease and persistence, any goal is achievable. In recent years, just as training methods for collegiate, professional, and Olympic sports have become more sophisticated, pageant contestants have eagerly embraced the tradition of intense competitive preparation. As a result, it has become increasingly common to see young women with eyes focused firmly on the crown—and aggressively campaigning to win it. "The contestants are much more prepared today than they were back in the forties and fifties," confirms Ruth McCandliss, retired national director of field operations. "And they're more ambitious!"

The seeds for that heightened level of competitive sophistication were sown in the early 1930s, when reporters observed that many contestants "showed the results of careful training for public appearances by chaperons selected for their experience in the teaching of poise." A decade later, a determined California beauty, Rosemary LaPlanche,

brought new depth to the art of pageant preparation. After finishing as first runner-up to Frances Burke in the 1940 Miss America Pageant, LaPlanche developed a painstaking strategy for winning the crown, reentered the next year—and easily walked away with the 1941 Miss America title. Shortly after her coronation, she informed reporters, "I worked awfully hard to get here this year for a second try. It meant studying and practicing night and day. To get here again, I had to overcome competition from five hundred other California girls picked in American Legion contests. And if I hadn't won the title here this year, I was determined to come back again next year!"

By the sixties, although such tenacity was still uncommon, growing numbers of competitors were beginning to appreciate that meticulous preparation could be the key to victory. Perhaps decades of her predecessors had won their titles almost accidentally, but Arizona's Vonda Kay Van Dyke determinedly carved her pathway to the Miss America throne with nine months of exhaustive training. "It was my project," she explains, "and every spare moment was spent on getting ready for Miss America. It was just my whole focus and I really lived and breathed it for nine months." She interjects with a laugh, "Just like having a baby!" Vonda perfected her ventriloquism routine by performing twelve shows a day six days a week at an amusement park. "I tried out different songs and thousands of jokes. I tried to get just the right psychological pitch to the jokes and I wrote time tables of how long each response was because the responses were part of my three minutes." Ironically, Vonda practiced so relentlessly that during national Pageant week she had to remind herself to *move* her lips when she spoke!

Despite her determined preparations, Vonda somehow failed to accept the possibility of actually *winning*. "I was committed to doing my best, but I didn't have any idea I was going to win." Yet, when Bert Parks announced her name as Miss America 1965, the realization suddenly dawned, "But you know, I'm sure I worked harder than anybody else this year."

Although Vonda's efforts had been unprecedented at the time, by the late seventies, such fervid preparative efforts were widely practiced—leading to measures that have been criticized as excessive. "I think there are a lot more superficial kinds of things that happen to young women now," explains former Miss America Rebecca King, who served as a national judge in 1984, "from plastic surgery to five-thousand-dollar evening gowns. I didn't have that kind of money," she says, "and most of us [Miss Americas] did not."

Although the increasing reliance on cosmetic surgery and costly apparel by overzealous contestants has received extensive media attention, such competitive tactics are _not_ necessarily the qualities that capture the judges' votes. Dorothy Benham, Miss America 1977, is a classic example. Although she is regarded as one of the finest titleholders ever, Dorothy won the crown with a bare-necessities wardrobe compiled from department store bargains. Her preparations were equally meager. "I didn't do anything special," she reports with a shrug. "I just had a nice summer. A lot of girls live with somebody who works with them," she acknowledges, "but I stayed right at home. I made my appearances every day and then I'd come home and go out in the evening with my friends. When I won my state pageant, my judges looked at my state people and said, 'Leave her alone. Just let her go as she is.' So they did. I have to tell you, I think it was a wonderful way to go because there was no pressure."

Another winner who proved that the crown isn't won with a huge bank account and a surgeon's skills, but with old-fashioned hard work, is Cheryl Prewitt, Miss America 1980. From all appearances, Cheryl was an improbable prospect to make it to the national throne. She still bore scars from a serious childhood car accident and she had competed for four years before winning her first _local_ title! When her parents couldn't afford a fancy competition wardrobe, she simply competed in clothes that were borrowed or homemade, including a cheap pair of sandals dipped in glue and red sparkles. Despite the inauspicious debut, Prewitt finally won the Miss Mississippi title in 1979.

She moved in with state officials Briggs and Pat Hopson, who reviewed Cheryl's strengths and weaknesses and designed a demanding daily schedule to prepare her for the national contest. Cheryl rose at 6:30 A.M. and launched into a three-hour exercise regimen alternated with studying television news programs, newspapers, and her Bible, followed by a lunch break, several hours of sunbathing, and a second round of exercise and study. After a light dinner, she would either practice walking and pivoting, working with microphones and timing her talent at a nearby high school auditorium, or participate in videotaped mock interviews. Finally, at 11:00 P.M., she logged a final hour of exercise and collapsed in bed. The schedule was grueling, but entirely _self-motivated_ by her desire to be at her very best in Atlantic City. "I kept _myself_ on that schedule," she explains. "I worked hard. I've always been very mentally and physically disciplined, and this was my one time to be the very best that I could be with no distractions."

Cheryl's triumph as Miss America 1980 disproved the misconception that big bucks and silicone are the winning qualities. Instead, she insists, the crown is earned through persistence, determination, and self-discipline. For those determined to forge their way to the national throne, she recommends a safer, more economical prescription for victory: each contestant should evaluate her strengths and weaknesses, and invest time and unrelenting effort to become her best—not necessarily reaching the status of "the best," but certainly achieving her *personal* best.

THE LAST LEG ON THE ROAD TO MISS AMERICA

The last leg on the road to Miss America is run during the two-month period immediately preceding September's national finals, when the fifty hopefuls enthusiastically volunteer for grueling schedules of last-minute preparations. "They work very, very hard," asserts Nora Chapman, Alabama's "Iron Maiden" executive director. "Until you have groomed a girl for Miss America and until you go through all of that with her, you truly cannot know how hard they do work." Nora offers each Miss Alabama a piece of advice. "The theory I teach my girls is that you can do anything that you want to do if you work for it and *earn* it. You can't ask for it to be given to you. You have to *earn* it—every ounce of the way."

Apparently, that willingness to pay the price of success is the quality that distinguishes winners from girls who merely drool over the crown. "So many girls don't take this seriously," asserts B. Don Magness. "They think, 'Boy, it'd be neat to be Miss America! Now I don't want to work my buns off to do it—but it would sure be neat to *be* Miss America!'" Magness laughs. "Hey, there's not any Santa Claus, regardless of what they might have read. Anything worth having, you have to *work* for."

And work they do. The preparations begin the morning after their state pageants, when, according to Tom Hensley, many state directors have a heart-to-heart chat with their contestants to determine exactly what each young woman hopes to accomplish in the next few months. The first question Hensley asks each new Miss Tennessee is "Do you want to be Miss America?," to which the immediate response is almost always a resounding "Yes!" At

that point, in order to ensure that the young lady understands that this is *her* decision, Hensley tells her, "We're not interested in being Miss America, per se, but if *you* want to be Miss America, then we will do everything in our power financially and physically to prepare you . . . but we are happy that you're Miss Tennessee and we want you to be the best Miss Tennessee we've got."

While state directors offer guidance and assistance to their titleholders, they realize that they do not *create* a Miss America. They provide the environment for personal development, but it is the young women who must harness those opportunities for growth. "We afforded Kellye Cash the opportunities to fine-tune what she had," Hensley explains, "but she had the initiative to do it on her own. She wanted to do it. We didn't 'make' Kellye Cash. You don't make a Miss America. They make themselves."

Once the young ladies have strengthened their talent performances, perfected their physiques, mentally prepared for the interview, compiled and organized their competitive wardrobes, and increased their confidence, it is time to put the months of hard work to the big test.

BALANCING THE WILL TO WIN

For the fifty aspiring Miss Americas, their shot at the crown is a once-in-a-lifetime opportunity that could dramatically alter the course of their lives. With so much at stake, the pressures of competition can be difficult to handle if the young woman has not prepared herself emotionally. According to former contestants, the key to maintaining a healthy competitive attitude—*whatever* the eventual outcome—is to view Pageant week as a remarkable experience few women have the privilege of sharing.

In essence, balancing their will to win with a desire to savor the experience.

What you *don't* want to do, says former Miss Mississippi Mary Donnelly, chuckling, is to step off the airplane in Atlantic City with the attitude, "This is it! This is my destiny. I will *be* Miss America!" A preoccupation with winning at all costs—as opposed to the healthier approach of working to perform at one's best—inevitably leads to disillusionment. "The end of it is that only *one* girl can have the crown," says Donnelly, "so, if you go up thinking that the only way you can win is to bring the Miss America crown home, then you're not going to win, and you're not going to be happy."

Conversely, many women who earned the Miss America title emphasize that, while they wanted to win, they refused to focus their energies and hopes specifically on that one goal. Instead, they concentrated on performing at their best and enjoying the experience. "I had a *wonderful* time," says Dorothy Benham, "and I think that made the difference. I went to have a good time and make friends." When enthusiastic supporters kept predicting, "We're going to be Miss America! We just know she's going to win!," Dorothy stopped them cold. "I told them, 'If you all want to say that, and if you want to believe that, you do it. But *I* don't want to hear it, because if I don't win, I'm not going to be disappointed. *You* will be. I'm not going to be a part of that. I'm here to have a good time and hopefully to gain more scholarship money.'" In retrospect, Dorothy says, "I think my faith was a lot of it. I was very calm and relaxed because I knew in my own mind, 'If I am meant to win this, it will happen.'"

Even enterprising competitors such as Phyllis George admit that once their rigorous preparations were completed, they relaxed and concentrated on having a wonderful time during Pageant week. "I remember thinking, 'I'm here, and I'm going to make this a great experience *whatever* the outcome,'" Phyllis recalls. "I loved being a part of the program—and, of course, the outcome was a very positive one for me."

And the outcome *should* be a positive one whether or not the young lady happens to win the Miss America title, says Jane Kubernus, chairman of the Convention Hall dressing room hostesses. "The girls who get the most fun out of the Pageant are the ones who come here thinking, 'I'm going to have fun!' If they have that feeling—and most of them *do*—it's a marvelous experience they will never forget for the rest of their lives."

CHAPTER 13

On to Atlantic City!

Every September, fifty young women depart for Atlantic City, where they will experience the most exciting adventure of their young lives. They have trained as diligently as Olympic athletes for this week of national competition, and as one would expect, they are full of expectation, anticipation—and a noticeable case of the jitters. They are *finally* on their way to the Miss America Pageant—and their chance at realizing "the dream of a million girls."

The experience of driving along the Atlantic City Causeway, sighting the resort's famed casino-dotted skyline for the first time, and arriving at a posh ocean-front hotel is an unforgettable prelude to Pageant week. "There's a lot of excitement!" exclaims Sarah Ann Evans, Miss Ohio 1988. "After all the preparation, when you finally get to Atlantic City, it's like, 'I can't believe it's here already.' You've worked for such a long time to get there, and suddenly you're in Atlantic City and it's Miss America week. That was the biggest shock I had—the realization that we were actually *there!*"

As contestants arrive at their host hotels, they are formally greeted and escorted to a private suite they share with a state traveling companion. After freshening up, the young ladies present themselves for preregistration in Convention Hall. There, they receive their identification badges, pose for promotional photographs for the corporate sponsors and NBC, and autograph a huge map of the United States.

STATE TRAVELING COMPANIONS AND ATLANTIC CITY HOSTESSES

Bert Parks once joked that during their stay in Atlantic City contestants "are supervised about as well as you're supervised in the army!" To ensure the young women's safety, two groups of approved chaperons accompany contestants at all times.

Fifty official state traveling companions, women who are screened and approved by the national office to accompany state titleholders to Atlantic City, stay with their charges in their hotel suites and are responsible for them during unscheduled hours of Pageant week.

When contestants leave their hotels to at-

Contestants arrive in Atlantic City. IRV KAAR

Arriving at the host hotels. IRV KAAR

Registering at Convention Hall.
MICHAEL KURTZ

tend Pageant functions, a second group of chaperons, the National Hostess Committee, assumes responsibility for their safety. For security reasons, organizers are finicky about whom they grant such close access to contestants. Qualified applicants are accepted only after they have been sponsored, interviewed, and carefully screened. The hostesses, 175 prominent New Jersey women, are responsible for the Convention Hall dressing room, contestants' transportation, arranging for rehearsal space, keeping the young women on schedule, and observing their interviews with reporters. Hostesses also offer contestants much-needed encouragement, guidance, and moral support during Pageant week. "These hostesses have been doing it for years," explains Leonard Horn, "and they know exactly

Hostesses lend support and encouragement.
IRV KAAR

how to handle each situation and how to help the young ladies enjoy their experience here. I think the hostesses do a particularly good job in letting them know what to expect, helping them to measure their time, and encouraging them to enjoy this week, because it's going to be something the young ladies will look back on as a high point in their lives."

Hostesses often develop close relationships with the young women they chaperon—bonds of affection that have led to comical situations on occasion. One such incident occurred in 1983, when Regina Hopper, Miss Arkansas, was assigned a new hostess who took her contestant's interests to heart. After helping Regina prepare for the swimsuit competition, the inexperienced chaperon watched anxiously from the wings while Miss Arkansas was introduced. As Regina strolled down the runway, her state rooting gallery saluted their

queen with a spirited Razorback cheer, "Whoooo Piiiigg Soooooeeeey!" Moments later, Regina returned backstage to find her hostess in tears. "Honey, you are *not* fat!" the woman wailed. "You are *not* a fat pig and I don't know who those people are calling you that! I think that's just *terrible!*"

While such amusing episodes cut the tension momentarily, the intense pressures of national competition can take their toll on contestants, according to Jane Kubernus, the Pageant's longtime chairman of the dressing room hostesses. Not surprisingly, the presence of an army of experienced, concerned caretakers makes all the difference. "The girls do appreciate our efforts," she asserts with a smile. "In the end, it's not a thankless job."

Autographing the Miss America map.
GEORGE SORIE

FAMILY, FRIENDS, AND PAGEANT DELEGATIONS

As the big day approaches, thousands of relatives, friends, and Pageant devotees pour in from around the nation. Because contestants' relatives are usually nervous newcomers to the Pageant week experience, the Parents' Activities Committee aids families with tickets, hotel information, maps, and schedules of Pageant events. In addition, the committee operates a hospitality room in Convention Hall where families and friends of the state queens can socialize before showtime.

While the schedule of events for contestants' families varies, activities usually include a get-acquainted brunch, a tour of Convention Hall's backstage area, a parents' reception, and tours of local attractions. The traditional highlight of the noncompetitive events is the parents' luncheon, where the reigning Miss America's parents address the excited couples who hope to take their place. Wylie King, father of Miss America 1974, Rebecca Ann King, recalls his experiences from both perspectives. "I can remember when Terry Meeuwsen's father stood up and I was sitting clear in the back. I said to myself, 'Well, *I'm* going to be there next year.' I felt confident about it." Sure enough, a year later, King took the podium as royal dad and quipped, "You fathers better be ready . . . because come Saturday night, one of you dads is going to be responsible for getting Miss America's taxes in!"

Although keeping families busy eases some of their anxiety, it can't entirely erase the sympathy pangs parents experience while their daughters are sweating to win a once-in-a-lifetime sweepstakes. As the mother of a recent Miss Mississippi admitted, "I was a nervous wreck! We mothers realize all the things that can go wrong. She could trip, her gown's hem could unravel, a heel could break off. I was in a fog the whole week. It was nerve-racking!"

Despite the nervous jitters parents endure that week, they are proud to watch their daughters participate in such a celebrated American tradition.

The experience is especially meaningful for those parents who have emigrated to the United States. Michele Passarelli, Miss Rhode Island 1972, recalls the excitement her European parents experienced watching her compete for the Miss America title. "My parents were born in Italy and I am a first-generation Italian-American, so it meant a lot to them to be there with all these people *living* the American dream." She adds softly, "It was very, very moving."

Contestants' families are not the only people captivated by the annual ritual. Thousands of local and state pageant volunteers flock to the Miss America Pageant each year. "There are three or four reasons most of us go to Atlantic City," says Bob Wheeler. "Number one, I go for my girl, and we're gonna do the hog call, and we're gonna scream and holler and show Miss Arkansas how much we appreciate her. The next thing you go for is the girls you judged. In other words, if *your* girl can't make top ten, then you're going to be pulling for one that

Miss America hopefuls pose with a Chevrolet Corvette. JOHN FRANK, CP NEWS

Visitors aboard Donald Trump's yacht **Princess.** GEORGE SORIE

Awarding the Allman Medical Scholarship. IRV KAAR

Making a splash with reporters. IRV KAAR

you judged along the way." The final reason people return year after year to observe the national finals, he says, is that the excitement of Pageant week "gets in your blood." For many supporters, the week in Atlantic City, socializing with fellow Pageant volunteers from around the country, is the highlight of their year.

Throughout the week, Pageant devotees enjoy a whirlwind schedule: roaming casinos, attending breakfasts, luncheons, Pageant rehearsals, the Miss America trade show, USO troupe performances, style shows, the Boardwalk Parade, and the gala regional and southern states hospitality parties. Still, the highlight of Pageant week is the opportunity to boisterously cheer for their favorite candidates during four evenings of onstage competition.

Having a noisy crowd of fans and family is one of the highlights for contestants, as well. "The nicest part of the week was probably the fact that my state [people] and a lot of relatives and friends were there," says Christi Taunton, Miss Arkansas 1985. "To know that I had a group of people who were sitting out there in the audience every night to root and cheer for

Celebrating a birthday. MICHAEL KURTZ

me, and who would be waiting to greet me at the end of the night whether I won a preliminary or not, was always so nice!"

REHEARSALS

When millions of viewers tune in for the Miss America Pageant, they see a meticulously choreographed telecast. What they *don't* see are the countless hours of rehearsals that have been poured into the production before the curtain is raised. From the time contestants arrive in town until a few hours before showtime, they strain to perfect every step they will take on the Convention Hall stage.

One of the most memorable moments of rehearsal occurs when the aspirants step onto the Convention Hall stage for the first time and scan the cavernous auditorium. "It was really overwhelming, to say the least," says Marian McKnight Conway. "How many football fields can you put in Convention Hall? There aren't many halls around the country that are that big. It's overwhelming in the beginning, but some-

how you warm up very fast and you fall into the routine of hard work."

It *is* hard work. There are rehearsals for production numbers, the talent, evening gown, and swimsuit competitions, and for the announcements of the top ten, runners-up, and the new Miss America. As chances would have it, rehearsals for "the moment you've all been waiting for" have spawned interesting coincidences over the years, as contestants who were randomly selected to practice the victory walk repeated it for real hours later. One of them, Laurel Schaefer, excitedly phoned her mother with the news that she had been called out to practice the role of the "pretend" Miss America during rehearsals. Eleanor Schaefer laughs at the irony of her daughter's remarks. "Believe me, Mother," Laurie said, "I know how it feels to be Miss America. They chose me to play the role blocking [for TV] because they knew *I* would never be chosen!"

It happened again a decade later, when new emcee Ron Ely nonchalantly announced Susan Powell's name as the practice Miss America during Saturday rehearsals. That evening, when he opened the judges' enve-

Days of rehearsals. GEORGE SORIE

lope and discovered Powell listed as the real-life winner, he was unnerved by the eerie coincidence. The two-time queen, however, was delighted. "I am a little superstitious," Powell joked to reporters, "but it was a wonderful rehearsal, wasn't it?"

While such coincidences occur innocently, organizers now exercise particular caution during rehearsals for the coronation of Miss America. "They are very careful about that," judges' co-chairman Ellen Plum explains. "They give a great many contestants a chance to rehearse."

The contestants' dressing room. GEORGE SORIE

Backstage encouragement. IRV KAAR

BACKSTAGE AT THE MISS AMERICA PAGEANT

When contestants aren't rehearsing onstage, they are backstage in the huge Convention Hall dressing room, where row upon row of cosmetic tables, mirrors, and portable wardrobe closets have been arranged. From early morning until late in the evening, the ladies dart in and out of the facility, making rapid wardrobe changes, setting and styling their hair, applying cosmetics, chattering, laughing, and fretting about their performances. "It's an *organized* madhouse," says Jane Kubernus, chairman of the dressing room hostesses, "but it's definitely under control, because my women *keep* it under control!" The huge dimensions of the dressing room and the necessity of contestants adhering to a rigid television time schedule oblige Kubernus to punch out her instructions over a microphone. "Sometimes during the week I have to 'crack the whip' and push them hard schedule-wise. I have a no-nonsense attitude to get things done." Still, her efforts to maintain strict control are balanced by the hostesses' occasionally "letting their hair down" for the benefit of contestants. "My hostesses try to put them at ease, and we do a lot of silly things," Jane confesses. Wearing comical hats and "boogying" at the front of the dressing room for starters. "This gets the contestants laughing at us, and then they realize that we're human, that we aren't just there to crack the whip. So, as the week goes on and I start saying, 'Okay, you have _exactly_ thirty seconds to do this!,' they're more willing to listen."

Because the dressing room can become the arena for every conceivable catastrophe, a team of veteran hostesses serves as a behind-the-scenes rescue squad. "I have a tremendous committee of ten women who are versed in everything you can think of," Jane explains. "Hems, pins, spots, buttons . . . three of them are hairdressers, three of them are cosmetologists, and a couple of them are real fine seamstresses. So I think we can cover just about every problem that comes up—and they _do_ come up!" the veteran hostess acknowledges. "A girl will get dressed, she's ready to go out onstage and trips on the hem of her dress and sticks her foot through it—which happened. Somebody has to be there to repair it very, very quickly. Or they don't like the way their hair looks. I've had hairdressers run behind a girl all the way to the wings of the stage fixing her hair, spraying, brushing, or putting it up." Then there was the year the zippers on contestants' identical designer gowns jammed. She winces at the memory. "On competition night, we were cutting them out of these magnificent dresses with scissors because the zippers just wouldn't go down! The women who run the dressing room just have to be ready for everything! Of course," she interjects with a relieved grin, "nobody in the _audience_ sees any of this."

The enormous pressures of competing for the crown have created the perception that the Convention Hall dressing room is a combat zone where contestants deviously wage their battles for the crown. Not so, says Debbie Riecks, Miss Colorado 1989. "I had been warned before I came that Miss America is 'different.' You can be friends, but Miss America is 'different.'" Instead, Debbie insists she found national contestants had a genuine respect and concern for one another. "I made wonderful lifetime friends. We are all here to compete and we are all very ambitious and goal-oriented young women, so certainly there is some tension in that respect. However, because we _are_ all goal-oriented, we have so much in common that we form fast friendships." The surprising truth, Debbie says, is that the atmosphere backstage was more like "Well, if I can't win, I hope _you_ do!"

MEETING THE MEDIA

Media coverage is an integral aspect of Pageant week, with close to four hundred newspaper, magazine, radio, and television representatives covering the event annually. Reporters' interviews with contestants are arranged and conducted at the "Press Center," an information clearinghouse in Convention

Endless press interviews. IRV KAAR

Hall. In addition to privately scheduled interviews, numerous "photo opportunities" are staged for the press throughout the week, followed by press conferences with the new Miss America on Saturday evening and Sunday morning.

While there are occasional frustrations with unbalanced media coverage, most reporters strive to present the Pageant objectively. "Most of us who have worked it have been fairly protective of the Pageant," says photographer Sid Stoen, who has covered the national finals since the 1930s. "It's just a great thing for America. It's part of our heritage."

THE MISS AMERICA BOARDWALK PARADE

Another long-standing tradition of Pageant week is the festive Miss America Boardwalk Parade, when "Pageant fever" is epidemic and every contestant feels like a queen. Although the parade, which is staged on either Tuesday or Friday evening, is televised regionally, a quarter of a million people still flock to the resort each year to personally witness the famous annual spectacle.

Over the decades, a number of celebrities have served as parade grand marshal, including Grace Kelly, Tom Jones, and Joan Crawford. However, the biggest star ever to shine on parade audiences was, unquestionably, Marilyn Monroe. The film legend's appearance as grand marshal in 1952 made headlines across the nation. "Wow, was it ever a big deal!" reminisces Neva Langley, who won that year's contest. During Monroe's highly publicized appearance, the star created a sensation when she appeared in a daring cut-to-the-navel dress. "It was embarrassing for the Pageant at the time," Neva explains, "because she wore the first dress anybody had ever worn, I suppose, that was cut down to her midriff. I actually think

she was rather *exposed* several times." She adds with a chuckle, "Well, the next year was *Grace Kelly* as the parade marshal. That's quite a big swing!"

Despite such illustrious grand marshals, the real stars of parade night are the fifty aspirants for the crown, who describe the evening as an unforgettable highlight of Pageant week. "It was wonderful!" remembers Terry Meeuwsen, who soared through the parade on her way to the 1973 Miss America title. "The parade was one of the best experiences of the whole week. I knew it was a time that I could enjoy without being judged for anything. I was stunned by the number of people who

A highlight of Pageant week—the Miss America Boardwalk parade. GEORGE SORIE

turned out for it. There were thousands and thousands and thousands of people. . . . They'd run up to the car, shake your hand, wish you luck, and tell you they were rooting for you. Or they'd call our names from the bleachers and wave madly." She sighs. "You just felt so loved by the time the parade was over. It was an unbelievable high!"

Former Miss Arkansas Christi Taunton adds, "Plus, you have to think about the environment. You're on the Boardwalk in Atlantic City, the ocean breeze is blowing, all the huge lights from the casinos are shining, and there are thousands upon thousands of people lined up cheering. You're riding in brand-new cars and you're all dressed up in Mardi Gras type clothes. It was really a neat experience—especially if you live in the Midwest or South like I do, because then it's something you've always heard about or looked at on a Monopoly board." In retrospect, having experienced that invigorating ride past the cheering crowds, she exclaims, "It's just the grandest parade of them all for Pageant girls!"

THE PRELIMINARY COMPETITIONS

The parade may be grand, but during Pageant week, contestants' minds are clearly focused on the competitive events that will determine the top ten and Miss America: the private interviews and the evening gown, swimsuit, and talent competitions. The candidates are divided into three preliminary groups, with seventeen young women to a group. Each group is designated with one of the titles of the Pageant sorority, Mu Alpha Sigma. In order to avoid having fifty talents presented on one evening, the three groups alternate days of competition. For instance, the official lineup in 1990 was as follows:

MU GROUP
Sunday—A.M. interview

Preliminary award winners. GEORGE SORIE

Tuesday—Evening gown
Wednesday—Swimsuit
Thursday—Talent

ALPHA GROUP
Monday—A.M. interview
Tuesday—Talent
Wednesday—Evening gown
Thursday—Swimsuit

SIGMA GROUP
Tuesday—A.M. interview
Tuesday—Swimsuit
Wednesday—Talent
Thursday—Evening gown

The first competitive event is the series of private interviews between contestants and judges. In 1989, "In an effort to lessen the tension and let the contestants see that [judges] are real caring people—not ogres," Leonard Horn arranged for the girls to informally greet the preliminary panel before the private interviews began. "We thought contestants appreciated it," he explains, "and it made them more relaxed before they actually entered the judges' interview room."

The fifty interviews are conducted prior to the onset of the onstage competitions, and are videotaped for review by the celebrity panel later that week. Each interview is supervised by the judges' chairman, a senior Pageant official, and a legal representative of NBC. Contestants are escorted to the site of the interviews—usually a Convention Hall or hotel conference room—and are seated in an adjacent room to await their opportunity to meet with the panel. To many jittery candidates, the wait seems like a lull before the hurricane. "I think they get more nervous over the judges' interviews than anything," says Jane Kubernus. "Their hands shake and they don't talk. They just get very quiet, because they want to do everything so perfectly, and it's only *one* shot!"

One by one, contestants are ushered into the interview chamber, introduced, and seated in the center of the room facing the panelists and a video camera. The judges, who are seated behind two draped banquet tables several feet away, immediately begin a barrage of questions. "You're sitting in front of nine people who are safely behind a table," says interview survivor Kim Boyce, "but *you're* out in the middle of the room exposed. Then there are TV lights and guys piddling around behind the camera, which is kind of distracting. It's definitely a bit intimidating, but one of the things that you're constantly told during preparations is, 'Don't let it intimidate you!' So you just walk in there and show 'em what you've got!" And that's what the judges want to see—a candidate who enters the interview session and radiates confidence and warmth *despite* the stress of the situation. As judge George Peppard, who studied the taped interviews in 1989, put it, "I think the interviews are the most important thing we see because it's a hot spot to be in for

all these ladies—and we're looking for grace under pressure."

At the conclusion of each round of interviews, judges' ballots are turned over to Price-Waterhouse certified public accountants for tabulation. Unlike the talent and swimsuit categories, the highest-scoring contestant in the interviews is not announced to the public.

Following the private interviews, the three evenings of preliminary competitions commence. On Tuesday, Wednesday, and Thursday nights, approximately twenty thousand spectators pack Convention Hall to watch the hopefuls compete. As the crowds rustle to their seats, fifty nervous contestants battle the butterflies backstage. "The pressure is pretty bad," affirms Mrs. Kubernus. "They're getting ready to go out on that stage in front of thousands of people who are sitting out there. It's hard on some of them, but I think the majority of them really enjoy it. It's very, very exciting! It's real big-time showbiz—and they *know* it! Sure they get nervous, but most of the girls handle it very well."

At 8:15 P.M., the curtain is raised and the master of ceremonies, the reigning Miss America, and the candidates for the crown flow onstage for the opening production number and parade of states. Each contestant walks to the microphone, introduces herself, and then proceeds down the runway. As the parade of states concludes, the reigning queen strolls down the runway to a standing ovation, the judges are introduced, and the competition begins in earnest.

The swimsuit competition is the first event, with seventeen contestants emerging onstage attired in modest swimsuits of their own choice. As each young lady is introduced, she pauses briefly and turns before the judges, then walks the runway ramp as the next contestant takes her position before the panel. After each of the ladies has been presented, she leaves the stage. There is no longer group modeling because comparative judging has been eliminated. Swimsuit ballots are collected by the judges' chairman and handed over to the auditors for tabulation.

Following the swimsuit competition, the next group of seventeen contestants perform in the talent competition. At the conclusion of each performance, judges immediately mark their ballots without comparing the contestant to previous candidates. As the last performer takes her bow, the ballots are collected and tabulated.

After a production number, the beautiful evening gown competition ensues. The event's format differs from years past in that the seventeen candidates now answer questions posed to them by the master of ceremonies. After responding extemporaneously, the young ladies individually model their gowns before the judges and then walk the runway. At the conclusion of the evening gown segment, the ballots are collected and tabulated, but in order to maintain suspense, the highest-scoring contestant in evening gown is not announced to the audience.

At the conclusion of each night of competition, the fifty hopefuls gather onstage for a closing production number. Then, the highest-scoring contestants in talent and swimsuit are announced as preliminary winners. As their names are called out, the thrilled award winners accept their trophies, assume their place on each side of the reigning queen, and victoriously parade down the runway and back. Preliminary trophy winners are then escorted offstage for interviews and publicity photos, while remaining contestants proceed to the press center for previously scheduled interviews with reporters. Soon after, the young women attend "States' Visitation" in the Convention Hall ballroom, where they unwind with their families and state supporters before returning to their hotels for the night.

By Friday, all fifty contestants have competed in interview, evening gown, swimsuit, and talent, their scores have been tabulated and double-checked, and the official list of semifinalists has been determined. The incoming celebrity judges have arrived and are undergoing orientation to prepare them for their critical responsibilities. Meanwhile, as the countdown continues, contestants are preparing for the evening they have dreamed about—the night when the names of ten lucky women will be announced to the nation during the coast-to-coast broadcast of the Miss America Pageant. . . .

CHAPTER 14

It's Pageant Day at Last!

Saturday. The morning they've been anxiously awaiting, when fifty hopefuls wake to the exciting realization that before the day is over, someone in their midst will hear her name announced as the new Miss America!

Pageant day is an exhausting capstone to the week, as contestants engage in television rehearsals from early morning until late afternoon: production numbers, the parade of states, and the announcements of the top ten, the court of honor, and Miss America. When rehearsals conclude, contestants break for a casual dinner in Convention Hall's Galley—and, then, it's time to dress for the evening they have dreamed about for years.

The last few nerve-tingling hours preceding the broadcast are unsettling for the young ladies. "Back in the dressing room, there's a lot of tension," explains Christi Taunton. "Everybody is wondering, 'Well, is it *me*—or is it *them?*,' because it can't be *all* of us. It seemed like during the last few hours before the Pageant started, most of the girls stuck to themselves. While you're getting dressed and getting your makeup and hair done, it's a time

to be by yourself and to think. You know the time has come that it's over, things are winding down, so before you go onstage you want to prepare yourself for whatever the outcome will be." Christi adds quietly, "And that's *not* the easiest thing in the world to do."

Contestants aren't the only people who are jittery. Network executives, stage and television producers, musical directors, camera teams, lighting and audio engineers, set designers, and a host of other instrumental workers are racing against time to ensure that all is in place by the moment the cameras roll, and the announcer's voice heralds . . .

"LIVE FROM ATLANTIC CITY! . . ."

"*. . . It's the Miss America Pageant!*" It has finally arrived. The long-anticipated evening when 55 million viewers tune in for the coast-to-coast broadcast of the Miss America Pageant. As the opening credits roll, the television host, a dance ensemble, the reigning Miss America, and the national finalists flow onstage from the wings and launch into the opening production number. Then the fifty women who hope to capture the crown are introduced to the nation, the reigning queen takes an emotional stroll down the runway to the accolades of the audience, the judges are introduced—and then it's time for the first major announcement of the evening.

The suspense heightens as the emcee slowly opens the envelope containing the list of ten women who will compete for the Miss America title. The nervous contestants and their families, friends, and fans tense optimistically as the semifinalists are divulged. As the ninth name is announced, their eyes betray a fading glimmer of hope. Only one more woman will be granted the opportunity to ad-

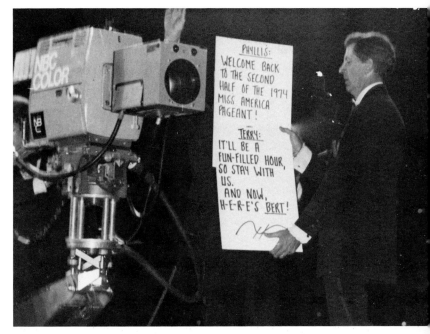

"Live from Atlantic City!..." IRV KAAR

Announcing the top ten. PAUL ABEL, JR.

vance to the semifinals. That last name is shouted to the audience, and the young lady visibly sighs with relief and moves forward to complete the top ten. The radiant faces of the finalists reflect the excitement of this long-sought moment in the spotlight. As the audience cheers their good fortune, forty women stand in the background applauding politely. For them, the moment is an enormously difficult one, when tantalizing hopes and expectations collide with reality.

THE NONFINALISTS' VIEW

"It's a pretty empty feeling," says Debra Cleveland, Miss South Dakota 1984, "because you've spent all this time preparing for that moment—and then it's done with. I really wanted to be in the top ten. Every girl there does. But you go there knowing that there can only be ten out of fifty." A former Miss Mississippi, Mary Donnelly Haskell, concurs. "It's a real letdown and I wouldn't be honest if I said otherwise. There's a surge of emotion and disappointment when—*boom!*—number ten is called out and you don't hear your name. 'Well, that's *it!*' Then they say, 'Thank you very much, ladies,' they cut to the commercials, and you walk offstage. The evening goes on and you're backstage watching the Miss America Pageant."

As dressing room supervisor, Jane Kubernus has observed the reactions of nonfinalists for eighteen years, and sees her role as a supportive one. "The emotions run the highest on Saturday night after the top ten are announced. There is deep disappointment amongst the other forty girls, but most of them handle it very well. Sometimes we have buckets of tears," she admits sympathetically. "I've been holding them on my shoulder and patting them and talking to them for a good many years now. That's sort of my job."

After offering her doses of encouragement, Jane flashes a smile and orders, "Hey, let's dry the eyes. Let's do the face over. You've got to get ready to go back out there. You're in a production number and millions of people are going to see you on TV!" Not surprisingly, Mrs. Kubernus is pleased to see the telecast's updated format involve all the contestants in production numbers. Besides placing all the girls before the cameras, she says, the numbers also keep them busy, "so they don't have much time to sit around and feel sorry."

Although the schedule varies from year to year, contestants usually return backstage, where they undress and relax until the next production number. As they watch the broadcast on a television monitor in the dressing room, a huge platter of refreshments is brought in for the ladies to snack on. In the sudden freedom from months of strict dieting, the snacks are usually devoured—much to the consternation of the hostesses, who have to squeeze the girls back into their slinky gowns. Mary Donnelly recalls with a laugh, "The hostesses kept running around pleading with the

girls, 'Pleeease make *sure* you can get back into your gowns for the finale at the end of the evening!'" And the nervous hostesses weren't overreacting, she points out with a giggle. "I mean, there were girls who had been *cinched* into their gowns before and here we are all stuffing our faces—but we had been starving all week long!"

The former Miss Mississippi also remembers the exemplary behavior of her fellow contestants despite their disappointment. "It was interesting. As we watched the Pageant, everybody *cheered*. They cheered and clapped for everybody. It wasn't a negative atmosphere at all. It was a real good feeling."

While the young ladies strive to be sportsmanlike, watching the top ten excitedly racing in and out of the dressing room is a difficult part of that evening. "They take those ten dressing tables and move them up to the front of the dressing room so the girls are closer to the entrances and exits of the stage," explains Regina Hopper. "So they're there getting ready for the finals while you're sitting there watching them prepare, and watching it on television. It's tough. I mean, it's awful, and you feel so sorry. But," she adds with a good-natured laugh, "I don't think it ever *killed* anybody!"

For Michele Passarelli, her disappointment at not making the top ten was tempered by a touching realization. As she stood waiting in the wings moments before the grand finale, her thoughts wandered back to what she had been doing a year ago that evening. "I had been sitting in my mother's house in a small town in Rhode Island watching the Miss America Pageant, as we always did. After the telecast, I went into the kitchen with my bathrobe tied around my neck singing, 'Therrrre She Is, Miss A-mer-i-caaaa!' And that *very next year* I was there on that stage, with God knows how many people watching, and millions of seventeen-year-old women sitting in their living rooms watching the Miss America Pageant. Well, I was so emotionally touched by the whole moment that I was hysterical crying! That I was *there,* and that there were millions of people watching me, dreaming about doing it someday. It turned the whole week around for me. I was so happy and excited just to *be* there that I wished I could have done the whole week over right there. Just being chosen to participate was such an honor for me!"

When the initial disappointment fades, the forty nonfinalists begin to realize that, win, lose, or place, being a participant in such a grand American tradition is an honor to be cherished. As Carrie Folks, Miss Tennessee 1988, put it, "Now that I've been here, I realize that regardless of how I did, I have been in the Miss America Pageant and nothing is going to take that away. I've been in the *Miss America Pageant!* Not many people *have* been—and it's all been worth it!"

Performing under pressure. PAUL ABEL, JR.

MAKING THE TOP TEN!

The announcement of the top ten is an intoxicating moment for the women lucky enough to hear their names announced. They have survived the narrowing of the huge nationwide pool of entrants to two thousand local titleholders, fifty state representatives, and finally to the last ten candidates for the coveted Miss America crown. It's a once-in-a-lifetime thrill according to Miss Florida 1987, Jennifer Sauder. "I'm sure being chosen for the top ten was the most exciting thing that has *ever* happened to me," she exclaims, "or probably will for quite some time!"

However, the expectation to perform at your peak potential with seven to twelve celebrity judges, twenty-five thousand Convention Hall spectators, and 55 million television viewers evaluating your every move practically defies description. "It's probably the most intense pressure any young woman could put

herself through," affirms Terry Meeuwsen, who found the stress overwhelming. "I don't remember very much about going through the show that night. I just *couldn't.* It was such a pressure-packed situation that I think I just functioned on automatic pilot."

The dressing room hostesses understand the pressure contestants are under, and they make every effort to ensure that the evening flows smoothly for them. "My women take care of everything," Jane explains. "We cover every base that we possibly can. My ten women work with the top ten on a one-to-one basis. We do just about everything for them that you can think of. We literally dress and undress them because with these gowns, with all these hooks and eyes and zippers, and the buckles on the shoes . . . There is no way they could ever get themselves dressed. We do their hair. We do their makeup. We don't leave anything to chance. We try our best to think of every possible thing we can."

The top ten, 1990. TERRY CHENAILLE

While the meticulous assistance from hostesses frees finalists to focus their energies on performing before a vast live audience, the moments of waiting before being introduced onstage can be utterly unnerving—especially when the previous candidate bowls the audience over. Former Miss Florida Marti Phillips, an amateur musician, remembers her reaction to following Cheryl Prewitt's stirring rendition of *Don't Cry Out Loud.* As she stood in the wings "getting goose bumps" from Prewitt's performance, her thoughts jolted back to an earlier college audition when she was so nervous she forgot how to finger her clarinet. "I thought, 'Oh my goodness. How in the world am I going to do this? How am I going to get up in front of millions of people knowing that just last year I blew an audition and couldn't play my clarinet?' Then," she adds with a groan, "I had to follow Cheryl!" Marti turned to a hostess standing nearby and gasped, "How in the world do you follow *that?*" Fortunately, like most contestants, Marti discovered that under the tremendous pressures of the moment, contestants often surprise themselves by summoning a strength from deep within. "I played the very best I've ever played!" she reports in barely concealed amazement. "It was a miracle!"

More experienced candidates often report that once their initial competitive jitters subside, the experience of performing during a coast-to-coast broadcast is exhilarating. "I just kept thinking, 'This is *it!* Girls *dream* about doing this their whole lives, so let's just have a good time and enjoy it,'" says Kim Boyce, a professional gospel singer, "and it was a wonderful, wonderful experience for me!" Terry Meeuwsen, who had toured with the New Christy Minstrels, also cites the talent competition as her favorite event. "It was the highlight of the competition for me," she exclaims. "To be twenty-three years old and have a thirty-some-piece orchestra of some of the finest musicians in the country playing your orchestration for you is just a dream come true. Then to have an audience of millions of people who are intent on listening to your talent . . . It was a wonderful experience!"

At the conclusion of the talent competition, contestants reappear for the evening gown competition. The segment used to breeze by with the young ladies uttering a brief introduction and then modeling before the panel. But now that the format has been revamped to include a question-answer exercise, it is considerably more challenging for the candidates. Even the usually unflappable Gretchen Carlson confesses that the segment was her biggest disappointment that night. "I'll admit I did not feel comfortable with my answer. It was not the best answer I've ever given onstage. When I got offstage, I thought that I had blown it, to be quite frank, but there wasn't enough time to get down

because we went back out onstage right away."

That's one of the blessings of live television. It proceeds at such a fast pace that there really isn't time to mope about a poor performance, or about who's going to win. "I was so excited being in the top ten that the rest of the evening just flew by," says Kaye Lani Rafko. "You don't even think about TV, you don't think much about being nervous, because it goes by so _fast!_"

Once the last round of competition concludes, the judges' ballots are collected, the auditors tabulate and double-check the results, and contestants return onstage for the grand finale. At long last, the "moment they've all been waiting for" has arrived. Within moments, the quest for the crown will end with a flourish as the master of ceremonies reaches for the auditor's envelope and announces the names of four runners-up—and a new Miss America!

CHAPTER 15

"And the Winner Is . . ."

I t is a scene that is indelibly impressed upon the American psyche, the climactic moment when the judges' verdict is proclaimed to the nation and a new Miss America takes her place in the spotlight. Although the famous annual ritual has been repeated for seven decades, it never ceases to leave audiences spellbound. Year in and year out, we watch in fascination as young women learn they have been singled out to live the "dream of a million girls." And, year after year, as they walk toward center stage to receive their glittering crowns and scepters, we wonder what it must be like to actually experience that glorious moment; to hear your name shouted out as the winner, to look into the eye of the camera knowing that millions of viewers are observing your every gesture, to hear the roar of the crowd as you embark on that heart-stirring walk down the runway.

THE CORONATION EVOLVES

While the dreamlike atmosphere that pervades the crowning of a new Miss America

hasn't changed much since the first production in 1921, the specific coronation procedures have evolved radically over the decades.

During the Roaring Twenties, when the Pageant was in its infancy, the event was a far cry from today's sophisticated television extravaganza. In 1925, for instance, judges' ballots for the two top-ranking candidates were hidden inside a tiny, hollow "golden apple" on Pageant morning. That evening, as the audience eagerly looked on, the apple was hacked open with a matching "golden ax." Officials withdrew the ballots, tallied the votes on a blackboard, and announced the winner to the cheering crowd. As the band launched into the strains of the national anthem, King Neptune inaugurated the new queen with a towering facsimile of Lady Liberty's crown, while four royal pages draped an ermine-trimmed coronation robe upon her fair shoulders.

During the period between the Pageant's revival in 1933 and its first live television broadcast in 1954, the actual announcement of the winner was made backstage. As five finalists huddled together in the wings, the runners-up would be led onstage until only one young woman remained offstage—the new Miss America. The method seemed logical at the time because many winners either convulsed into tears or swooned upon receiving the good news.

Evelyn Ay, the last queen to be crowned backstage, recalls that the stage theme used in 1953, *Gems of the Ocean,* introduced Miss America and her court to the audience by elevating them onstage on a tiny hydraulic lift, "like Neptune out of the sea." As Evelyn and her fellow finalists waited in a hall beneath the stage, officials escorted four of the girls into the lift, raised them through a trapdoor, and presented them to the audience. Evelyn, who was left standing alone, surmised she must have won. "For Heaven's sake!" she exclaims with a laugh. "I just realized I must be the winner because I was the only one left!" Suddenly a swarm of officials rushed at her, frantically adjusting the robe, banner, and crown, handing her roses, and shoving smelling salts in her face. When they ushered Evelyn toward the tiny elevator—which, she recalls, "had no handles or sides to hold onto while it would rise up one story"—her trembling legs nearly buckled under, and she refused to budge. As good fortune would have it, a jovial policeman Evelyn had befriended during the week happened to wander by at that moment. Surmising her predicament, he wisecracked, "Listen, 'Pennsyltucky'—if you got this far, the *least* thing you can do is *go up!*" She grins. "I'll tell you—it put a brace in my knees and I went right on up!"

As Evelyn "rose up from the depths" as the new queen, she was greeted with thunderous applause and a standing ovation—a glorious moment in the spotlight she still savors. "I

The Pageant's only two-time winner, Ohio's Mary Campbell, was inaugurated with suitable regalia: an ermine-trimmed robe, jeweled diadem, and pronged tiara. MISS AMERICA PAGEANT

King Neptune, the Pageant's amphibious monarch, traditionally bestowed the emblems of royalty upon each queen. Here, Neptune poses with Miss America 1938, Marilyn Meseke.
MISS AMERICA PAGEANT

don't know that I was able to really record that feeling at that time, but the reason I have returned to Atlantic City for over thirty years is because when I see that young woman go down that runway, I feel what I must have felt then. I guess I walk with that girl every year," she sighs, adding with a laugh, "and I like it because I can feel it now, but I don't have all the trauma!"

The following year, the first live telecast of the Pageant allowed millions of viewers to observe the coronation of Miss America for the first time. According to Lenora, because the television crew had been "so decent" under her iron command, she invited a cameraman to follow her backstage and film the winner's reaction. But, she sternly warned, no one was

to know a camera was present. As three of the five finalists were escorted onstage, only Florida's Ann Daniels and California's Lee Meriwether remained seated in the wings. Suddenly the director leaned toward Lee and warmly informed her, "Congratulations! *You* are Miss America!" According to Lenora, she then placed the robe and banner on Meriwether and ushered her toward the stage curtains. There, she recalls, Lee paused for a moment of solitude, gazed toward heaven, and whispered, "You know, *I* know how happy you are!" "That was the first we knew," Slaughter says, "that her father had died two weeks before. They kept it to themselves until that minute when the cameras caught her looking up toward heaven speaking to her father. It was so beautiful! The cameras caught the whole scene and ABC won the prize that year for the best television shot on the air."

Lee's recollections of the incident differ. Although she recalls waiting backstage with Miss Florida as the runners-up were introduced, she lapsed into shock when Lenora informed her she was Miss America. Her memories of the subsequent moments are fleeting, but since she viewed the original kinescope of the telecast (since lost) on several occasions, she has the coronation scene "engraved" in her mind's eye. What she observed on tape, she laughs, was "wild." A bulky television camera rolled over her gown and she was "crying hysterically." Then, she says, "they had me go out to the microphone and Bob Russell, the emcee, asked me how I felt. Although I was crying, I remember from the telecast that I said, 'I hope Daddy knows and I hope he's proud.' "

The funniest part of the broadcast occurred moments later when officials hauled her shell-shocked mother out of the audience for an on-air chat with co-anchor Bess Myerson. *"Poor thing!"* Lee exclaims sympathetically. "She almost died! She was covered with *hives!"* When Lee, who was still sobbing uncontrollably, was ushered over to join the televised interview, her mom momentarily forgot her surroundings and barked, "Stop your sniveling, Lee!" "That snapped me out of it," she says, laughing. "I mean, she really knew the right thing to say. Then my mother realized that she was *on television,"* Lee recalls, convulsing with laughter at the memory, "and she got *more* hives!"

Not surprisingly, the first live broadcast of the coronation of a Miss America mesmerized the television audience and garnered astronomical ratings for ABC. Clearly, TV executives gloated, the coronation of an American queen had possibilities.

From that point on, for the benefit of the television cameras, finalists were seated onstage to await the judges' verdict. Bert Parks would announce the runners-up until only two contestants remained seated—the eventual Miss America and her first runner-up. During the commotion of the ensuing announcement, young women occasionally misunderstood who had actually won. Laurie Lea Schaefer, the last Miss America to be announced from the top five, remembers how as she and Idaho's Karen Heard awaited the news of which would wear the crown, Laurie somehow misunderstood Bert's instructions and thought that the *first* name called out would be Miss America. When Karen Heard's name was announced, Laurie assumed Miss Idaho had won.

"But, suddenly," Laurie recalls with a laugh, "Phyllis George grabbed *me* and they started putting all this stuff on me: the robe, the banner, the crown—and I was *arguing* with her! I kept saying, 'Are you making a mistake? Are you *sure?'* I was positive they were crowning the wrong girl!" Rather than making a scene on national television, Laurie reasoned, "Well, I might as well walk the runway and we can straighten this mess out afterwards." Until she reached the end of the runway she didn't shed a tear because she was thoroughly enjoying "pretending to be Miss America."

"I *loved* it!" Laurie laughs. "I mean, the flashbulbs were flashing and all—but it still hadn't hit me that I was Miss America. I truly felt, as I was walking away from the stage, that at any moment Bert Parks was going to tap on my shoulder and say, 'Gosh! I'm really sorry, could you come back? We've made a mistake.' " As she reached the halfway point and looked into the camera lens, she snickered. "Boy, if they made a mistake, they're gonna *live* with it!"

The realization that she was indeed the winner finally dawned when she turned to walk back toward the stage. "I saw the entire Convention Hall [audience] standing on its feet, the photographers en masse clamoring to get that one picture of me, my other forty-nine colleagues applauding and Bert Parks singing, and I thought, 'I guess I *am* the new Miss America!'—and *that's* when I started crying. I think the picture of those girls in their salute, applauding, 'We're happy you're the one,' was the best feeling I could have ever felt. It was a feeling of acceptance, of accomplishment, and of tremendous satisfaction. But I'm sure these feelings are felt by any girl who has felt the crown of Miss America placed upon her head."

While most Miss Americas have experienced a predictable array of emotions upon accepting the coveted crown, one winner's impressions were decidedly different. In 1970, when the Pageant celebrated its fiftieth anniversary, Phyllis George was crowned Miss America with a specially designed commemorative golden crown—which she promptly *dropped* on live television! "They put the crown, the scepter, the banner, and the robe on you then," Phyllis recalls with barely concealed exasperation. "That's a lot of stuff to balance! As I nodded to the judges, my crown wobbled and fell off onto the floor and stones splattered all over the place!" To complicate matters, she says, "the robe fell around my elbows and the banner unpinned! It was quite a sight!" Phyllis remembers returning to her hotel room that night and crying, "This is so embarrassing! My big moment, I've won Miss America—and my crown is in my *hand!*"

While Phyllis was embarrassed by her memorable debut, her predecessor, Pamela Eldred, was mortified to have contributed to the unfortunate incident. "Oh, I just wanted to die! You see, I had been telling everybody, 'There's no way I'm gonna crown this girl. I'm not giving up the crown!' When the crown fell off I thought, 'Oh nooo! They're gonna think I did that on purpose!'" Actually, as Pamela had attempted to fasten the crown upon her successor's head, its side combs somehow wouldn't penetrate Phyllis's hair. "I didn't know *what*

Phyllis George made a memorable debut in 1971, when her crown tumbled off and rolled down the runway during the broadcast. "I guess my head wasn't made to have a crown on it," she joked. MISS AMERICA PAGEANT

was happening!" Pam laughs. "It wasn't until after the Pageant that she told me that she had a *fall* on!"

As Pam fidgeted with the crown, officials urgently signaled her, "Come on, we'll be off the air before you get the crown on! Cut it!" Obediently, she nudged Phyllis toward the runway and watched with stunned disbelief as the crown crashed to the stage floor. "I thought, 'I can't believe this happened. My final act and I had to completely blow it!' I was just devastated! But," she reports, grinning, "Phyllis loved it! It gave her something for the rest of the year." In fact, a few days later, when Phyllis appeared on *The Tonight Show,* Johnny Carson welcomed her onstage with the remark, "Phyllis, it's good to see you, but where's your crown? Afraid you'd drop it again?" Phyllis's response, "Yeh, funny Johnny, I'm the klutzy one!," disarmed the gibe and turned the incident to her advantage. "From that moment on, the story that I had been so embarrassed about turned out to be a funny human interest story, and I used it all year—'I'm the klutzy one who dropped the crown and had to pick it up and carry it.' But," she recalls in amusement, "I kept dropping that thing all year. It just wouldn't stay on. I guess my head wasn't made to have a crown on it."

In 1972, officials altered the announcement of Miss America in order to improve the scene's dynamics. "In the old days," Bill Caligari explains, "when we used to have the two sitting up there, there was suspense for the winner, but I've always felt that the first runner-up got a poor shake in that case, because nobody ever gave a damn who she was. When they said, 'The first runner-up is . . .' everybody would look at the girl who had become Miss America." With the new procedure, Miss America and her court would be announced directly from the top ten, rather than from a final five.

Wisconsin's Terry Meeuwsen was the first winner to be crowned under the new system. "Instead of just having the two girls there when they announced the winner," she recalls, "they kept all ten of us up there, so after they announced the runners-up there were still six of us standing there—so it could have been anybody in that group. As I stood there I was praying and asking God to help me be a gracious loser, because winning in front of a bunch of people isn't that hard—but losing *is* because you're up there and you feel so naked. Everybody is watching you and watching for your reaction." In Terry's case, because she had won two preliminaries and was heavily favored to win, the audience would be especially interested in her reaction if she lost. When Bert

Parks finally shouted her name as Miss America 1973, Terry instinctively buried her face in her hands for several seconds. "It was so emotional and too private a moment to have so many people looking at me! I just had to have at least ten seconds when I was behind my hands all by myself going, 'I *really did this!*'"

Many winners have grappled with the isolation of victory. "At that moment, it's kind of like dying," philosophizes Terry Meeuwsen, Miss America 1973. "You're alone. *There's nobody that can do it for you."* EARLE HAWKINS

A MOMENT IN MISS AMERICA'S GLASS SLIPPERS

Despite delight at having accomplished such a difficult feat, many Miss Americas have grappled with the unsettling isolation of the experience. "You're up there by yourself," Terry explains. "It's a moment of aloneness. Not loneliness, but aloneness—because there isn't anybody out there who can quite understand what you're feeling at that moment." She chuckles as she offers an unusual analogy: "They could be happy and thrilled for you, but at that moment it's kind of like dying—you're *alone*. There's nobody that can do it for you."

Apprehension at the thought of remaining isolated throughout the coming year is another

Upon winning the 1975 title, Shirley Cothran paraded down the runway, looked into the eye of the television camera, and mused, "Hmmm, look who's watching *me—Johnny Carson!" EARLE HAWKINS*

When Bert asked Shirley how it felt to win, she responded, "How can you ask me questions at a time like this!?" *Bert managed a polite titter, but later growled to a reporter, "God, I'd like to have punched her one!" EARLE HAWKINS*

common reaction. "I don't know if you can print this," admits Shirley Cothran, Miss America 1975, "but it's the honest truth. As I walked the runway, I looked out there and saw my Texas delegation, my friends, my family, my mom and dad, and my boyfriend standing out there, and this feeling of complete panic overtook me like, *'What have I done!?* Not only have I won this pageant, but tomorrow my friends and family are going to leave and go back home to Texas and I'm going off with a bunch of Yankees that I haven't even met yet!' "

Shirley didn't dwell on that thought long because she soon reached the end of the runway, where she had been instructed to pause before the television camera. "I remember looking into the eye of that camera and *knowing* that there were millions of people watching, and I thought, 'Look who's watching me—Johnny Carson!' " She laughs. "You know, so many people watch Johnny Carson and I thought, 'Huh, I bet he's watching *me* now!' It was kind of a neat feeling!"

What Shirley and Terry did not look upon with such pleasure was the experience of being interviewed by Bert Parks moments after their coronations. Meeuwsen remembers the shock of seeing the emcee rushing toward her with a microphone as she returned from her victory walk. Stunned by this unexpected development, she silently gasped, "He can't ask me anything *now!* I don't even know my middle name!" As it turned out, the program had run short and Parks had been ordered, "Quick, go ask her something! Just fill some time!" Terry recalls the emcee asked something like "What does it mean to you to be Miss America?" She remarks with a laugh, "I love Bert dearly, but as I look back on it now—how would I *know?* I'd only been Miss America for thirty seconds! I mean, how can I *answer* this question?" Yet, with amazing composure, Terry responded with a Biblical parable. "Love is like a basket of five loaves and two fishes. It never begins to multiply until you give it away, and on behalf of fifty girls I want to say thank you for giving it to us this week."

Two years later, the tables were turned on the emcee when, as a live audience of millions looked on, Parks posed a similar question to a barely crowned Shirley Cothran. With a hint of exasperation behind her composed smile, she replied, "How can you ask me questions at a time like *this?!*" Parks managed a polite titter, but later growled to a *Chicago Tribune* reporter, "God, I'd like to have punched her one!"

THE REACTIONS BEHIND MISS AMERICA'S SMILE

While the "moment you've all been waiting for" has never failed to provide viewers with a host of amusing, endearing, and memorable responses, the reaction that has quietly intrigued fans for decades is whether, during those last few moments before the big announcement is made public, eventual winners somehow sense that the crown will be theirs. The intriguing subject was addressed in Frank Deford's book *There She Is—The Life and Times of Miss America.* "It is claimed by someone who has made a study of the moment, that when there are two girls left in the running, and they clasp hands to await Bert Parks' declaration of their fate, the girl whose hand is on top will always win. . . . Unconsciously, it seems, the winner realized who she was and . . . was permitted to take symbolically a position of authority even in advance of her crowning."

National judges' co-chairman Ellen Plum takes issue with the suggestion that every queen subconsciously realizes she will win. "I've never found a set pattern for that," she insists. "I think it depends on the girl. Every attitude is a little different. Some girls may be a little more sure of themselves than others. I think some girls may not be totally surprised because, if she's won two preliminaries, I think a girl knows she's got a very good chance." While every Miss America's response to her victory is unique, Mrs. Plum is convinced there *is* one reaction that every winner shares. "I've never seen a Miss America who wasn't *thrilled.*"

Former titleholders acknowledge that Plum's assessment that each winner has different expectations is accurate. While some were apparently quite certain of victory, others were surprised even to be among the top ten, and had no inkling they were about to win the title. However, a modest admission of surprise has been the tradition among titleholders for decades. "None of the girls I talked to—nobody—really thought they had a chance," insists Marian McKnight Conway, who won the crown in 1956. "It seemed that everybody was pulling for somebody else. I never talked to anybody who thought they had a chance at all of winning. I don't think anybody even *thought* about that!" She adds with a laugh, "Or if they did, they would never—*ever*—let anybody know! I know I never expected to win. In fact, I remember thinking that at least forty-six girls were better than I was. I was so thrilled just being announced in the top ten that I thought it was the highlight of my life!" She giggles. "Little did I know . . ."

Marian's successor, Marilyn Van Derbur, a reluctant participant who had been drafted by her college sorority, was also stunned to learn the crown was hers. The thought of winning the Miss America title had been the farthest thing from her mind. "It never *occurred* to me that I might win," she recalls. "I just wanted to get through it without embarrassing myself—or Colorado—in front of eighty million people!" Unfortunately, because of her complete confidence that she would never become Miss America, Marilyn hadn't paid much attention during the coronation rehearsals. When her name was announced as the winner and she was gently nudged down the runway, she silently panicked. "'What did they say to do? I wish I had listened more carefully! I have no idea what I'm supposed to be doing now that I'm on this runway in front of everybody in America that I know!' I was really just trying to put all that together." She offers an off-beat analogy. "There's a very famous poet who wrote, 'I heard a fly buzz as I died.' The idea of it was you think of such everyday things during these ultraimportant moments in your life—and that's what I was doing. I was thinking of something quite functional."

Even in today's increasingly sophisticated Pageant environment, there are still young

Kaye Lani Rae Rafko was so absorbed in her thoughts that Gary Collins's announcement of her victory didn't register. "He got through my first three names"—she laughs—"and that's a long name to get through! But I didn't even react until 'Rafko'!" ©PRO PHOTOGRAPHICS/ JOE PROFETTO

"I had a premonition that day that I would win," admits Jacquelyn Mayer, Miss America 1963 (shown here with Lenora Slaughter and her predecessor, Maria Fletcher). *"I think the good Lord kind of showed me what was in store for me."* EARLE HAWKINS

women who are shocked to win the crown. Kaye Lani Rae Rafko, Miss America 1988, is the most recent example. Kaye Lani admits that she was absolutely dumbfounded to hear her name announced as the winner. The best she had dared hope for was a runner-up trophy. "I prayed I would be one of the top five, and when I heard Patricia Brandt's name announced as first runner-up, I guess I was kind of consoling myself, 'That's okay. My goodness, I made the top ten. That's better than I thought I would.'" Absorbed in her thoughts, Kaye Lani somehow missed most of Gary Collins's dramatic announcement, "And our new Miss America is—Kaye . . . Lani . . . Rae . . ." "He got through my first three names," she recalls, "and that's a long name to get through, but I didn't even react until 'Rafko.' Then I thought,

'There's no way! You mean I've just won the *title?!'*" She shakes her head in disbelief. "I had no idea I would win. No idea at all."

While most Miss Americas report that they were surprised by the big announcement, other winners candidly admit they *did* have an idea the crown would be theirs. "I had a premonition that day that I would win," says Jacquelyn Mayer Townsend, Miss America 1963. "I tried to get it out of my mind, although I did tell my aunt, who was with me, that I would be Miss America that night." She chuckles at her aunt's skeptical reaction: "Oh, you silly girl, why would you say *that?*" Jackie admits that there really hadn't been any indication during the week of competition that the judges were favoring her. After all, she hadn't won a preliminary award. Still, the premonition persisted. "It was a strong-enough premonition that I was surprised, yet I wasn't. I think the good Lord kind of showed me what was in store for me."

Similarly, Miss America 1980, Cheryl Prewitt, who shares Mayer's deep faith, candidly admits that she knew she would earn the title months before she arrived in Atlantic City. Nothing unethical was in the works, the Mississippi gospel singer explains—she simply had an unquenchable conviction that God had a purpose for her to win the crown. Cheryl, whose left leg had been crushed in a horrifying car accident during her childhood, had been told by doctors that she would never walk again. After her leg was miraculously healed during a prayer meeting, Cheryl sensed that a victory in Atlantic City was part of a divine plan. "I *knew* God had called me," she says softly, "and I knew it was to win for His glory."

Strengthening that conviction was a startling phone call. "A little old lady in my home town had called me before the Miss Mississippi Pageant, and she was crying her eyes out. She said, 'Cheryl, you're going to be Miss Mississippi.'" Cheryl politely thanked her for the vote of confidence, but her elderly caller continued, "I mean, you're going to *be* Miss Mississippi. I just had a vision. I was sitting here with my eyes wide open and I saw you being crowned." When Cheryl interjected a "Praise the Lord!," the lady added an unexpected footnote. "The reason I know you are going to be Miss Mississippi is because *Bert Parks* crowned you!" Cheryl pauses for emphasis. "I was still Miss Starkville at the time."

Indeed, within the year, Prewitt was standing on the Convention Hall stage listening to Bert Parks rattle off the names on the judges' list—and there wasn't a doubt in her mind that the last name announced would be her own. "As I stood on that stage, I really believed in my heart that I would be Miss America." In fact, Cheryl was *so* confident of victory that when

After a car crash crushed her leg, a divine healing enabled Cheryl Prewitt to pursue the crown. "Halfway down the runway the thought hit me that I could have been home watching that 1980 Miss America Pageant from a wheelchair—but praise the Lord—I wasn't!" IRV KAAR

Bert turned to face the remaining contestants for the big announcement, she reminded herself, "Now, don't step out until Bert calls your name!" She confesses with a giggle that when he *did* name her as the winner she thought, "Okay, now put your hands over your face so they'll think you're surprised." Cheryl admits with infectious laughter that behind those pretty hands she was actually grinning from ear to ear.

Moments later, as she was gliding down the famous 125-foot runway with millions of people looking on, she gestured her thanks toward the heavenly emcee who had made the ethereal announcement months earlier. "When I won the Pageant, about halfway down the runway the thought hit me that I *could* have been home watching that 1980 Miss America Pageant from a wheelchair—but praise the Lord I *wasn't!* I knew that I had won, not on my own strength, but totally and completely on His strength, and I was very thankful and humbled by it."

It wasn't a heavenly nudge that tipped off another national titleholder to her impending

Dorothy Benham sensed the 1977 crown would be hers. "All of a sudden something comes over you. Before my name was announced, I thought, 'Uh-oh! I can already feel where that crown is going to go—on my head!'" IRV KAAR

"I was very conscious of it being an extremely humbling experience," recalls Debra Maffett, Miss America 1983, "because I realized that so many of those girls would have been great Miss Americas." EARLE HAWKINS

victory. It was the analytical mental gears of a future lawyer. "I thought I could win," admits attorney Rebecca King Dreman, Miss America 1974. "I could see the judges watching me a great deal." Becky was so confident of her ability to size up the judges' preferences that she drew up a list of four other contestants she suspected would do well. "I thought, now, if *these* young women are runners-up, then I'll win." On Saturday night, Bert Parks's announcement of the court of honor accurately mirrored Becky's predictions. "I started to panic, thinking, 'Boy, this could really happen!' I really *did* have a feeling that I would win."

Still, by the late 1970s, such admissions remained sufficiently uncommon that for a decade after her reign, Miss America 1977, Dorothy Benham, hesitated to divulge that she had been overwhelmed by a strong hunch that she

"I believe that anybody can be anything they want, if they work hard enough and never give up," advises Debbye Turner, Miss America 1990. *"It took me seven years and four state tries to get here, and I'm so glad I didn't stop trying . . . I am living proof that dreams do come true!"*
©*PRO PHOTOGRAPHICS/JOE PROFETTO*

would win. "You know, I never told anybody that for years and years because I thought, 'Oh, you can't tell people that. They'll think you're crazy.' " But when other queens publicly told of their experiences, Dorothy decided, "Gee, they're saying it. I guess I can, too." Dorothy recalls that as Parks named the runners-up, she was impressed with an unshakable certainty that the crown would be hers. "All of a sudden something comes over you. Before my name was even announced, I thought, 'Uh oh! I can already feel where that crown is going to go—on *my* head!' " She adds with a giggle, "But it's true. All of a sudden you just *know* it's going to happen."

Whatever individual reactions new Miss Americas have exhibited, there is one reaction that every winner has experienced—a deep sense of awe and gratitude that such a coveted honor has been bestowed upon her. "I was very conscious of it being an extremely humbling experience," explains Debbie Maffett, Miss America 1983, "because I realized that so many of those girls would have been great Miss Americas—and the fact that I had been singled out by that panel of judges didn't make me any better than them. I was also aware that I had a big responsibility to those girls onstage, to the Pageant, and to all of those other young women out there who look up to the Miss America Pageant." Debbie pauses and then expresses the heartfelt sentiments seven decades of Miss Americas have shared: "I remember feeling very grateful and very honored—and realizing that it was just the beginning of my life."

Facing page: *Gretchen Carlson (1989) accepts flowers from a four-year-old boy.*
DOUG RUMBURG

PART IV

LIFE AFTER THE PAGEANT

CHAPTER 16

Almost Miss America—Returning Home Without the Crown

The verdict of the national judges has ended the quest for the crown and one lucky young woman has emerged from the crowd as the new Miss America. For the winner, it is an unforgettable moment when the course of her life is instantly and dramatically changed. As she savors the thrill of victory, forty-nine pensive competitors look on wistfully, slowly adjusting to the fact that the dreams they had harbored within their hearts have been extinguished by the reality of this moment. As contestants observe another young woman accept the glittering crown and scepter and maneuver down the runway, they experience a flood of emotions. "It's a very mixed feeling," explains Michele Passarelli, "a feeling that part of you is there with her because you were part of that year. She will forever be *your* Miss America and she sort of becomes the embodiment of your dreams." Michele adds softly, "But you also realize that it is *only* her and not you. You feel a part of it—yet so far away at the same time."

When the broadcast ends and the winner is whisked away to her first press conference,

the forty-nine young ladies who were *almost* Miss America gather their belongings, greet their supporters during States' Visitation in the Convention Hall ballroom, and then return to their respective hotel suites to pack for the trip home the next morning. Once they reach the solitude of their rooms, there is time to ponder the events of the past week and an acute sense of disappointment sets in. "When you're brought back to your hotel room and you say good-bye to your Atlantic City chaperon who has been with you all week long, it hits you that it's over," says former Miss Mississippi Mary Donnelly. "It's *over!* It's not so much the disappointment of not making the top ten or not becoming Miss America," she explains. "Rather, "It's like climbing a mountain. You get back down and you go, 'Oh, that's where I *was*. That's what all that intense preparation was for.'" Meanwhile, she adds, "You are trying to remember it all. You want your senses to hold onto *everything* and not forget a thing."

The next morning, when contestants depart for their respective states, they face several adjustments. First, Donnelly says, "There is a definite 'gear change' that occurs after the Pag-

Pageant week ends as contestants return home to complete their reigns. IRV KAAR

eant. You've been at hyper-speed for weeks preparing for Atlantic City, and all of a sudden it's back to 'real' time." She adds with a laugh, "Life is not a continuing pageant—thank goodness—or we'd all be worn out! No one can give one hundred and ten percent every day of their lives."

Then, there are the concerns some contestants experience about having disappointed their supporters. Fortunately, Mary explains, people are quick to reassure the young ladies that they have represented their states well and made their loved ones proud. "People are not that superficial that they would think any less of the girl they were thrilled to send up to Atlantic City just because she comes back home without another crown." After all, she points out, "She was one of only fifty girls a year who represent their states—out of *thousands* that try! A girl would be doing herself an injustice—and her state an injustice—to think that she

was any less of a state queen because she didn't become Miss America."

But returning home without the crown can be a melancholy experience—at least initially. "You're *ultra* disappointed," says former Miss New Jersey Christina Chriscione, "because it's something you've dreamed about. But you have to learn that there is life after the Miss America Pageant." Christina explains that once contestants have a chance to mull over the events of Pageant week, the significance of their accomplishment suddenly dawns. "Hey, you got to the *Miss America Pageant!* You were one of only fifty girls who came out of eighty thousand across the country—and you realize that it was such an *honor!*"

That's the message Leonard Horn stresses each year as fifty ambitious aspirants arrive for Pageant week. "Success is not in the winning," he reminds the candidates. "Success is in the *trying*. I keep trying to get that message across,

The court of honor poses with trophies. IRV KAAR

Miss America's court of honor hams it up backstage. DOUG RUMBURG

peted before, and you realize that yes, you *can* handle this situation."

Therefore, Blakely recommends that contestants view the Pageant as a step toward future successes. "If you don't win Miss America, that's okay," she says reassuringly, "because Miss America is a wonderful goal—but it's not the *final* goal. The final goal is to become a great attorney or a great governor, or whatever. Be mature enough to look at what it gave you contact-wise and experience-wise. Look at the girls who didn't win Miss America, and what they're doing. You know, those girls didn't just evaporate. The majority of them are very successful in what they've done."

However, according to Leonard Horn, the public is often unaware of the impressive professional accomplishments and credentials of

that the very fact they have had the courage to go through a program like this—for whatever their goals are—puts them far and above most people. Even if they don't win the crown, they should feel extremely good about the fact that they *tried*."

TURNING PAGEANT "LOSSES" INTO CAREER VICTORIES

In fact, whether or not contestants walk away with the crown, they inevitably look back upon their participation in the Super Bowl of pageants with an appreciation for the inner strength and confidence the experience developed within them—qualities that will benefit them throughout their professional careers. "It's all worthwhile," says attorney Regina Hopper Blakely, Miss Arkansas 1983, "because you've competed on the national level with fifty of the best girls in the country. You've competed against the best—and then later on in your career, let's say when you go into court, a strength comes from inside, from having com-

Runners-up accept their trophies at a post-coronation reception. IRV KAAR

former state queens because many of these women have gone into fields that are less visible, "the types of things that you're not going to hear about—doctors, lawyers, engineers. These are the type of people that we attract." In fact, Horn asserts, the program can cite examples of "literally hundreds of young women who have competed in this program over the years who have never been Miss America, who have gone on with the scholarship money and done something meaningful with their higher education . . . and have developed very interesting, important professional careers."

WHAT THEY'RE DOING TODAY

Debra Cleveland, *Miss South Dakota 1984.* Physics degree/nondestructive aerospace engineer, MacDowell Aircraft Company.

Mabel Bendiksen Pina, *Miss Massachusetts 1965.* Harvard M.P.A./serves on boards of educational institutions.

Dr. Carla Huston Bell (Berta Huebl), *Miss Montana 1955.* Columbia University doctoral degree/author/financial planner/Wall Street stockbroker.

Janet Ward Black, *Miss North Carolina 1980.* Graduate, Duke University Law School/former state assistant district attorney/senior law partner, Wallace, Whitley, Hope and Black.

Katherine Karlsrud, *Miss New York 1970.* Medical doctor/graduate of Albany Medical College/clinical instructor in pediatrics at Cornell University/New York Hospital pediatric physician.

Marti Phillips, *Miss Florida 1979.* Magna cum laude law degree, Florida State University/clerked with federal judge/attorney with Bostwick and Tehin.

Cloris Leachman, *Miss Chicago 1946.* TV, film, and stage actress/recipient of four Emmy Awards and an Academy Award.

Barbara Jennings, *Miss Maryland 1976.* Doctor of optometry/professor of optometry (lectures worldwide on disorders of the eye)/fellow, American Academy of Optometry.

Sandra Adamson Fryhofer, *Miss Georgia 1976.* Medical doctor/magna cum laude degree in chemical engineering/graduate, Emory University School of Medicine/first woman diplomate, American Board of Internal Medicine.

Veronica Clark, *Miss Maryland 1975.* Former assistant state attorney in Baltimore.

Nancy Moore, *Miss South Carolina 1965.* Author, *Mother's Medicine*/wife of U.S. senator Strom Thurmond.

Margo Ewing Bane, *Miss Delaware 1969.* State senator.

Kathleen Callahan Bousquet, *Miss Massachusetts 1986.* Biology degree with minor in physics and chemistry/chief technologist in nuclear medicine, AdvaCare, Boston.

Jeanne Swanner Robertson, *Miss North Carolina 1963.* Award-winning humorous speaker/author.

Charmaine Kowalski, *Miss Pennsylvania 1978.* Phi Beta Kappa graduate of Penn State/Harvard Medical School graduate/psychiatrist at New York City hospital.

Angela Baldi Bartell, *Miss Wisconsin 1964.* Attorney/county court trial judge named to Wisconsin State Supreme Court.

Mary Hart, *Miss South Dakota 1970. Entertainment Tonight.*

Vera Ralston Miles, *Miss Kansas 1948.* Film star, *Psycho.*

Susan Anton, *Miss California 1969.* Recording artist, actress, *Golden Girl.*

Zoe Ann Warberg, *Miss Idaho 1952.* Stanford law degree/Idaho Probate Court judge.

Rebeccah Bush, *Miss Illinois 1983.* Actress, *Jake and the Fatman, The Men's Club, Sydney.*

Joan Blondell, *Miss Dallas 1926.* Film actress.

Lex Ann Haughey, _Miss Texas 1979_. Assistant vice president, Merrill Lynch/past E. F. Hutton Broker of the Year.

Nancy Stafford, _Miss Florida 1976_. Actress, _St. Elsewhere, The Doctors, Matlock_.

Delta Burke, _Miss Florida 1974_. Attended the London Academy of Music and Dramatic Arts/Emmy-nominated actress, _Designing Women, Filthy Rich_.

Marlyse Reed Stapleton, _Miss Minnesota 1955_. Expert show-woman and breeder of Spanish Arabian horses.

Lisa Kleypas, _Miss Massachusetts 1985_. Author of five novels.

Sonya Pleasant, _Miss Tennessee 1985_. White House staff member, Office of Legislative Affairs.

Kathleen Ennis, _Miss Arizona 1969_. L.P.N./co-author of book on child abuse.

Cynthia Sikes, _Miss Kansas 1972_. TV and film actress, _St. Elsewhere, L.A. Law, Arthur 2— On the Rocks, Love Hurts_.

Paula Pope Webster, _Miss New York 1978_. Attorney, New York law firm Webster & Webster.

Mary Beth Haroth Neill, _Miss Maryland 1984_. D.D.S., Navy dentist, U.S.S. _Vulcan_.

Idell Hulin, _Miss Minnesota 1953_. Alcohol and drug abuse counselor and lecturer.

Linda Moulton Howe, _Miss Idaho 1963_. Stanford graduate/documentary filmmaker/ winner of three Emmy Awards.

Regina Hopper Blakely, _Miss Arkansas 1983_. Attorney/corporate law practice with Arnold, Grobmyer and Haley.

Anita Bryant, _Miss Oklahoma 1958_. Singer/ spokesperson.

Kristi Reindl Vetri, _Miss Maryland 1973_. Mayor, O'Fallon, Illinois/attorney.

Dorothy Lamour, _Miss New Orleans 1935_. Film actress.

Rebecca Graham, _Miss Indiana 1972_. Operates Florida state lottery/formerly ran Illinois state lottery.

Linda Hitchens, _Miss Delaware 1970_. Holds B.A., M.B.A., and law degrees/practices international law.

Linda Hall Daschle, _Miss Kansas 1976_. FAA's director of federal legislation for government affairs/vice president, American Association of Airport Executives.

Whatever the particular career paths chosen by former contestants, they each share a certain intangible confidence, according to Michele Passarelli. "Every former contestant I have ever spoken to has gone through life from that point on with a feeling that whatever they attempt will be successful. It really does make you feel that you have that special something that set you apart that year and made you one of fifty." Michele adds with a laugh, "There _is_ life after the Miss America Pageant—and it can be very successful and productive!"

CHAPTER 17

On the Road with Miss America

hile the forty-nine national contestants who have narrowly missed the Miss America throne return home to complete their reigns as state queens, one slightly awed and understandably nervous young woman embarks on an extraordinary experience others only dream about—a whirlwind year that, former Miss America Debra Maffett advises, "no one can be totally prepared for."

As the winner is escorted offstage at the conclusion of the television broadcast, officials take her aside for a few moments of privacy to collect her thoughts and compose herself before being introduced to the national media during her first press conference. "I must tell you that when I came back and we started getting ready for the press conference, my mind was just *swirling!*" exclaims Kaye Lani Rae Rafko. "You can't possibly imagine the different emotions that you feel. Of course, you're elated that all the hard work has paid off and you're thinking, 'Oh, what an exciting year!,' but you're also nervous and sad because you know that you'll be away from your family. And

you're very frightened because all these people that you've never met before are suddenly *tugging* at you and guarding you from the world. I was a nervous wreck because I immediately knew that I would be representing the eighty thousand women who compete each year for this title, the Pageant sponsors, my home state of Michigan, and the nursing profession. I knew it was a big responsibility, and that anything I would say or do would be representing them—and I was afraid that I would say the wrong thing." She adds with a laugh, "Now, in a matter of three minutes, all these thoughts were going through my mind at once!"

MISS AMERICA'S FAMILY

While the new Miss America adjusts emotionally to her good fortune and prepares to begin her reign, her loved ones are drawn into the glamour and excitement of the magical evening. The winner's parents are escorted to the press center, where they are immediately mobbed by television, radio, and newspaper

162

What began as a dream is now reality. Marjorie Vincent, Miss America 1991.
TERRY CHENAILLE

all hours of the morning—and there were these two little boys taking all these calls!" An amusing footnote to the commotion was a message from the workers who handled the deluge of congratulatory messages to Terry. "The last telegram was so cute!" she recalls with a laugh. "It said something like, 'Best wishes and good luck in your year ahead—from two very tired Western Union girls!'"

On occasion, the winner's parents have not been able to attend the national Pageant, like the year Nonnie and Ron Maffett watched daughter Debbie's victory from their home in Cut 'n Shoot, Texas. "I don't remember experiencing anything quite like it!" Mrs. Maffett says, chortling. "From that evening, everything was different—and is *still* different! The telephone started ringing immediately after the Pageant and didn't stop until four in the morning. The next morning we were deluged by the press. All three major networks, NBC, CBS, and ABC, converged on us. There were newspaper

Miss America's reign begins as she is escorted offstage. TERRY CHENAILLE

reporters. Other members of her family who are in attendance in Convention Hall are also inundated by press and well-wishers. Sometimes the crowd can become overenthusiastic, like the year Rebecca King's brother was so deluged that a team of police officers was sent to escort him away from the mob.

Even those members of the new queen's family who have watched her selection at home aren't exempted from the ensuing bedlam. In 1972, when Terry Meeuwsen won the national title, her two younger brothers watched the telecast from their DePere, Wisconsin, home. Terry giggles that her brothers' experiences in the hours following her coronation "must have been a riot! The phone just went crazy with people calling, people were coming over, and cars were driving by our house honking until

Marjorie Vincent addresses reporters at her postcoronation press conference in 1990.
PAUL ABEL, JR.

MISS AMERICA'S REIGN BEGINS

The morning after her coronation, after only a few hours of sleep, Miss America wakes to a morning packed with appointments: her second press conference, official photographs with her state director and parents, a presentation of the keys to her new Corvette, and press photo sessions along the beach and Boardwalk.

That afternoon, the new titleholder is driven by limousine to New York City, where she prepares for the Monday-morning onslaught when her reigns begins in earnest.

The changing of the guard: Kylene Barker (1979) crowns Cheryl Prewitt (1980).
IRV KAAR

and radio stations calling from all over the United States wanting interviews. The *National Enquirer* called. We actually had a helicopter from a station in Houston land in our yard! The mailbox was just absolutely deluged with all kinds of gifts, portraits people had painted, and letters—constantly letters from people wanting autographs and things of this sort. Just all kinds of things going on the whole year." However, during those first few days after Debbie's triumph, Nonnie reports, the onslaught was so intense that the Maffetts "actually had to leave the house to get away from the telephone and to get some rest." She admits with a laugh, "It was pretty nerve-racking, I'll have to say!"

"It was really overwhelming," says Marian McKnight Conway, "because after you're crowned, you're whisked away to New York and you're having press conferences and TV news and radio interviews. It's just one, two, three! It isn't until a few days later that it sort of sinks in. Then you realize that it's a big responsibility! But you really have to experience it to know how it feels because words can't describe it. It's just that simple."

According to Karen Aarons, those first few days in New York, although harried, provide an ideal opportunity for the new titleholder to gain confidence in "a controlled situation where she has a lot of different appearances, but where there are some Pageant people there to explain what's going on and to answer any questions." Miss America's hair is coiffed by a world-class hairstylist, she appears on major talk shows, selects her "Made in the U.S.A." wardrobe, is introduced to the national sponsors, and gets a taste of the responsibilities she will carry throughout the upcoming year.

MISS AMERICA'S SCHEDULE

During Miss America's reign, her schedule, which is arranged by business manager Robert Bryan, involves over two hundred appearances a year and close to thirty thousand miles of air travel per month. Travel expenses, including first-class airfare, meals, and private accommodations for both Miss America and her traveling companion, are borne by the booking party. Appearances range from commercial and sponsor bookings to charity and civic events, and include autograph sessions, fund-raisers, conventions, club luncheons, preliminary pageants, parades, visits to children's and veterans' hospitals, and speeches before student groups and political conferences.

In arranging Miss America's schedule, Bryan attempts to ensure a reasonable balance, allowing the winner to take full advantage of the myriad opportunities her reign provides while protecting her health. His "every other day" policy arranges for Miss America to travel

Sharlene Wells, 1985, and court of honor (from left to right—Miss Minnesota, Miss Mississippi, Miss America, Miss Ohio, Miss Texas). IRV KAAR

Dorothy Benham (1977) with her mother and stepfather. IRV KAAR

and rest one day, while making her appearance the following day. "It's hectic," he acknowledges, "but I try to keep it from being *too* hectic. I try to protect her health, and I feel they're much better off." Even so, Bryan finds that most winners are eager to take advantage of the year's career and publicity opportuni-

Marjorie Vincent's parents, Lucien and Florence Vincent, answer reporters' questions at a Sunday-morning press conference. PAUL ABEL, JR.

ties. "If she's worked that hard, if she's that ambitious to work for it in the first place, she's certainly not going to let it slip away. She's going to take full advantage of it while it's there." He interjects with a grin, "And she's certainly going to be well fixed financially."

In fact, today's queens make over $150,000 in personal appearance fees. When combined with the $35,000 national scholarship, Miss America's financial nest egg may reach $200,000—and with the exception of a small administrative charge, the winner keeps it all.

The Vincent family, Lucien, Florence, and sister Carla, watch with pride as Marjorie is introduced to the national press as Miss America 1991. PAUL ABEL, JR.

MISS AMERICA MEETS THE PRESS

One of the new titleholder's first and most stressful assignments is her introductory press conference in New York City, which, Kaye Lani Rafko advises, "is very, very important because it really sets you up for the rest of the year." The pressure of facing the podium clustered with microphones, and a sea of inquiring faces and camera lenses, can be unnerving for a suddenly famous college coed. "All I remember about that is that it was just a blur of faces and a *lot* of questions," recalls Shirley Cothran-Barret. "It dawned on me that second that I had better be precise in what I said. There was a real inkling of 'Shirley, questions are going to come fast and fierce and you'd better have some idea of what you're going to say!'"

Unlike past decades when winners were forbidden to discuss politics or religion, today's queens are free to comment on any issue they wish. "What was so nice was that Pageant officials never once told me to say 'No comment,' or to stifle myself on certain issues," says Kaye Lani, "so I was very open and spoke my opinions, and was right away branded the most outspoken Miss America ever. I think that changed people's minds a little bit about who Miss America is and that she *can* speak and she does feel comfortable voicing her opinions."

Whatever the titleholder decides to say to the press that year is her prerogative, but Albert Marks used to offer a bit of fatherly advice to each winner. "I'd tell them, 'Just remember before you answer that whatever answer you give, you are the one who has to live with it. So guide yourself accordingly.'"

Marjorie Vincent discusses her issues platform with reporters. PAUL ABEL, JR

THE OFFICIAL TRAVELING COMPANIONS

As Miss America embarks on her whirlwind year, she is accompanied by one of two official traveling companions who alternate month-long stints. According to Karen Aarons, the traveling companions' responsibilities are to "take care of all the details of traveling so that Miss America has only to worry about her own health and being ready for each appearance. It's a twenty-four-hour-a-day job," she stresses, "and they work hard at it." In fact, the position is so demanding that veteran escort Ellie Ross admits she works her shift "and then

I go home and *recuperate* while the other lady is with her!"

From the titleholder's perspective, having a mature woman to accompany her during her travels is a reassuring safeguard. "The first thing I was grateful for was a chaperon, a traveling companion," affirms Marilyn Van Derbur. "It was so wonderful to never be put in any kind of situation that was uncomfortable because you had someone with you at all times. There could be no innuendos, nothing uncomplimentary written about any Miss America, because everyone knew that she was *always* chaperoned. As I looked back on it later, I was really grateful for that."

Gretchen Carlson (1989) with her mother and father at Sunday-morning breakfast.
DOUG RUMBURG

Tawny Godin (1976) and her parents toast her victory. IRV KAAR

American royalty. PAUL ABEL, JR.

With the women being in such close contact for twelve months, a warm relationship is critical and chaperons emphasize their supportive role. "You want to be her cheerleader and make her feel great because they have their down times," Midge Stevenson explains. "I avoid saying 'mother' because we really are not trying to supplant her mother. You're a friend."

Mature friend, travel agent, or chaperon, the position calls for unfailing energy, enthusiasm, and diplomacy, not to mention the considerable responsibility of ensuring the safety of an American symbol. It's not the easiest role to play, but, as Ellie Ross points out with a relieved smile, "We haven't lost one yet!"

MISS AMERICA MEETS THE PUBLIC

After her debut in New York, Miss America embarks on her year-long whirlwind tour of the nation, where she meets the American public. Becoming acquainted with the people her title represents is inevitably one of the most fascinating aspects of a Miss America's reign.

First, she discovers that a large segment of the population regards her with a surprising degree of familiarity. "It's amazing." Ellie Ross laughs. "But they think that Miss America _belongs_ to them! That they can touch her and give her a kiss on the cheek—or even on the lips! People just think it's wonderful that a celebrity is among them, but I doubt that if Eliz-

Gretchen Carlson during an appearance for national Pageant sponsor "Made in the U.S.A." DOUG RUMBURG

Marjorie Vincent poses with Susan Stautberg (to her right) and other members of the Miss America Women's Advisory Council. PAUL ABEL, JR.

abeth Taylor or any other celebrity was in their home town they would feel they could hug or kiss her." She shrugs. "But Miss America belongs to the public."

One overly imaginative fan took that attitude more seriously than most during Debra Maffett's reign. It seems the young man became enamored of Debbie during the live broadcast. "As I was being crowned and was walking down the runway with my scepter, someone said, 'I love you! Will you marry me?' And while I'm just being crowned Miss America, I supposedly told him 'Yes,' so he packed up all his stuff and moved to California and in the process I guess dropped and broke his television set. So a few months after I was crowned, he was suing me for breach of promise. He had it all itemized, with the television set he had dropped and broken while moving—and he was trying to make me pay for all of his moving expenses! It was wild!"

As Debbie discovered, fame can be a two-edged sword. The adoring public not only assumes that Miss America belongs to them, but they also harbor lofty expectations for their youthful queen. "I found the most difficult part of that year was living up to the public's image of Miss America," says Terry Meeuwsen. "I think they had very *un*realistic expectations. They expected me to look like I had just walked off a runway every time I arrived in town. You know—the same dress and a dozen roses that hadn't wilted. The hardest part of the year was trying to stay fresh and look fresh."

Terry recalls one time when her travels whisked her through three states in one day. By the time her last flight landed at nine that evening, Terry felt "exhausted and bedraggled. I felt like my makeup was on my ankles, my hair was just hanging, my face felt oily, and my feet felt like they were swollen over the sides of my high heels. I just wanted to go to bed!" She glanced out the window and noticed a small high school band standing in salute and a red carpet rolled out to welcome a dignitary. "My first reaction was, 'Oh, who's on board with us?'" Then she noticed a gentleman cradling a huge bouquet of roses. "Oh, noooo!" she groaned. "You must be kidding!" To make matters worse, the reigning state queen, "who looked like she had spent the entire day preparing for this," was on hand to greet her. "She looked like a *million dollars!*" Terry sighs, adding with a laugh, "I remember getting out of the plane thinking, 'The poor kid is probably looking at me saying, "I *knew* I should have won!"'—and so was everyone around her! That's the kind of pressure you're under," she explains. "They're really paying for you to be Cinderella everywhere you go."

Kaye Lani Rafko agrees that the public's expectations can be pretty lofty. "When you're crowned Miss America, they put you up on a pedestal. People really look up to you and they think you're perfect. They think that you have everything that you've ever wanted or dreamed about in life, and that you don't have to work hard. They have this image of you being untouchable and unapproachable, and I wanted to change that. I wanted them to know that, my goodness, it took me six and a half years to get here. Nothing was handed to me on a silver platter. I've worked hard at everything I've achieved. I'd sit down and really *talk* to them and say, 'Don't treat me like a goddess because

Debbie Maffett (1983) responds to a reporter during an interview near the end of her reign. IRV KAAR

I'm not. There's no one in the world that's perfect. I'm human."

Still, most Miss Americas give their best to fulfill the public's expectations, but the effort can become tedious. "People would try to hold you up to their ideals," explains Judi Ford. "You can't possibly live up to everybody's ideal—especially everybody's idea of an ideal. You just can't do it. I tried for a while, but it just didn't work." Sometimes the public would openly express disappointment. "You'd get these guys who'd say, 'Aaaah, my *sister's* better looking!,' but I really don't let it bother me." Even so, there were occasions when she wearied of the game and let her impatience show. Once, during an autograph session, a young fellow raved about Ford's first runner-up. "He went on and on about how Miss Massachusetts shuddawon, how he couldn't *believe* she had lost, how wonderful she was, and blah, blah, blah." After tolerating the tirade politely, Judi finally blurted out in exasperation, "Yeah? Well, I *beat* her!"

Posing with admirers: Kaye Lani Rae Rafko with Ann-Marie Bivans and Ann-Marie's sons, Chris and David. K. BIVANS

Kylene Barker, Miss America 1979, addresses the Miss Philadelphia Pageant contestants.
IRV KAAR

Such encounters *could* be discouraging to the young women who wear the crown, but Evelyn Ay Sempier points out reassuringly, "Maybe you don't measure up the way they want you to, but you have to be confident that for the *majority* you are all right." She shakes her head slowly and chuckles, "It's an interesting phenomenon being Miss America."

ADVENTURES IN TRAVELING

One of the most exciting opportunities provided the national titleholder is the chance to travel extensively—over 200,000 miles of air travel alone. In fact, travel is such an integral aspect of the year that, Robert Bryan says, laughing, "if a girl gets airsick or homesick, she'd better not run for Miss America!" Dorothy Benham affirms, "It's constant travel. You're in a different city, town, or state every day or every other day, so you're flying constantly. But it happens so fast you don't have time to really think about it." Besides, she exclaims, "It's so exciting."

Sometimes *too* exciting. On rare occasions, Miss Americas have experienced unnerving brushes with airborne disaster. "The most terrifying experience was the time I was on an airplane where one of the engines caught fire and we had to turn around and go home again," Dorothy recalls. "As we took off, something didn't feel right. I looked at my traveling companion and she looked at me—and we didn't say a word. We knew something was

Kaye Lani Rae Rafko (1988) poses with Leonard Horn and Miss America 1959, Mary Ann Mobley. MICHAEL KURTZ

Encouraging an aspiring Miss America: Kaye Lani Rae Rafko (1988) and a teen pageant winner. DOUG RUMBURG

wrong. About ten minutes into the flight, the pilot announced on the intercom, 'We are afraid that we have to turn around and go back to O'Hare. We think one of the engines has caught fire or lost power.' That did shake me," she admits. "I was a nervous wreck. When I got off for the appearance, I said, 'All I want to do is get to our room so I can lie down!'"

One of the less dangerous, but undoubtedly aggravating, problems with constant travel is lost luggage. Anita Puhala reports that during her travels with Kaye Lani, there were several occasions when pieces of her luggage mysteriously disappeared. "One time, we really had a panic," she exclaims, "because Kaye Lani's

gowns, fur coat, and crown were in the missing suitcase!" Apparently, as her luggage came off the turnstile, another limo driver assumed an unmatched suitcase belonged to his passengers and tossed it into his trunk. She chuckles: "Well, as soon as they got to their destination and realized that they had *Miss America*'s luggage, they called the airport and brought it back!"

Despite the adventures and mishaps of constant travel, there are also amusing incidents scattered throughout the year. Judi Ford recalls a comical episode that occurred during a flight to a major appearance. Ford, who happened to be glamorously attired in a mink coat that day, noticed a little girl scrutinizing her intently throughout the flight. As the plane landed, passengers watched in curiosity as a high school band, an official with a lavish rose bouquet in hand, and a cluster of camera crews rustled toward the plane. The little girl peered at the ensemble outside and then back at the fur-clad blonde seated nearby. Finally, she inquired skeptically, "Are you *Miss America?*" Assuming she wanted an autograph, Judi admitted that she was indeed Miss America. "Well, gollyyy!" the little girl exclaimed in a suddenly impressed tone. "I thought you were just a rich ol' girl!"

From Judi's experience, life on the road as Miss America involves much more than inquisitive passengers, hijacked luggage, and aircraft engine trouble. The frenetic schedule with its early-morning flights, daily hotel hopping, and midnight laundry sessions requires a definite adjustment. "It was one of those things where we were up until two in the morning, we had to get up at five, and my chaperon would come in and start singing *There She Is—Miss America*—and there I would be, standing in the bathroom with my hair in curlers, washing my underwear out in the sink!" She adds with a grin, "But that's life on the road! It takes a while to get used to it, and it's not quite the glamorous life. But it was a job for which I was well paid, and I got to see almost all of the United States."

THE RESPONSIBILITY THAT GOES WITH THE CROWN

The fact that life on the road as Miss America can be less than glamorous at times comes as a surprise to some winners. "It's a job," explains Shirley Cothran-Barret. "The glamour wore off in about a week and a half, and then it was a job. A very enjoyable job—but a hard one. It's very demanding traveling and meeting people every day." She laughs. "There are some days when you just want to get up and stick your tongue out at everyone! But you can't do that when you're Miss America. You have to be nice and congenial and enthusiastic. What makes that so difficult is you have to be nice, congenial, and enthusiastic three hundred and sixty-five days in a row! That's the real pitch—*in a row!* You can't have a day off because if someone has invited you to come, they have paid an honorarium, they've paid expenses for you and your traveling companion, and it has not been an inexpensive endeavor for them, so you have to be gracious. Or at any rate," she suggests, chuckling, "you *should* be gracious and accommodating."

In fact, the young woman's attitude during her reign is so critical that Lenora Slaughter discussed the issue in depth with three decades of winners. Marilyn Van Derbur recalls that the morning after her coronation, Lenora advised her, "You know, I've spent my entire adult life building the Miss America Pageant. . . . Because you, as Miss America, represent everything I have worked for, you *are* the Miss America Pageant. If you go into Columbus, Ohio, or Roanoke, Virginia, when you're so tired you think you can't go another minute, and you're not charming and eager to please, they will

think that Miss America is not all that we say she is. On the other hand, if you are gracious, dynamic, eager to please, and happy to sign autographs, then you build in that city what the Miss America Pageant is." Marilyn adds, "She left me with a belief larger than myself. I would have done my best anyway, but in those times—and there were many—when I thought 'I can't go another minute! I can't smile for one more picture!,' I really did remember what she had said to me, and I knew that she was right."

When those challenging moments of fatigue and frustration strike, many titleholders put them into perspective by focusing on the honor of the crown. As Kaye Lani Rafko puts it, "I kept in mind that the minute it got too rough, the minute the fourteen-hour days became too long, the minute people started to be naggy and frustrating, I knew that I could walk away and there were over seventy-nine thousand women who would trade shoes with me in a second! So despite all the work, I always kept in mind that there were so many people who wanted this position—who *dreamed* of holding the position I had—and who was I not to appreciate it? So I decided to enjoy *every single minute*—and that's what I did."

A TREASURE CHEST OF ROYAL MEMORIES

It's not hard to appreciate the reign when one stops to consider the treasure chest of memories Miss Americas collect over the year. "Oh, you get to do some wonderful things," exclaims Becky King. "The glamorous side is that you get to *do* some of those things that you dream about. I emceed the Rose Bowl Parade with Ed McMahon and John Davidson, and I got to do a layout for *Vogue* magazine!" Many of the opportunities handed to Miss Americas are well beyond the reach of other young women their age: performing with Bob Hope on a TV special, chatting privately with the president in the Oval Office, dining with senators, addressing a congressional subcommittee, appearing on television's _The Love Boat, Family Feud, Hollywood Squares,_ or _Bloopers and Practical Jokes,_ performing on _The Tonight Show_ and during the Macy's Day Parade, being featured on magazine covers, and hobnobbing with celebrities.

One of the highlights of any titleholder's reign is her "Homecoming," conducted a month after her victory, when her state welcomes back their champion with suitable fanfare. In 1973, Terry Meeuwsen was honored with _three_ homecomings: Appleton, home of her local pageant, saluted her with a parade and formal luncheon; Oshkosh, home of the Miss Wisconsin Pageant, transformed the airport into a ballroom, saluted her with a military honor guard, and gave her a new car and wardrobe; and DePere, her hometown, toasted Terry with a "This is your life, Miss America" banquet featuring a parade of her past acquaintances. The most poignant moment of the evening was the introduction of a surprise guest—the wife of a Wyoming serviceman Terry was supporting by wearing a POW bracelet. "It was the first time we ever laid eyes on each other," she explains, "and it was a very emotional experience—for everyone there, really." Her Homecomings added a "very personally meaningful" touch to an already extraordinary year.

Kaye Lani found her Michigan Homecoming equally exhilarating. "The highlight of my year was Homecoming. It was so phenomenal they're _still_ talking about it!" she says, giggling. "When we arrived at the airport, there were hundreds of people there and over a dozen limousines waiting for us. Out of about twenty-five thousand people in Monroe, over fifteen thousand showed up for a parade in my honor. They even dedicated a street to me—'Kaye Lani Avenue'! It was so exciting, I cried through the whole thing!"

Another thrilling highlight of the Miss America experience is the opportunity to meet heads of state. Lee Meriwether remembers the fascinating conversation she had with Argentine president Juan Perón during a Bancroft fashion tour of South America. Desiring to put Miss America at ease, Perón chatted with her in broken English during a private tour of his collection of rare artifacts. The president paused before his most prized curio, a giant condor, and shared his philosophy of life. "I try to live my life like the condor," he mused. "He can fly over the Andes, but it doesn't go to his head." Lee chuckles. "It didn't exactly work out that way" for the soon-to-be-exiled leader, "but what he was, at least, _trying_ to tell me was that he was trying to keep his head, not above the clouds, but down on earth."

Two decades later, Laurel Shaefer and her mother, Eleanor, spent an afternoon visiting with President Nixon in the Oval Office. Despite their awe at "standing in the presence of the most important man in the world," they found the president "delightful to talk with and a charming host." Mrs. Schaefer recalls with amusement that as Nixon chatted with Laurie about how his daughters had always stayed up late to watch the Pageant, she noticed his eyes "twinkling" and realized, "Why, you're just a great big teddy bear!" For both Miss America and her mom the day was unforgettable. "Oh, we just had the best time!" Eleanor sighs nostalgically.

Cheryl Prewitt enjoyed an equally memorable visit with Jimmy Carter shortly after her victory. As she was presented to the president, he welcomed her with a bear hug and smiled: "I understand we have the same 'Father'!" Carter then inquired about the childhood auto accident that had crushed Cheryl's leg and how that limb had been divinely healed. "I understand that you had a miracle and your leg grew an inch and a half. How do people react when you say that to them?" Cheryl's answer—"I just tell 'em, 'Well, take a look yourself!' "—elicited a mischievous grin from the president. "And I bet they do!" he replied, laughing.

Despite the excitement of such high-profile appearances, Miss Americas also enjoy a host of delightful but less glamorous experiences that color their reign with the unforgettable flavors of traditional America: snowmobiling through shoulder-deep snow in a Minnesota farmyard, being dubbed an honorary American Indian in full regalia, being initiated into the *Boy* Scouts, serving as the inspiration for a Miss America Girl Scout badge, ordering lunch at a McDonald's drive-through in a stretch limo. In fact, many queens insist that some of the most memorable experiences of their reigns were those unusual slices of American life.

"There's a lot to choose from," says Shirley Cothran-Barret. "Going to Hawaii for the first time—and," she interjects with a laugh, "eating raw fish and hot Coke! Going to Disney World for the first time, seeing Mount Rushmore, and going to Maine during the peak season when the leaves were falling. I got to see America the way very few people get to see America!" One of her favorite memories is of the night when she attended a "Rattlesnake Round-up" in the deep South, where a toothless septuagenarian named Zeke served as her tour guide. "I remember it being so totally down-home and I guess there was something about the allure of rattlesnakes. I went out on their hunt and we caught a six-foot rattlesnake. It was thrilling and a sight to behold!" she exclaims. "They're all very poignant memories in my mind."

Unfortunately, there have also been rare occasions when a Miss America's reign has been touched by catastrophe. Two of the most tragic instances occurred during Donna Axum's reign. On November 22, 1963, Donna and her traveling companion arrived at the Pepsi-Cola National Bottlers Convention in Dallas, Texas. Pepsi, then a Pageant sponsor, had invited Donna and film star Joan Crawford, wife of Pepsi chairman Alfred Steele, to attend a lavish luncheon. As the guests arrived shortly before the meal, they were greeted with the horrifying news that an assassination attempt had been made on John F. Kennedy only miles away. "When we first heard that he had been shot," Donna says, "we said a prayer for President Kennedy and then they dismissed the convention." Soon after, they learned of the president's death. "It was a very somber day," Donna recollects softly, "as you can well imagine."

A month later, during a trip to the Gator Bowl in Jacksonville, Florida, the Roosevelt Hotel, where Donna and her chaperon were staying, erupted into flames. Twenty-one guests perished, and Donna, who dragged her unconscious chaperon to safety, was rushed to the hospital with chemical burns of her throat and bronchial tubes from smoke inhalation. She admits that in the face of impending tragedy, a disconcerting vision flashed through her mind—the image of a newspaper headline: MISS AMERICA PERISHES IN FIRE! FIRST RUNNER-UP TAKES OVER.

FALLING OFF THE THRONE

While few Miss Americas have encountered such sobering occasions during their year, many queens have experienced situations that left them blushing—and wishing they could somehow hide behind their famous crown. Embarrassed titleholders have been pelted with apple crisp by school kids, had soiled babies plopped on their laps at autograph sessions, climbed out of a limousine's sunroof when its doors froze shut, had an evening gown ripped off by a mall escalator, and fallen off stages and runways. Traveling companion Midge Stevenson admits that "because everyone notices Miss America," queens are not at all amused to find themselves in the public spotlight when things go haywire. "They just hope that's not how people will remember them!"

Those were undoubtedly Marilyn Van Derbur's sentiments back in 1957, when Colorado saluted her victory with a massive Homecoming ceremony. The festivities were to conclude with a dramatic grand finale as Miss America regally descended a flight of stairs to a standing ovation. Despite the fact that the stairs lacked a railing, organizers couldn't find a gentleman "honorable enough" to escort Miss America down the stairs, so they instructed Marilyn to descend alone. "I was standing at the top of the stairs," she recalls, "carrying roses, and wearing my crown and this big red cape, and tall, spiky heels. The choir was singing *There She Is—Miss America,* there was a spotlight on my face, and," she gasps in mortification, "I *fell down the stairs!* Everyone, everyone I ever knew was there, and I just humiliated myself!"

Still, Marilyn manages to find a shred of humor in the memory. It seems her sorority sisters (who had drafted her into the Pageant in the first place) had been pestering her father, "Has she changed, has she changed?" So in the moments following Marilyn's unforgettable grand entrance, Mr. Van Derbur settled the matter. "Well, now they *know* you haven't changed!" he wisecracked.

Laurie Shaefer experienced a similar public plunge. During her reign, Laurie's hectic schedule included appearances at preliminary pageants around the country. Usually, she would arrive at the auditorium only moments before her introduction and walk onstage without a practice walk. Fortunately, she points out, most runways are well illuminated, "so while you've never been on that runway before, you can play it by ear and know that if you use your peripheral vision, you'll be fine."

However, at one particular pageant, no one thought to inform the newly arrived Miss America that there were no lights marking the *end* of the runway. It proved to be a disastrous oversight. As they introduced her, Laurie found herself onstage in a velvet black auditorium with only a narrow spotlight beam and a few dim bulbs along the sides of the runway to guide her. She remembers "walking and walking and walking" and *still* not seeing any lights to mark the end of the ramp. "So, here it's this pitch-black room except for this tight spotlight on my face and the crown—and suddenly I just literally *fell off the runway!*"

The only thing that saved her from serious injury was the man she landed on. "I fell into a man's lap. I mean I *smashed* the poor man, but luckily he was a big man so he didn't care—but it knocked the wind out of *me!*" Laurie explains that, at this point, the audience had only an unsettling suspicion of what had happened to their celebrity guest. "I just disappeared out of the spotlight"—she laughs—"only to *climb* back up onto the runway, ask for my shoe back, put it on, stand up, and straighten out my clothing." Her crown was cockeyed, her gown torn and splattered with blood from a badly skinned leg, and one of her delicate shoes was missing the heel. Down but not out, Miss America smiled weakly at the audience and limped back toward the stage. "It was not a pretty picture, to say the least!" she jokes.

Safely back onstage, Laurie grabbed a microphone from the emcee and quipped to the startled audience, "I don't think I was expecting your runway to *not* go further. I don't know if you noticed, but you lost me for a few minutes there. The cameraman at the end of the runway, who is now about three inches shorter than he was before, can tell you the story at intermission." In retrospect, she says, "Miss America must always be 'perfect,' so it was a disastrous thing!"

It's nearly impossible to conceive of a more embarrassing scenario, but Laurie manages to recall one—her incomparable hospital fiasco. It seems that, during her reign, poor Laurie became extremely ill and was hospitalized. When word spread that Miss America had been admitted, a privacy problem quickly developed. "I'm sure every single doctor, resident, intern, and lab technician came in to say, 'Well, I saw your lungs, but I'd like to see your face.'" To Laurie's relief, a strict no-visitors rule was invoked to alleviate the problem. A few days later, a no-nonsense woman technician entered her room, instructed her to disrobe, attached a cluster of electrodes to her chest, and sternly ordered, "This will take about twenty minutes from the start to finish, but I need you to lie *perfectly* still, because if you move, the electrodes could come unattached and we'd have to start the whole procedure over again."

As the technician absorbed herself in reading the electrocardiogram results, a gentleman wearing a white medical coat confidently strode into the room and greeted Laurie with a cheerful "Good morning!" Assuming he was a physician, Laurie managed a polite smile. "But," she says, chuckling, "you have to picture this. I am lying there on my back, fully exposed, with all these attachments to my body, and he's standing at the bottom of my bed. Although I was terribly uncomfortable with the fact that I was completely undressed and he was getting a good eye's worth, I was still trying to do what the technician had asked me to do." As they engaged in a bit of awkward conversation, Laurie inquired, "Are you a doctor here?" To her astonishment, the "doctor" answered, "*Oh, noooo.* I'm just visiting my mom down the hall and came in to say hello. Are you *really* Miss America?" Laurie violently yanked the sheet over her torso and gasped, "Wa wa wa . . . well, pleeease get out! Get out now!" At this point, she reports, the technician turned from the machine and chided the still-shell-shocked Miss America, "I can't *belieeeve* this!

We were three minutes away from being done and you couldn't follow my instructions. Now we have to do the whole thing over again." Laurie shrugs off the episode with self-deprecating humor. "Well, I can honestly say that he *truly* knows whether I should have won swimsuit or not! That was the most unbelievable situation I ever faced!"

From her wealth of experience surviving Miss America mishaps, Laurie understands that when titleholders are faced with the startling surprises their reigns inevitably dish out, they learn to "just keep on going. You get to a point where you just *defy fate* to throw something at you that you can't handle. You just *defy* it—and, somehow, you always come through to meet the challenge. It's an almost unbelievable energy that you utilize—which is probably the reason we age so badly that year! Because about ninety percent of the adrenaline that has been designated for a lifetime is used in that one year. You talk about crisis living! This is it," she declares, laughing, "but it certainly prepares you for anything you could possibly get involved with after that year."

Despite the reign's responsibilities and hectic pace, the endless seas of eager fans awaiting autographs, the cumbersome packing and unpacking, and embarrassing encounters with unlit runways and ogling hospital visitors, Miss Americas display an overwhelming sense of respect, even reverence, for the once-in-a-lifetime journey in Cinderella's glass slippers. "It's an absolutely humbling experience," Laurie explains, "to have literally hundreds of people looking at you with their eyes telling a story of their own hopes and dreams. It's a humbling experience and one that only someone who has looked into the faces of those people would understand." She continues, "There's a feeling that what you have attained for yourself—although only relatively short-lived, for a year—is a lifetime venture. It's a feeling of *destiny.*"

CHAPTER 18

A Farewell to Miss America

As swiftly as it began, the glorious year in the national spotlight approaches its conclusion. For 365 days, Miss America has lived a once-in-a-lifetime experience filled with non-stop travel, personal appearances, media interviews, visits with dignitaries and celebrities, and unparalleled opportunities to acquaint herself with the nation she has represented. Her reign has included moments of excitement, glamour, and public acclaim, but there have also been moments of self-doubt, frustration, and fatigue. "It's a busy year," says Vonda Kay Van Dyke. "I never thought of it as being anything but *wonderful,* but I remember being tired, and my smile not wanting to work. I was *ready* to move on to something else, but I loved it while it lasted." She adds with a laugh, "I think that it only lasts a year because that's just enough of something great." As the experience draws to an end, Miss America returns to the Atlantic City stage where her unforgettable reign began a year earlier.

Throughout Pageant week, the retiring queen is lauded by the Pageant "family" she has represented, and prominently featured in lavish production numbers. Her return to the Convention Hall spotlight is one of the most cherished moments of a titleholder's reign. "That week is something a Miss America looks forward to for months," explains Terry Meeuwsen. "It's her chance to say good-bye to all of the wonderful people she visited throughout the year, and her chance to end her year saying and doing something she feels is meaningful."

During the live broadcast, the retiring queen proudly takes her final walk down the runway that launched her on the most exciting year of her life. The farewell is always a poignant moment when Miss America acknowledges the audience's standing ovation and thanks the individuals who have made her reign so meaningful. In the parting words of Susan Akin, Miss America 1986:

Yes, tomorrow is yours.
Only in America can eighty thousand young women have the right not just to dream of becoming Miss America, but the right to pursue that dream.
For me it became a reality because of so many friends, family, and loved ones.

179

> Dreams should be more than dreams.
> They should and *can* be realities.

Like generations of Miss Americas, Marilyn Van Derbur describes the experience of concluding her reign in triumph as "one of the highlights of my life." As she looks back on that thrilling evening years ago when she strolled the Convention Hall runway for the final time as the reigning titleholder, she says, "I had so much pride walking down the runway. I knew I had done the best job that I could possibly do every single day. There are a few things—and *only* a few things—I've done in my life that I can say I could not possibly have done any better—and that was such a wonderful feeling to have." Marilyn recalls being aware of the appreciation the Pageant audience had for her efforts that year. "I knew the people in Atlantic City had respect and warmth for me. They follow their Miss Americas very closely in Convention Hall, and they really do know what kind of job you've done as Miss America. You are not a stranger in that auditorium of twenty-five thousand people. I felt the warmth, appreciation, and acceptance from the Pageant and from the people who were sitting there—and I felt it within myself."

The farewell walk is an especially emotional moment for the retiring Miss America's parents. Eleanor Schaefer reminisces about the night her daughter Laurie relinquished her crown. "I thought I'd never make it because I was just reduced to tears. I had a man-sized hanky right in front of me, and I was really mopping up. It was so emotional because I knew it was the culmination of a year of many challenges, the culmination of a year that probably was the most important year in her life."

When the moment finally arrives for Miss America to crown her successor, it is inevitably marked by a flurry of emotions: deep appreciation, relief and sadness, but happiness for the lucky winner. "It wasn't strange for me to see a new girl crowned because I knew going into this that it would only be for twelve months," remarks Marian McKnight Conway. "As I looked at Marilyn Van Derbur, whom I crowned, I knew that she was going to have the same experiences that I had and I was thrilled for her. It was really almost a relief to pass on the crown, although I sobbed. It was a very emotional experience because it's a major part of a young woman's life at that stage of the game."

While the first moments as a *former* Miss America are understandably emotional, there have been occasions when the unexpected has interjected a comical touch—like the year Terry Meeuwsen literally concluded her reign with a bang. "I remember Phyllis [George] had said to me, 'They'll take the crown away from you and push you out of the way and you'll be forgotten as quickly as you were crowned.'" It took one preoccupied cameraman to demonstrate Phyllis's point. "After I crowned Becky [King], I was applauding when this giant camera moved across the stage to get a shot of Becky from the rear as she walked down the runway. Well, the camera's huge cable *ran right over me!* It knocked me back about ten feet! It was a riot because I had a very tight dress on, and I had to really stumble around just to stay on my feet! Of course, the guy never saw me because he had one eye closed and the other one was looking in the camera. I had to laugh because she was right. There's some truth to it. It's easy come—easy go!"

While Terry's departure was undoubtedly more comical than most, the coronation of a new Miss America signals an abrupt conclusion to the retiring queen's year of public adoration. Cheryl Prewitt got a foretaste of that change during a television rehearsal when she inquired where she should stand after crowning her successor that evening. The producer nonchalantly shrugged, "Oh, you just leave the stage." Surprised, Cheryl persisted, "But the

Debbye Turner (1990) waves good-bye to the audience moments before crowning Marjorie Vincent. TERRY CHENAILLE

Pageant's not _over_ yet." He explained with a grin that as the retiring queen, she should accustom herself to no longer being the center of attention. Cheryl laughs at the recollection. "All of a sudden, man—life's over!—'_Off the stage!_'"

"You just get off the stage," concurs Dorothy Benham, "because it's no longer your limelight at that point. There is now a new Miss America." Dottie explains that while she was delighted to pass the crown on to Susan Perkins, and excited about the thrilling year her successor would soon experience, she was also keenly aware of the abrupt departure of the spotlight. "When that crown was taken off my head, and I crowned the new Miss America, people just _evacuated_ Convention Hall so quickly that I was left standing onstage alone, and I thought, 'Where did everybody _go?_'" As Dorothy and a traveling companion gathered her belongings and toted them out of the auditorium, they were spotted by a few lingering spectators in the stands. "This one little boy pointed to me and yelled, 'Hey! There goes the _old_ one!'" Dorothy enjoyed a hearty chuckle at her new moniker, but the incident illustrated the change that every Miss America must eventually face. "It's a wonderful year," she says, "but it ends as abruptly as it begins."

As each titleholder faces the conclusion of her reign, she hopes that the young woman who follows in her steps will uphold the values of the program and contribute to its image. "I don't know how this is going to sound," Kaye Lani Rafko offers hesitantly, "but I was very nervous about who would be taking over my position. I had worked so hard trying to represent the people across the country well and the three hundred thousand volunteers who are involved in the system. I tried so hard to do the best I could, and I wanted my successor to continue representing the system well. It's a big responsibility—something women dream about—and I didn't want her to take it lightly."

Kaye Lani had the opportunity to spend several days with her successor, Gretchen Carlson, shortly after the Pageant, and she informed her half jokingly, "Gretchen, the minute you feel this starts to be a burden to you, the minute you want to quit, don't worry, because if they can't find anyone else, _I'll_ take over the spot and go another year." Kaye Lani admits that getting better acquainted with her successor

Debbie Maffett (1983) waves at fans a final time as she leaves Convention Hall. A.M. *BIVANS*

relieved any lingering anxiety and she warmly offered Carlson her blessing. "I told her, 'I am so relieved, because you are representing us so well. I'm relieved that they've chosen someone like you to represent young women, to represent me, to represent your sorority of former Miss Americas, and to represent the people who competed with you." Rafko affirms with a smile, "She's just what I had hoped she would be. She's a wonderful lady, and I'm very, very proud to have her follow in my footsteps."

While the crown inevitably must be passed on to another, its glory never entirely fades. "With every day that goes by, there is *always* some reference to the Miss America title and my being a former Miss America," says Laurie Schaefer. "It was—and has remained — totally humbling to me, and every time I think about it, I feel so blessed and so unbelievably *grateful.* To this day, when I am asked to make a presentation to a group of people and I have to describe and relive those moments when Bert Parks made that announcement, I choke. Can you believe after seventeen years I still shed tears? But it just thrills my heart that out of all the young women across the nation who would love to step into those glass slippers, I was the one given the distinction that year!"

Laurie and Kaye Lani would undoubtedly appreciate the gracious sentiments another proud queen, Colleen Kay Hutchins, shared with the *Atlantic City Press* on the eve of her retirement. Today, her timeless advice for those who seek the coveted Miss America crown remains as appropriate as when she offered it four decades ago:

"Tell the girl who wins the title this year to remember that she only borrows the crown for a year. Tell her she doesn't create it, and tell her every Miss America who has gone before has added to it a jewel. Tell her she is taking on a great responsibility. A responsibility to herself, to her people, to the Miss America Pageant, the people of Atlantic City, her state and her nation. Tell her the country and the world will judge America by her."

Facing page: Rose Veronica Coyle, Miss America 1936. MISS AMERICA PAGEANT

PART V

CLOSING

CHAPTER 19

The Tradition Continues

America's "Queen of Femininity" has certainly blossomed since 1921, when the Pageant's original contestants frolicked along the shore in Atlantic City's bathing beauty contest. Since Miss America's humble birth that year, the public has watched her remarkable transformation from a flirtatious seaside "National Beauty Tournament," to a Hollywood-struck "Showmen's Variety Jubilee," to a golden-era television extravaganza, and finally to the status of the modern-day "Miss America Organization"—the world's largest private scholarship program for women and the *grande dame* of pageants.

Despite that occasionally turbulent history, the splendid tradition has proven itself remarkably resilient. "It's an American institution," remarks Phyllis George, "a tradition which has gone on for seventy years. The Pageant has survived wars, depressions, social movements, scandals, crisis, and tough critics—and it's *still* here. They must be doing something right, because fifty-five million people watch it, and it's one of the top-rated shows every single year!" She pauses reflectively. "It's

a part of Americana that will continue—because America loves it."

So do its participants, who laud the program for making significant contributions to their lives. "I've talked to so many women who have competed," says former Miss America Pamela Eldred, "and they have all said that they have never done anything which has influenced their lives as much as being a part of the Miss America program. It's a unique experience," she says enthusiastically, "and I hope that the Miss America Pageant goes on and on to provide young women with opportunities they might never, ever have in any other way."

As the Miss America Organization and its family of volunteers and contestants enter a new decade and approach the twenty-first century, they share a growing confidence that the Pageant's accomplishments and contributions will eventually receive recognition. "The Miss America Organization is a social organization," explains Gretchen Carlson, "and like any social change in our society—whether it's women becoming equal or minorities becoming equal—it takes a long time for those changes to come about." Still, she predicts, the day will come

185

Pamela Eldred, Miss America 1970.
MISS AMERICA PAGEANT

when "this program will gain the type of recognition in our society that it deserves."

Whether or not the Pageant has received the recognition its contributions to American women warrant, more young women than ever are lining up for the chance to compete in the Super Bowl of pageants. Indeed, the program's increasing popularity among young women bolsters the prophetic lyrics of Bernie Wayne's tribute to Miss America: "The dreams of a million girls,/Who are more than pretty/May come true in Atlantic City. . . ." Only today, the dream isn't simply to win a crown. It is to cultivate a successful future by utilizing the scholarships, friendships, professional contacts, and opportunities for personal development made available through the Miss America Pageant program.

THERE SHE IS—THEN AND NOW

1921, Margaret Gorman, Miss Washington, D.C.
Gorman was selected from fifteen hundred entrants to represent the *Washington Herald.* The daughter of an executive with the Department of Agriculture, Margaret starred in a U.S. government film. After her victory, she married real estate investor Victor Cahill.

*1922–23, Mary Katherine Campbell, Miss Columbus.**
Campbell, the only two-time Miss America, was offered movie contracts after her reign, but turned them down to care for her invalid mother. In 1933, she married Du Pont executive Frederick Townley.

*1924, Ruth Malcomson, Miss Philadelphia.**

* Deceased.

Ruth, the gal who ended Campbell's winning streak, married Carl Schaubel, a military tactics instructor and printing company president. Ruth's niece and grand-niece competed as Miss Pennsylvania 1956 and Miss Delaware 1981.

*1925, Fay Lanphier, Miss California.**
The first winner from the West Coast, Fay appeared in a Laurel and Hardy film and in *The American Venus,* before marrying engineer Winfield Daniels and raising their two daughters. She died of pneumonia in 1959.

*1926, Norma Smallwood, Miss Tulsa.**
Norma married George Bruce, a wealthy petroleum executive, after a scandalous divorce from oilman Thomas Gilcrease. She had two children, one of whom was named Des Cygnes l'Amour (of the swans of love).

*1927, Lois Delander, Miss Illinois.**
The last queen chosen before the pageant was discontinued, Lois won on her parents' anniversary. She later married Ralph Lang, a stockbroker, and raised three daughters.

1928–32, No pageants held.

1933, Marian Bergeron, Miss Connecticut.
A gifted singer, Marian signed with Columbia Broadcasting Company and appeared with Rudy Vallee and Guy Lombardo. She married executive Donald Ruhlman, with whom she had three children, Donald, Robert, and Donna. Widowed, she has remarried and now has eleven granddaughters.

1934, No pageant held.

1935, Henrietta Leaver, Miss Pittsburgh.
A salesclerk prior to her victory, Henrietta was nicknamed "the million-

dollar babe from the five-and-ten-cent store." She married John Thomason and had two daughters, Patricia and Frances.

1936, Rose Veronica Coyle, Miss Philadelphia.

Rose later appeared with celebrities including Abbott and Costello, married Leonard Schlessinger, a top Warner Brothers executive, and had a daughter, Diane. Widowed, she married Robert Dingler, an executive.

1937, Bette Cooper, Miss Bertrand Island (New Jersey).

Best known as the "missing" Miss America, Bette made only rare appearances during her reign, and dated her hero-chaperon for several years before marrying William Moore, an engineer. The couple has two children.

1938, Marilyn Meseke, Miss Ohio.

A dance instructor, Marilyn won her title the year talent became mandatory. She later married Major Stanley Hume, a commercial pilot, with whom she had one son. Widowed, she married Benjamin Rogers, also a pilot.

1939; Patricia Donnelly, Miss Michigan.

Pat, remembered for her bass fiddle rendition of *Ol' Man Mose,* later appeared on Broadway and in the movie *Cover Girl.* She married Robin Harris, a publicist, and had two children, Stephen and Amanda.

1940, Frances Marie Burke, Miss Philadelphia.

Frances became a prominent East Coast fashion model and married Lawrence Kenney, a funeral supply firm owner. The couple has four children, Missy, Larry, Bill, and Wendy.

1941, Rosemary LaPlanche, Miss California.*

After losing to Frances Burke in 1940, she reentered and won the 1941 crown. Later, Rosemary signed with RKO Pictures, appeared in eighty-four films, and married TV producer Harry Koplan, with whom she had two children. Rosemary also achieved nationwide recognition as an oil painter.

1942, Jo-Carroll Dennison, Miss Texas.

The first Texan winner, Jo-Carroll signed with 20th Century-Fox and married comedian Phil Silvers. After their divorce, she worked at CBS, where she met and married TV executive Russell Stoneham. Jo-Carroll has two sons, Peter and John.

1943, Jean Bartel, Miss California.

The first college girl to win the crown, Jean starred on Broadway, hosted a TV series, produced documentaries, and currently owns her own international travel consulting firm. She reportedly did U.S. intelligence work in Lebanon during the forties. She is married to Bill Hogue.

1944, Venus Ramey, Miss Washington, D.C.

A native of Kentucky, Venus worked as a secretary in Washington, D.C., prior to her victory. She later performed as a singing comedienne, ran unsuccessfully for the Kentucky legislature, and married a Kentucky automobile dealer, with whom she had two sons.

1945, Bess Myerson, Miss New York City.

The first winner from New York, the first Jewish Miss America, and the first scholarship recipient, Bess built an illustrious career in television and government service and ran unsuccessfully for the U.S. Senate before becoming embroiled and acquitted in the scandalous "Bess mess" trial.

1946, Marilyn Buferd, Miss California.
Marilyn studied at Berlitz in Rome, signed with MGM Studios, appeared in fifteen Italian motion pictures, and was romanced by Roberto Rossellini. Now widowed, she has one son, Nicky.

1947, Barbara Jo Walker, Miss Memphis (Tennessee).
Barbara Jo wed John Hummel, a Memphis obstetrician (who, ironically, delivered future Miss America Kellye Cash), during her reign. She later earned her bachelor's degree, hosted a daily television show, and raised three children. Today she is an active churchwoman.

1948, BeBe (Beatrice) Shopp, Miss Minnesota.
A graduate of Manhattan School of Music, BeBe performs with musical groups, and is a licensed lay minister, popular pageant judge, and drug prevention volunteer. She is also the proud mother of four daughters.

*1949, Jacque Mercer, Miss Arizona.**
Jacque married during her reign and divorced soon after. A descendant of Daniel Boone and President James Polk, Jacque graduated from Arizona State College, married Richard Curran, an all-American football player and advertising executive, and had two children, Richard and Shannon.

1950, Miss America title postdated.

1951, Yolande Betbeze, Miss Alabama.
Yolande's refusal to pose in swimsuits prompted sponsor Catalina to pull out and start the Miss Universe Pageant to promote its swimwear. The widow of movie tycoon Matthew

Fox, she has one daughter, Yolande, and has produced musicals for the theater.

1952, Colleen Kay Hutchins, Miss Utah.
Until recently the tallest and oldest winner, Colleen won her crown with a portrayal of Elizabeth I. She married former New York Knick and prominent pediatrician Ernest Vandeweghe. Their son Kiki also played in the NBA.

1953, Neva Jane Langley, Miss Georgia.
A graduate of Wesleyan Conservatory, Neva was also awarded an honorary doctorate in fine arts. Neva is an editor with *Southern Accents* magazine, a governor's appointee to the Georgia Council of the Arts, and a recipient of the "Lady Bird Johnson Award." She and her husband, William Fickling, a real estate investor, have four children.

1954, Evelyn Margaret Ay, Miss Pennsylvania.
The last pre-TV queen, Evelyn later married Navy lieutenant Carl Sempier and had two daughters, Carlyn and Stacy. Today, she serves on corporate boards, raises funds for hospitals, and is a popular lecturer.

1955, Lee Ann Meriwether, Miss California.
Lee, the first winner crowned on live television, studied with Lee Strasberg, appeared in fourteen films, twenty-one stage productions, and twenty-eight TV programs, including *Barnaby Jones* and *The Munsters Today.* An Emmy and Globe Award nominee, Lee was awarded a 1980 Genii Award. She is married to Marshall Borden and has two daughters, Kyle and Lesley.

1956, Sharon Kay Ritchie, Miss Colorado.

The first winner to be crowned to the tune *There She Is,* Sharon later married golfer Don Cherry. Today, she is the wife of Robert Fomon, chairman of E. F. Hutton, serves as a trustee of the Boy Scouts of America, and has two sons, Shaun and Steven.

1957, Marian Ann McKnight, Miss South Carolina.
Marian, a one-time "Clairol Girl," is married to actor Gary Conway and has two children, Kathleen and Gareth. She enjoys public speaking and charity work, and owns a dinner theater in California. A devoted marathon runner, Marian carried the Olympic torch in 1984.

1958, Marilyn Elaine Van Derbur, Miss Colorado.
Marilyn graduated Phi Beta Kappa, developed the Marilyn Van Derbur Motivational Institute, and has produced award-winning film series. She is married to attorney Larry Atler, has one daughter, Jennifer, and is the only woman to receive the Speakers Hall of Fame Award.

1959, Mary Ann Mobley, Miss Mississippi.
After training under Lee Strasberg, Mary Ann appeared in theater, television, and movies, including two films with Elvis Presley. Most recently, she has appeared on *Different Strokes* and *Falcon Crest,* and filmed documentaries in Cambodia and Africa. Mary Ann and husband Gary Collins have one child, Mary Clancy.

1960, Lynda Lee Mead, Miss Mississippi.
One of Mississippi's famous back-to-back Miss Americas, Lynda now resides in Memphis, where she serves as director of the city's Development Foundation. Lynda is married to a surgeon, John Shea. She has three

children, Peter, Susanna, and Paul.

1961, Nancy Ann Fleming, Miss Michigan.
The last high school student to win the crown, Nancy went on to work in broadcasting with shows such as *A Whole New You* and *A.M. San Francisco.* She is married to TV's Jim Lange and has two children, Ingrid and Steig, from a previous marriage.

1962, Maria Beale Fletcher, Miss North Carolina.
A Radio City Music Hall Rockette, Maria danced her way to the Miss America title. Now a songwriter, she recently recorded a gospel album with husband Dr. James Growden. The couple has two children, Robyn and Jim.

1963, Jacquelyn Jeanne Mayer, Miss Ohio.
Jackie is widely respected for her inspiring recovery from a massive stroke at age twenty-eight. She is a spokesperson for the American Heart Association and National Stroke Association, which awarded her its "Hope and Courage Award." She and husband John are proud parents of children Bill and Kelly, and raise Standardbred horses.

1964, Donna Axum, Miss Arkansas.
A "Distinguished Alumnus of the University of Arkansas," Donna holds a master's degree and has taught on the university level. She has also produced and hosted television programs, and is a professional speaker and author. Remarried to Bryan Whitworth, Donna has two children, Lisa and Gus Mutscher.

1965, Vonda Kay Van Dyke, Miss Arizona.
The only Miss America to win the Miss Congeniality award, Vonda is a well-known Christian speaker, singer, and ventriloquist. She has re-

corded four albums and written five books. Vonda is the wife of David Scoates, a minister, and has one daughter, Vandy.

1966, Deborah Irene Bryant, Miss Kansas.
The queen who dreamed of becoming a pediatrician has a similar practice today—mother of five handsome children: Kristen, Brock, Bryant, Brigitte, and Brent. Debbie, whose husband, Brent Berge, is a Phoenix auto dealer, once served as anchor of Miss America broadcasts.

1967, Jane Anne Jayroe, Miss Oklahoma.
Jane earned a master's degree from Tulsa University and is working on a Ph.D. A co-anchor for *5 Alive News* in Oklahoma, she was named "Outstanding News Personality." Jane and husband Wayne Robinson have three children, Tyler, Brett, and Laura.

1968, Debra Dene Barnes, Miss Kansas.
A gifted piano pedagogy major, Debra won her title with a piano rendition of *Born Free*. Now married to her college sweetheart, Mitchell Miles, she has two daughters, Kristi and Karla, and enjoys performing for Christian ministries.

1969, Judith Anne Ford, Miss Illinois.
A champion trampolinist, Judi earned her degree in physical education and was appointed to the President's Council on Physical Fitness. The mother of sons Brad and Bryan, she now works as a product spokesperson and part-time PE teacher.

1970, Pamela Anne Eldred, Miss Michigan.
Pamela, the only ballerina to win the Miss America title, now writes two newspaper columns, operates a cosmetics business, The Paint Shop, in West Bloomfield, Michigan, and is the proud mother of one child, Hilary.

1971, Phyllis George, Miss Texas.
Phyllis became the pioneer female sportscaster on CBS's *NFL Today,* a co-anchor of CBS *Morning News,* and frequent co-host of the Miss America Pageant. She and husband John Y. Brown, former governor of Kentucky, have two children, Lincoln and Pamela. Phyllis developed a gourmet chicken firm, Chicken by George.

1972, Laurel Lea Schaefer, Miss Ohio.
Laurel has worked extensively in theater and television, including roles on *Three's Company, Rockford Files, Falcon Crest,* and *Quantum Leap.* She also works in directing and casting and owns a consulting firm, Schaefer Associates.

1973, Terry Anne Meeuwsen, Miss Wisconsin.
Terry, who has recorded an album, written her autobiography, produced documentaries, and hosted several television talk shows, frequently guest-hosts *The 700 Club.* She and husband Andy Friedrich have four children, Drew, Tory, J. P., and Tyler.

1974, Rebecca Ann King, Miss Colorado.
Rebecca King, the first Miss America to earn a law degree, currently has a legal practice in Denver and is a corporate spokesperson and career development consultant. Becky and husband George Dreman, a banker, have two daughters, Emily and Diana.

1975, Shirley Cothran, Miss Texas.
Shirley, who holds a doctoral degree in educational guidance, is a motivational speaker, serves on her school board, and writes for Christian publications. She and husband Richard Barret are parents of four children: David, Julia, John, and Martin.

1976, Tawny Elaine Godin, Miss New York.

Tawny, who uses the professional name Tawny Little, is a news anchor for KABC-TV *Eyewitness News* and co-host of *AM Los Angeles.* She has also hosted *The Love Report* and written and produced award-winning news documentaries. Tawny and her husband, Tom Corsini, have two sons, "J.J." and Christian.

1977, Dorothy Kathleen Benham, Miss Minnesota.

A gifted classical singer, Dorothy has performed in *Jerome Robbins' Broadway,* on television, and with several opera companies. Dorothy and her children, Adam, Russell, Ben, and Mia, live in Connecticut.

1978, Susan Yvonne Perkins, Miss Ohio.

Susan has served as a spokesperson for Du Pont swimwear, and as a television guest host and reporter. She and husband Alan Botsford own a chain of retail stores called Ingear and have two children.

1979, Kylene Barker, Miss Virginia.

Kylene, who owns exclusive d. Kylene boutiques in Palm Beach and Boca Raton, Florida, has written a beauty book, recorded an exercise album, and served as a fashion consultant for the *Today* show. She is married to businessman James Brandon.

1980, Cheryl Prewitt, Miss Mississippi.

Remembered for her inspirational story of divine healing, Cheryl has since recorded seven albums, written six books, and produced three exercise videos. She also owns a pageant attire firm, and performs regularly on Christian television. Cheryl and husband Harry Salem, a TV producer, have two sons, "Lil' Harry" and Roman.

1981, Susan Powell, Miss Oklahoma.

Susan has pursued an opera career, performing with such major companies as the New York City Opera and the Seattle Opera in productions of *Die Fledermaus, Pirates of Penzance,* and *Guys and Dolls.* She resides in New York with husband David Parsons.

1982, Elizabeth Ward, Miss Arkansas.

Elizabeth has gone on to enjoy success as an entertainer, actress, and model. She has been a featured performer for Miss America telecasts, appeared in the Vista film *Pass the Ammo,* and is currently concentrating on developing a film career.

1983, Debra Sue Maffett, Miss California.

Debbie has recorded an album, co-hosted *World of Guinness Records* and *P.M. Magazine,* co-starred in the film *Pass the Ammo,* and worked with the President's Council on Physical Fitness and Sports. She is spokesperson for LIFE, an organization that feeds twenty thousand people weekly.

1984, Vanessa Williams, Miss New York.

The first black woman to win the Miss America crown, Vanessa Williams has since appeared in several television programs, a TV movie, and three feature films. Her debut album, *The Right Stuff,* earned Vanessa two Grammy nominations. Vanessa and husband-publicist Ramon Hervey have two daughters, Melanie and Jillian.

1984, Suzette Charles, Miss New Jersey.

Following her brief reign, Suzette Charles pursued a career in entertainment. She has appeared on *Lov-*

ing, recorded an album, headlined at major casinos, and performed with Sammy Davis, Jr., Liza Minnelli, Bill Cosby, and Stevie Wonder.

1985, Sharlene Wells, Miss Utah.

Sharlene Wells, who graduated summa cum laude from Brigham Young University in 1987, now works as a sportscaster for ESPN, where she covers major sporting events. Sharlene and her husband, Robert Hawkes, reside in Boston.

1986, Susan Diane Akin, Miss Mississippi.

Susan is the national spokesperson for the Down's Syndrome Association and lobbies state lawmakers for mandatory seat-belt laws. She is also pursuing an entertainment career and frequently tours with Bob Hope.

1987, Kellye Cash, Miss Tennessee.

Kellye, grand-niece of country singer Johnny Cash, attends San Diego State University and is married to Todd Sheppard, a math teacher and athletic coach. She served as a spokesperson for the Governor's Alliance for a Drug-Free Tennessee and now tours the nation as a gospel singer.

1988, Kaye Lani Rae Rafko, Miss Michigan.

Kaye Lani Rae Rafko Wilson is the national spokesperson for nursing and hospice and travels worldwide promoting the nursing profession and medical research. She plans to earn a master's degree in oncology-hematology and to open a hospice.

1989, Gretchen Elizabeth Carlson, Miss Minnesota.

Gretchen received her degree in organizational behavior from Stanford University and is developing a career in corporate public relations and television. She hopes to attend law school eventually, possibly at Harvard.

1990, Debbye Lynn Turner, Miss Missouri.

Debbye Turner, the Pageant's third black winner, will receive her doctorate in veterinary medicine in 1991 and plans to specialize in small-animal internal medicine. She continues her motivational work with youth groups and Christian youth ministries.

1991, Marjorie Judith Vincent, Miss Illinois.

A third-year law student at Duke University, Marjorie plans to complete her legal education and pursue a career in international law. The daughter of Haitian-born parents, she is a first-generation American and the Pageant's fourth black Miss America.

Photos on pages 193–212 courtesy of the Miss America Pageant (Kathleen Frank, John Reilly, Joe Profetto, Sid Schrier, Hess Photos, Central Studios, Earle Hawkins).

1921, Margaret Gorman.

1922–23, Mary Katherine Campbell.

1924, Ruth Malcomson.

1925, Fay Lanphier.

1927, Lois Delander.

1926, Norma Smallwood.

1933, Marian Bergeron.

1935

1935, Henrietta Leaver.

1936, Rose Veronica Coyle.

1937, Bette Cooper.

1938, Marilyn Meseke.

1939, Patricia Mary Donnelly.

1940, Frances Marie Burke.

1941, Rosemary LaPlanche.

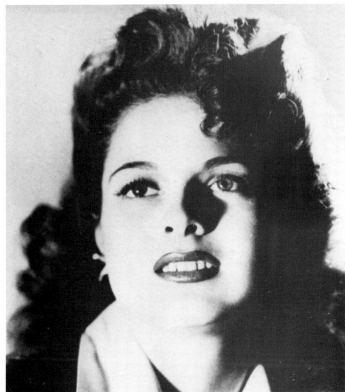

1942, Jo-Carroll Dennison.

1943, Jean Bartel.

1944, Venus Ramey.

1945, Bess Myerson.

1946, Marilyn Buferd.

1947, Barbara Jo Walker.

1948, Beatrice (BeBe) Shopp.

1949, Jacque Mercer.

1951, Yolande Betbeze.

1952, Colleen Kay Hutchins.

1953, Neva Jane Langley.

1954, Evelyn Margaret Ay.

1955, Lee Ann Meriwether.

1956, Sharon Kay Ritchie.

1957, Marian Ann McKnight.

1958, Marilyn Elaine Van Derbur.

1959, Mary Ann Mobley.

1960, Lynda Lee Mead.

1961, Nancy Anne Fleming.

1962, Maria Beale Fletcher.

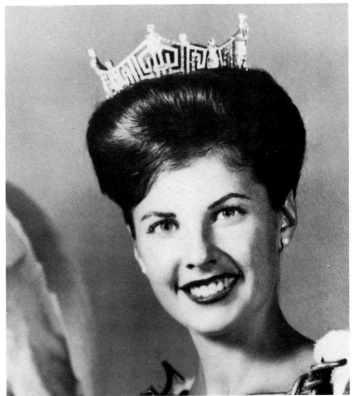

1963, Jacquelyn Jeanne Mayer.

1964, Donna Axum.

1966, Deborah Irene Bryant.

1965, Vonda Kay Van Dyke.

1967, Jane Anne Jayroe.

1968, Debra Dene Barnes.

1969, Judith Anne Ford.

1971, Phyllis George.

1970, Pamela Anne Eldred.

1972, *Laurel Lea Schaefer.*

1974, *Rebecca Ann King.*

1973, *Terry Anne Meeuwsen.*

1975, Shirley Cothran.

1976, Tawny Elaine Godin.

1977, Dorothy Kathleen Benham.

1978, Susan Yvonne Perkins.

1979, Kylene Barker.

1981, Susan Powell.

1980, Cheryl Prewitt.

1982, Elizabeth Ward.

1983, Debra Sue Maffett.

1984, Vanessa Williams.

1984, Suzette Charles.

1985, Sharlene Wells.

1986, Susan Diane Akin.

1987, Kellye Cash.

1988, Kaye Lani Rae Rafko.

1989, Gretchen Elizabeth Carlson.

1990, Debbye Lynn Turner.

1991, Marjorie Judith Vincent.

APPENDIXES

Miss Americas

1921 Margaret Gorman, Washington, D.C.
1922 Mary Katherine Campbell, Columbus, Ohio
1923 Mary Katherine Campbell, Columbus, Ohio
1924 Ruth Malcomson, Philadelphia, Pennsylvania
1925 Fay Lanphier, Oakland, California
1926 Norma Smallwood, Tulsa, Oklahoma
1927 Lois Delander, Joliet, Illinois
1933 Marian Bergeron, West Haven, Connecticut
1935 Henrietta Leaver, Pittsburgh, Pennsylvania
1936 Rose Veronica Coyle, Philadelphia, Pennsylvania
1937 Bette Cooper, Bertrand Island, New Jersey
1938 Marilyn Meseke, Marion, Ohio
1939 Patricia Mary Donnelly, Detroit, Michigan
1940 Frances Marie Burke, Philadelphia, Pennsylvania
1941 Rosemary LaPlanche, Los Angeles, California
1942 Jo-Carroll Dennison, Tyler, Texas
1943 Jean Bartel, Los Angeles, California
1944 Venus Ramey, Washington, D.C.
1945 Bess Myerson, New York City
1946 Marilyn Buferd, Los Angeles, California
1947 Barbara Jo Walker, Memphis, Tennessee
1948 Beatrice (BeBe) Shopp, Hopkins, Minnesota
1949 Jacque Mercer, Litchfield, Arizona
(Postdated hereafter)
1951 Yolande Betbeze, Mobile, Alabama
1952 Colleen Kay Hutchins, Salt Lake City, Utah
1953 Neva Jane Langley, Macon, Georgia
1954 Evelyn Margaret Ay, Ephrata, Pennsylvania
1955 Lee Ann Meriwether, San Francisco, California

1956 Sharon Kay Ritchie, Denver, Colorado
1957 Marian Ann McKnight, Manning, South Carolina
1958 Marilyn Elaine Van Derbur, Denver, Colorado
1959 Mary Ann Mobley, Brandon, Mississippi
1960 Lynda Lee Mead, Natchez, Mississippi
1961 Nancy Anne Fleming, Montague, Michigan
1962 Maria Beale Fletcher, Asheville, North Carolina
1963 Jacquelyn Jeanne Mayer, Sandusky, Ohio
1964 Donna Axum, El Dorado, Arkansas
1965 Vonda Kay Van Dyke, Phoenix, Arizona
1966 Deborah Irene Bryant, Overland Park, Kansas
1967 Jane Anne Jayroe, Laverne, Oklahoma
1968 Debra Dene Barnes, Pittsburg, Kansas
1969 Judith Anne Ford, Belvidere, Illinois
1970 Pamela Anne Eldred, West Bloomfield, Michigan
1971 Phyllis George, Denton, Texas
1972 Laurel Lea Schaefer, Bexley, Ohio
1973 Terry Anne Meeuwsen, DePere, Wisconsin
1974 Rebecca Ann King, Denver, Colorado
1975 Shirley Cothran, Denton, Texas
1976 Tawny Elaine Godin, Saratoga Springs, New York
1977 Dorothy Kathleen Benham, Edina, Minnesota
1978 Susan Yvonne Perkins, Columbus, Ohio
1979 Kylene Barker, Roanoke, Virginia
1980 Cheryl Prewitt, Ackerman, Mississippi
1981 Susan Powell, Elk City, Oklahoma

1982 Elizabeth Ward, Russellville, Arkansas
1983 Debra Sue Maffett, Anaheim, California
1984 Vanessa Williams, Millwood, New York
1984 Suzette Charles, Mays Landing, New Jersey
1985 Sharlene Wells, Salt Lake City, Utah
1986 Susan Diane Akin, Meridian, Mississippi

1987 Kellye Cash, Memphis, Tennessee
1988 Kaye Lani Rae Rafko, Monroe, Michigan
1989 Gretchen Elizabeth Carlson, Anoka, Minnesota
1990 Debbye Lynn Turner, Columbia, Missouri
1991 Marjorie Judith Vincent, Oak Park, Illinois

Miss Americas and
Their Courts of Honor

1921 Washington, D.C., Margaret Gorman
  (1) Camden, New Jersey, Kathryn Gerron
    (amateur winner)
  (1) New York, New York, Virginia Lee (professional winner)

1922 Columbus, Ohio, Mary Katherine Campbell
(inter-city winner)
  (F) Washington, D.C., Margaret Gorman
    (Miss America 1921)
  (F) New York, Dorothy Knapp (professional winner)
  (F) West Philadelphia, Gladys Greenamyer
    (amateur winner)

1923 Columbus, Ohio, Mary Katherine Campbell
  (1) Brooklyn, New York, Ethelda Kenvin
  (F) Coney Island, New York, Heather Walker
  (F) Philadelphia, Pennsylvania, Marian Green
  (F) St. Louis, Missouri, Charlotte Nash

Note: Results prior to 1936 incomplete.
* Discontinued award.
(BR) Bathers' Revue Award*
(MP) Most Popular*
(F)   Finalist
(EG) Best Evening Gown Award*
(T)   Preliminary Talent Winner
(BM) Best Model*
(S)   Preliminary Swimsuit Winner
(MC) Miss Congeniality*
(QL) Quality of Life Award

1924 Philadelphia, Pennsylvania, Ruth Malcomson
(BR)(MP)
  (1) Columbus, Ohio, Mary Katherine Campbell (Miss America 1923) (MP)
  (F) Santa Cruz, California, Fay Lanphier
  (F) Chicago, Illinois, Margaret Leigh
  (F) Manhattan, New York, Beatrice Roberts
    (EG)(MP)
  (F) Los Angeles, Lillian Knight

1925 California, Fay Lanphier
  (1) Los Angeles, California, Adrienne Dore

1926 Tulsa, Oklahoma, Norma Smallwood (EG)
  (1) Washington, Marjorie Joosting

1927 Illinois, Lois Eleanor Delander
  (1) Dallas, Texas, Mozelle Ransome
  (F) Philadelphia, Pennsylvania, Kathleen Coyle
  (F) Tulsa, Oklahoma, Virginia Howard
  (F) Hammond, Indiana, Anne Howe

1933 Connecticut, Marian Bergeron
  (1) California, Blanche McDonald
  (2) New York State, Florence Meyers (EG)
  (3) Virginia, Evangeline Glidwell

1935 Pittsburgh, Pennsylvania, Henrietta Leaver
  (1) Missouri, Edna Smith
  (2) Kentucky, Jeane M. Megerle

216

1936 Philadelphia, Pennsylvania, Rose Veronica Coyle (T)
    (1) California, Phyllis Dobson (T)
    (2) Connecticut, Tillie Gray
    (3) Cook County, Illinois, Arlene Causey (BM)
    (4) Birmingham, Alabama, Gloria Levings (T)

1937 Bertrand Island, New Jersey, Bette Cooper (EG)
    (1) Texas, Alice Emerick
    (2) North Carolina, Ruth McLean Covington
    (3) California, Phyllis Randall (T) (tie)
    (3) Miami, Florida, Irmigard Dietel (tie)

1938 Ohio, Marilyn Meseke (BM)
    (1) California, Claire James (EG)
    (2) Utah, Muriel La Von Goodspeed (T)
    (3) Asbury Park, New Jersey, Ruth Brady (T)
    (4) Jacksonville, Florida, Gloria Smyley (T)

1939 Michigan, Patricia Donnelly
    (1) Oklahoma, Bettye Cornelia Averyt
    (2) Washington (state), Annamae Schoonover
    (3) California, Marguerita Louise Shris (T)
    (4) Virginia, Rosa Marie Elliot

1940 Philadelphia, Pennsylvania, Frances Burke (S)
    (1) California, Rosemary LaPlanche (S)
    (2) Michigan, Monnie Drake (T)
    (3) Massachusetts, Polly Connors
    (4) Kentucky, Dorothy Slatten (S)

1941 California, Rosemary LaPlanche (S)
    (1) Western Pennsylvania, Roselle Marie Hannon (T)
    (2) Washington, D.C., Jean Fidelis Cavanaugh
    (3) Westchester County, New York, Lillian Helen O'Donnell (S)
    (4) North Carolina, Joey Augusta Paxton (S)(T)

1942 Texas, Jo-Carroll Dennison (S)(T)
    (1) Chicago, Illinois, Bette Brunck (S)
    (2) Michigan, Patricia Uline Hill
    (3) New Jersey, Madeline Layton
    (4) California, Lucille Lambert

1943 California, Jean Bartel (S)(T)
    (1) Florida, Muriel Elizabeth Smith
    (2) Boston, Massachusetts, Helena Frances Mack (S)(T)
    (3) New York City, Milena Mae Miller
    (4) District of Columbia, Dixie Lou Rafter (S)

1944 District of Columbia, Venus Ramey (S)(T)
    (1) Boston, Massachusetts, Paulina McKevitt
    (2) Florida, Virginia Warlen (S)(T)
    (3) Chicago, Illinois, Elaine Steinbach
    (4) Birmingham, Alabama, Betty Jane Rase (S)(T)

1945 New York City, Bess Myerson (S)(T)
    (1) San Diego, Phyllis Mathis
    (2) Birmingham, Alabama, Frances Dorn (T)
    (3) Florida, Virginia Freeland
    (4) Minnesota, Arlene Anderson (T)

1946 California, Marilyn Buferd (S)
    (1) Arkansas, Rebecca Jane McCall
    (2) Atlanta, Georgia, Janey Miller (S)(T)
    (3) Louisiana, Marguerite McClelland (T)
    (4) Utah, Amelia Carol Ohmart

1947 Memphis, Tennessee, Barbara Jo Walker (T)
    (1) Minnesota, Elaine Mary Campbell (T)
    (2) Canada, Margaret Marshall (S)
    (3) Alabama, Peggy Jane Elder
    (4) California, Laura Jean Emery

1948 Minnesota, Beatrice (BeBe) Shopp (S)
    (1) Wyoming, Carol Held
    (2) Alabama, Martha Ann Ingram
    (3) Kansas, Vera Ralston (S)
    (4) Oklahoma, Donna Jane Briggs

1949 Arizona, Jacque Mercer (S)(T)
    (1) Mississippi, Katherine Wright
    (2) Illinois, Trudy Germi (S)
    (3) Colorado, Sylvia Canaday (S)
    (4) California, Jone Ann Pedersen (S)

1950–51 Alabama, Yolande Betbeze (S)
    (1) South Dakota, Irene O'Connor (T)
    (2) Florida, Janet Ruth Crockett
    (3) Arkansas, Mary Jennings (S)
    (4) Oklahoma, Louise O'Brien

1952 Utah, Colleen Kay Hutchins (T)
 (1) Indiana, Carol Mitchell
 (2) North Carolina, Lu Long Osborn (S)(T)
 (3) Arkansas, Charlotte Rosalie Simmen (S)
 (4) Florida, Mary Elizabeth Godwin

1953 Georgia, Neva Jane Langley (S)(T)
 (1) Indiana, Ann Marie Garnier
 (2) California, Jeanne Shores (S)(tie)
 (2) Alabama, Gwen Harmon (S)(tie)
 (3) Chicago, Illinois, Jo Hoppe (S)

1954 Pennsylvania, Evelyn Margaret
Ay (S)
 (1) New York City, Joan Cecilia Kaible
 (2) Virginia, Anne Lee Ceglis (T)
 (3) Alabama, Virginia McDavid
 (4) Mississippi, Susanne Dugger

1955 California, Lee Ann Meriwether (S)
 (1) Florida, Ann Gloria Daniel (S)
 (2) South Carolina, Polly Rankin Suber (S)
 (3) Pennsylvania, Barbara Sue Nager
 (4) Michigan, Janice Hutton Somers (T)

1956 Colorado, Sharon Kay Ritchie
 (1) Oregon, Dorothy Mae Johnson
 (2) Chicago, Illinois, Florence Gallagher
 (3) North Carolina, Clara Faye Arnold (S)
 (4) Oklahoma, Ann Campbell (S)

1957 South Carolina, Marian Ann McKnight
 (1) District of Columbia, Margo Zita Sandra
   Lucey
 (2) Alabama, Anne Stuart Ariail (T)
 (3) Arizona, Barbara Patricia Hilgenberg
   (tie)
 (3) Kansas, Mary Ann McGrew (tie)

1958 Colorado, Marilyn Elaine Van Derbur
 (1) Georgia, Jody Elizabeth Shattuck (S)
 (2) Oklahoma, Mary Nancy Denner
 (3) California, Lorna Anderson
 (4) Florida, Dorothy Maria Steiner

1959 Mississippi, Mary Ann Mobley (T)
 (1) Iowa, Joanne Lucille MacDonald
 (2) Oklahoma, Anita Bryant (T)
 (3) California, Sandra Lee Jennings (S)
 (4) North Carolina, Betty Lane Evans (S)

1960 Mississippi, Lynda Lee Mead
 (1) Wisconsin, Mary Alice Fox (S)
 (2) Washington (state), Sharon Joyce Vaugh
   (S)
 (3) California, Susan Diane Bronson
 (4) Arizona, Patricia Anne Allebrand

1961 Michigan, Nancy Ann Fleming (S)(T)
 (1) California, Suzanne Marie Reamo
 (2) North Carolina, Ann Farrington Herring
 (3) District of Columbia, Ruth
   Rea (S)
 (4) Indiana, Tommye Lou
   Glaze (T)

1962 North Carolina, Maria Beale
Fletcher (S)
 (1) Arkansas, Frances Jane Anderson (S)
 (2) Utah, Carolyn DeAnn Lasater (T)
 (3) Texas, Linda Jacklyn Loftis (T)
 (4) Minnesota, Nancee Ann Parkinson (S)

1963 Ohio, Jacquelyn Jeanne Mayer
 (1) Wisconsin, Joan Mary Engh (S)
 (2) Texas, Penny Lee Rudd
 (3) South Carolina, Evelyn Keith Ellis
 (4) Hawaii, Patricia Lei Anderson (T)

1964 Arkansas, Donna Axum (S)
 (1) District of Columbia, Rosanne Tueller
   (S)(T)
 (2) Hawaii, Susan Dee Pickering
 (3) Tennessee, Martha Ellen Truett
 (4) Arizona, Susan Jean Bergstrom

1965 Arizona, Vonda Kay Van Dyke (MC)
 (1) Arkansas, Karen Elizabeth Carlson
 (2) West Virginia, Ella Dee Kessel (S)
 (3) Texas, Sharon McCauley
 (4) Minnesota, Barbara Phyllis Hasselberg
   (T)

1966 Kansas, Deborah Irene Bryant (S)
 (1) Mississippi, Patricia Alice Puckett (S)
 (2) Indiana, Eileen Mary Smith (T)
 (3) Florida, Carol Lynn Blum
 (4) Wisconsin, Sharon Mae Singstock

1967 Oklahoma, Jane Anne Jayroe (T)
 (1) California, Charlene Diane Dallas (S)(T)

(2) Tennessee, Vicki Lynn Hurd
(3) Ohio, Sharon Elaine
Phillian (T)
(4) New Hampshire, Nancy Anne Naylor (S)

1968 Kansas, Debra Dene Barnes (S)
(1) Mississippi, Joan Stephanie Myers
(2) Wisconsin, Barbara Burk Baugh
(3) Rhode Island, Marilyn Gail Cocozza (T)
(4) Florida, Dawn Lauree Cashwell (T)

1969 Illinois, Judith Anne Ford (S)(T)
(1) Massachusetts, Catherine Monroe
(2) Iowa, Susan Alane Thompson (S)
(3) Oregon, Marjean Kay Langley
(4) Indiana, Katherine Virginia Field

1970 Michigan, Pamela Ann Eldred (S)
(1) Ohio, Kathy Lynn Baumann (S)(T)
(2) California, Susan Anton (tie)
(2) New Jersey, Cheryl Carter (tie)
(3) Minnesota, Judy Mendenhall (T)

1971 Texas, Phyllis George (S)
(1) South Carolina, Claudia Turner (S)
(2) Maine, Karen Johnson
(3) Mississippi, Chris McClamrock
(4) Pennsylvania, Maggie Walker

1972 Ohio, Laurel Lea Schaefer (S)
(1) Idaho, Karen Herd
(2) Massachusetts, Deborah O'Brien
(3) Pennsylvania, Maureen Victoria Wimmer
(T)
(4) Maine, Allyn Warner (T)

1973 Wisconsin, Terry Anne Meeuwsen (S)(T)
(1) North Carolina, Constance Anne Dorn
(2) Pennsylvania, Linda Kay Olsen
(3) Texas, Mae Beth Cormany
(4) Indiana, Rebecca Sue Graham (S)

1974 Colorado, Rebecca Ann King
(1) Wisconsin, Judy Hieke (S)
(2) New Jersey, Suzanne Plummer (S)
(3) Louisiana, Debbie Ward (T)
(4) Pennsylvania, Tina Thomas (T)

1975 Texas, Shirley Cothran (S)
(1) California, Lucianne Buchanan (S)

(2) Illinois, Jean Ahern (T)
(3) Kentucky, Darlene Compton (T)
(4) Louisiana, Libby Lovejoy

1976 New York, Tawny Elaine Godin
(1) North Carolina, Susan Lawrence
(2) California, Janet Jay Carr (S)
(3) Ohio, Susan Kay Banks (T)
(4) Arizona, Stacey Peterson

1977 Minnesota, Dorothy Benham (S)(T)
(1) South Carolina, Lavinia Merle Cox (S)
(2) Texas, Carmen McCollum (S)(T)
(3) California, Linda Michelle Mouron
(4) New York, Sonja Beverly Anderson
(T)

1978 Ohio, Susan Yvonne Perkins (T)
(1) Indiana, Barbara Mougin
(2) South Carolina, Catherine Amelia Hinson (S)
(3) New Jersey, Mary D'Arcy
(3) Florida, Cathy LaBelle (T)

1979 Virginia, Kylene Barker
(1) Alabama, Teresa Cheatham (S)(T)
(2) Florida, Carolyn Cline (T)
(3) Ohio, Sher Lynette Patrick
(4) Washington, Laurie Nelson

1980 Mississippi, Cheryl Prewitt (S)
(1) Ohio, Tana Kay Carli (T)
(2) Kansas, Michelle Elaine Whitson
(3) Missouri, Susan Wilson
(4) Florida, Marti Phillips

1981 Oklahoma, Susan Powell (T)
(1) Alabama, Paige Phillips (T)
(2) Mississippi, Donna Pope (S) (tie)
(2) New Jersey, Therese Hanley (tie)
(3) Arkansas, Lencola Sullivan (S)

1982 Arkansas, Elizabeth Ward (S)
(1) Illinois, Sandra Truitt (T)
(2) Georgia, Kristi Anne Evans
(3) Indiana, Pamela Carlberg
(4) Texas, Sheri Ryman (T)

1983 California, Debra Sue Maffett (S)(T)
(1) Tennessee, Desiree Denise Daniels (S)

(2) Mississippi, Dianne Evans (T)
(3) Oklahoma, Nancy Chapman
(4) Alabama, Yolanda Teresa Fernandez

1984 New York, Vanessa Williams (S)(T)
1984 New Jersey, Suzette Charles (T)
(2) Alabama, Pam Battles
(3) Mississippi, Wanda Gayle Geddie (S)
(4) Ohio, Pamela Helean Rigas (S)

1985 Utah, Sharlene Wells (S)
(1) Ohio, Melissa Bradley
(2) Mississippi, Kathy Manning (S)
(3) Minnesota, Lauren Susan Green (T)
(4) Texas, Tamara Hext (S)

1986 Mississippi, Susan Diane Akin (S)
(1) South Carolina, Sherry Thrift
(2) Texas, Jonna Fitzgerald (T)
(3) Washington, Honey Castro
(4) Alabama, Angela Tower (S)

1987 Tennessee, Kellye Cash (S)(T)
(1) Virginia, Julianne Smith (S)
(2) South Carolina, Dawn Elizabeth Smith
(S)

(3) Michigan, Kelly Garver (T)
(4) Missouri, Tamara Tungate (S)

1988 Michigan, Kaye Lani Rae Rafko (S)
(1) Louisiana, Patricia Brandt (T)
(2) Nevada, Stacie James (T)
(3) Colorado, LaTonya R. Hall
(4) Mississippi, Toni Seawright

1989 Minnesota, Gretchen Carlson (T)
(1) Colorado, Maya Walker
(2) Oklahoma, Lori Lee Kelley (T)
(3) California, Marlise Sharlene Ricardos
(4) Alabama, Jenny Lee Jackson

1990 Missouri, Debbye Lynn Turner (S)
(1) Maryland, Virginia Cha
(2) Colorado, Debbie Riecks
(3) Illinois, Jeri Lynn Zimmerman (S)
(4) Ohio, Kristin Huffman (T)

1991 Illinois, Marjorie Judith Vincent (T)
(1) South Carolina, Mary Waddell Gainey
(2) Tennessee, Dana Brown
(3) Texas, Suzanne Lawrence (T)(QL)
(4) Louisiana, Linnea Marie Fayard

Miss Americas' Statistics

YEAR	STATE	NAME	AGE	HEIGHT	WEIGHT	FIGURE	EYES	HAIR
1921	DC	Gorman	16	5'1"	108	30-25-32	blue	blond
1922/1923	OH	Campbell	16	5'7"	140	35-26-36	blue	auburn
1924	PA	Malcomson	18	5'6"	137	34-25-34	violet	brown
1925	CA	Lanphier	19	5'6"	138	34-26-37	hazel	blond
1926	OK	Smallwood	18	5'4"	118	33-25-34	blue	brown
1927	IL	Delander	17	5'5½"	115	33-25-34	blue	brown
1933	CT	Bergeron	15	5'4½"	112	32-26-37	blue	blond
1935	PA	Leaver	17	5'6"	120	33-23-35	blue	brown
1936	PA	Coyle	22	5'6"	114	34-23-34	brown	black
1937	NJ	Cooper	17	5'6½"	120	32-26-36	blue	blond
1938	OH	Meseke	20	5'7"	128	34-26-36	blue	blond
1939	MI	Donnelly	19	5'7"	126	36-25-34	brown	brown
1940	PA	Burke	19	5'9"	120	34-23-35	green	brown
1941	CA	LaPlanche	18	5'5½"	120	34-24-36	hazel	blond
1942	TX	Dennison	18	5'5"	118	34-22-34	brown	brown
1943	CA	Bartel	19	5'8"	130	36-23-35	blue	brown
1944	DC	Ramey	19	5'7"	125	36-25-37	blue	red
1945	NY	Myerson	21	5'10"	135	35-25-35	hazel	black
1946	CA	Buferd	21	5'8"	123	35-25-36	blue	brown
1947	TN	Walker	21	5'7"	130	35-25-35	hazel	black
1948	MN	Shopp	18	5'9"	140	37-27-36	hazel	brown
1949	AZ	Mercer	18	5'3"	106	34-22-34	brown	black
1951	AL	Betbeze	18	5'5½"	119	35-24-35	brown	black
1952	UT	Hutchins	25	5'10"	143	36-24-36	blue	blond

Figures rounded to nearest number.

YEAR	STATE	NAME	AGE	HEIGHT	WEIGHT	FIGURE	EYES	HAIR
1953	GA	Langley	19	5'6¼"	118	35-23-35	green	brown
1954	PA	Ay	20	5'8"	132	37-24-36	green	blond
1955	CA	Meriwether	19	5'8½"	124	34-22-35	blue	brown
1956	CO	Ritchie	18	5'6"	116	35-23-35	blue	auburn
1957	SC	McKnight	19	5'5"	120	35-23-35	blue	blond
1958	CO	Van Derbur	20	5'8¼"	130	35-25-36	green	blond
1959	MS	Mobley	21	5'5"	114	34-22-35	brown	brown
1960	MS	Mead	20	5'7"	120	36-24-36	green	brown
1961	MI	Fleming	18	5'6"	116	35-22-35	green	brown
1962	NC	Fletcher	19	5'5½"	118	35-24-35	hazel	brown
1963	OH	Mayer	20	5'5"	115	36-22-36	hazel	brown
1964	AR	Axum	21	5'6½"	124	35-23-35	brown	brown
1965	AZ	Van Dyke	21	5'6"	124	36-24-36	brown	brown
1966	KS	Bryant	19	5'7"	115	36-23-36	blue	brown
1967	OK	Jayroe	19	5'6"	116	36-24-36	green	brown
1968	KS	Barnes	20	5'9"	135	36-24-36	blue	brown
1969	IL	Ford	18	5'7"	125	36-24-36	green	blond
1970	MI	Eldred	21	5'5½"	110	34-21-34	green	blond
1971	TX	George	21	5'8"	121	36-23-36	brown	brown
1972	IL	Schaefer	22	5'7"	118	36-24-36	green	auburn
1973	WI	Meeuwsen	23	5'8"	120	36-25-36	brown	brown
1974	CO	King	23	5'9"	125	36-24-36	blue	blond
1975	TX	Cothran	21	5'8"	119	36-23-36	brown	brown
1976	NY	Godin	18	5'10"	128	36-24-36	brown	brown
1977	MN	Benham	20	5'7"	120	35-23-35	hazel	blond
1978	OH	Perkins	23	5'5"	105	34-24-35	brown	brown
1979	VA	Barker	22	5'4"	108	35-24-35	green	blond
1980	MS	Prewitt	22	5'7"	114	35-23-36	blue	brown
1981	OK	Powell	21	5'4"	110	35-24-35	green	brown
1982	AR	Ward	20	5'9"	129	36-24-36	brown	brown
1983	CA	Maffett	25	5'7"	115	35-22-35	blue	blond
1984	NY	Williams	20	5'6"	110	34-24-34	green	brown
1984	NJ	Charles	20	5'3"	100	33-22-33	brown	brown
1985	UT	Wells	20	5'8"	120	35-25-36	aqua	blond
1986	MS	Akin	21	5'9"	114	35-22-35	blue	blond
1987	TN	Cash	21	5'8"	116	N/A	green	blond
1988	MI	Rafko	24	5'10"	131	N/A	green	brown
1989	MN	Carlson	22	5'3"	108	N/A	green	blond
1990	MO	Turner	23	5'8"	118	N/A	brown	brown
1991	IL	Vincent	25	5'6"	110	N/A	brown	brown

Additional Awards

NATIONAL FRUIT OF THE LOOM QUALITY OF LIFE AWARD ($10,000)

For exceptional commitment to improving the quality of life for others through volunteerism.

1989, Michelle Kline, Miss Pennsylvania. Promoting organ transplant donations.

1990, Suzanne Lawrence, Miss Texas. Founder of "Smiles Against Cancer" program.

DR. DAVID B. ALLMAN MEDICAL SCHOLARSHIP AWARD ($5,000)

Dr. David B. Allman was past president of the American Medical Association and a past Pageant president as well. Mrs. Ann Allman established this scholarship for medical studies in honor of her husband.

1970, Katherine Karlsrud, M.D., Miss New York, $3,000.
1974, Susan Sadlier, Miss Massachusetts, $1,000.
1974, Cynthia Erb, Miss New Hampshire, $1,000.

1974, Carol Ann Schmitt, Miss Wisconsin, $1,000.
1974, Cheryl Johnson, Miss Wyoming, $2,000.
1975, Ann Schmalzried, Miss Florida, $1,000.
1975, Patricia Ann Cyr, Miss Maine, $1,000.
1975, Julie Ann Beckers, Miss Michigan, $1,000.
1975, Cathy Marie Woell, Miss North Dakota, $1,000.
1975, Gina Campbell, Miss South Dakota, $1,000.
1976, Sandra Adamson, M.D., Miss Georgia, $4,000.
1976, Barbara Jennings, D.O., Miss Maryland, $3,000.
1976, Janice Frankino, Miss Montana, $1,000.
1977, Libby Kawaikikilani Lee, Miss Hawaii, $1,000.
1978, Charmaine Kowalski, M.D., Miss Pennsylvania, $3,000.
1981, Juliana Marie Zilba, Miss Ohio, $2,000.
1984, Kelly Lin Brumagen, Miss Kentucky, $5,000.
1985, Christi Lynn Taunton, Miss Arkansas, $5,000.
1985, Honey Castro, Miss Washington, $5,000.
1986, Kris Beasley, Miss Tennessee, $5,000.
1987, Julie Reil, Miss Montana, $5,000.
1988, Sophia Symko, Miss Utah, $5,000.

As of 1989, medical scholarships became available at the local and state levels as well. Since then, there have been eleven winners. The funds are awarded when the recipient starts her medical studies.

Index

References to photographs are given in *italics*.

About the Author

Ann-Marie Bivans has been a part of the beauty and pageant industries for more than a decade. She has competed successfully in pageants on the local, state, national, and international levels and is a Miss America preliminary judge. An accomplished lecturer, Ann-Marie Bivans lives in Miami, Florida, with her husband, who is a real estate investor, and their two sons.

Additional copies of *Miss America: In Pursuit of the Crown* may be ordered by sending a check for $27.50 (please add the following for postage and handling: $1.50 for the first copy, $.50 for each added copy) to:

MasterMedia Limited
16 East 72nd Street
New York, NY 10021
(212) 260-5600
(800) 334-8232

Ann-Marie Bivans is available for speeches and workshops. Please contact MasterMedia's Speakers' Bureau for availability and fee arrangements. Call Tony Colao at (908) 359-1612.

Other MasterMedia Books

THE PREGNANCY AND MOTHERHOOD DIARY: Planning the First Year of Your Second Career, by Susan Schiffer Stautberg, is the first and only undated appointment diary that shows how to manage pregnancy and career. ($12.95 spiral-bound)

CITIES OF OPPORTUNITY: Finding the Best Place to Work, Live and Prosper in the 1990's and Beyond, by Dr. John Tepper Marlin, explores the job and living options for the next decade and into the next century. This consumer guide and handbook, written by one of the world's experts on cities, selects and features forty-six American cities and metropolitan areas. ($13.95 paper, $24.95 cloth)

THE DOLLARS AND SENSE OF DIVORCE: The Financial Guide for Women, by Judith Briles, is the first book to combine practical tips on overcoming the legal hurdles with planning finances before, during, and after divorce. ($10.95 paper)

OUT THE ORGANIZATION: How Fast Could You Find a New Job?, by Madeleine and Robert Swain, is written for the millions of Americans whose jobs are no longer safe, whose companies are not loyal, and who face futures of uncertainty. It gives advice on finding a new job or starting your own business. ($11.95 paper, $17.95 cloth)

AGING PARENTS AND YOU: A Complete Handbook to Help You Help Your Elders Maintain a Healthy, Productive and Independent Life, by Eugenia Anderson-Ellis and Marsha Dryan, is a complete guide to providing care to aging relatives. It gives practical advice and resources to the adults who are helping their elders lead productive and independent lives. ($9.95 paper)

CRITICISM IN YOUR LIFE: How to Give It, How to Take It, How to Make It Work for You, by Dr. Deborah Bright, offers practical advice, in an upbeat, readable, and realistic fashion, for turning criticism into control. Charts and diagrams guide the reader into managing criticism from bosses, spouses, children, friends, neighbors, and in-laws. ($9.95 paper, $17.95 cloth)

BEYOND SUCCESS: How Volunteer Service Can Help You Begin Making a Life Instead of Just a Living, by John F. Raynolds III and Eleanor Raynolds, C.B.E., is a unique how-to book targeted to business and professional people considering volunteer work, senior citizens who wish to fill leisure time meaningfully, and students trying out various career options. The book is filled with interviews with celebrities, CEOs, and average citizens who talk about the benefits of service work. ($9.95 paper, $19.95 cloth)

MANAGING IT ALL: Time-Saving Ideas for Career, Family, Relationships and Self, by Beverly Benz Treuille and Susan Schiffer Stautberg, is written for women who are juggling careers and families. Over two hundred career women (ranging from a TV anchorwoman to an investment banker) were interviewed. The book contains many humorous anecdotes on saving time and improving the quality of life for self and family. ($9.95 paper)

REAL LIFE 101: (Almost) Surviving Your First Year Out of College, by Susan Kleinman, supplies welcome advice to those facing "real life" for the first time, focusing on work, money, health, and how to deal with freedom and responsibility. ($9.95 paper)

YOUR HEALTHY BODY, YOUR HEALTHY LIFE: How to Take Control of Your Medical Destiny, by Donald B. Louria, M.D., provides precise advice and strategies that will help you to live a long and healthy life. Learn also about nutrition, exercise, vitamins, and medication, as well as how to control risk factors for major diseases. ($12.95 paper)

THE CONFIDENCE FACTOR: How Self-Esteem Can Change Your Life, by Judith Briles, is based on a nationwide survey of six thousand men and women. Briles explores why women so often feel a lack of self-confidence and have a poor opinion of themselves. She offers step-by-step advice on becoming the person you want to be. ($9.95 paper, $18.95 cloth)

THE SOLUTION TO POLLUTION: 101 Things You Can Do to Clean Up Your Environment, by Laurence Sombke, offers step-by-step techniques on how to conserve more energy, start a recycling center, choose biodegradable products, and proceed with individual environmental cleanup projects. ($7.95 paper)

TAKING CONTROL OF YOUR LIFE: The Secrets of Successful Enterprising Women, by Gail Blanke and Kathleen Walas, is based on the authors' pro-fessional experience with Avon Products' Women of Enterprise Awards, given each year to outstanding women entrepreneurs. The authors offer a specific plan to help you gain control over your life and include business tips and quizzes as well as beauty and lifestyle information. ($17.95 cloth)

POWER PARTNERS: How Two-Career Couples Can Play to Win, by Jane Hershey Cuozzo and S. Diane Graham, describes how two-career couples can learn the difference between competing with a spouse and becoming a supportive Power Partner. ($19.95 cloth)

DARE TO CONFRONT: How to Intervene When Someone You Care About Has an Alcohol or Drug Problem, by Bob Wright and Deborah George Wright, shows the reader how to use the step-by-step methods of professional interventionists to motivate drug-dependent people to accept the help they need. ($17.95 cloth)

WORK WITH ME! How to Make the Most of Office Support Staff, by Betsy Lazary, shows how to find, train, and nurture the "perfect" assistant and how best to utilize your support staff professionals. ($9.95 paper)

MANN FOR ALL SEASONS: Wit and Wisdom from The Washington Post's *Judy Mann,* by Judy Mann, shows the columnist at her best as she writes about women, families, and the politics of the women's revolution. ($19.95 cloth)

THE SOLUTION TO POLLUTION IN THE WORKPLACE, by Laurence Sombke, Terry M. Robertson, and Elliot M. Kaplan, supplies employees with everything they need to know about cleaning up their workspace, including recycling, using energy efficiently, conserving water, and buying recycled products and nontoxic supplies. ($9.95 paper)